UNCOMPROMISED

THE RISE, FALL, AND REDEMPTION OF AN ARAB AMERICAN PATRIOT IN THE CIA

NADA PROUTY

palgrave
macmillan

UNCOMPROMISED
Copyright © Nada Prouty, 2011.
All rights reserved.

First published in 2011 by PALGRAVE MACMILLAN® in the United
States—a division of St. Martin's Press LLC, 175 Fifth Avenue, New
York, NY 10010.

Where this book is distributed in the UK, Europe and the rest of the
world, this is by Palgrave Macmillan, a division of Macmillan Publishers
Limited, registered in England, company number 785998, of Houndmills,
Basingstoke, Hampshire RG21 6XS.

Palgrave Macmillan is the global academic imprint of the above
companies and has companies and representatives throughout the world.

Palgrave® and Macmillan® are registered trademarks in the United
States, the United Kingdom, Europe and other countries.

ISBN 978-0-230-11386-2

Library of Congress Cataloging-in-Publication Data
Prouty, Nada.
    Uncompromised : the rise, fall, and redemption of an Arab American
patriot in the CIA / Nada Prouty.
        p.   cm.
    Includes index.
    ISBN 978–0–230–11386–2 (hardback)
    1. Prouty, Nada.   2. Intelligence officers—United States—
Biography.   3. Women intelligence officers—United States—
Biography.   4. United States. Central Intelligence Agency—Officials
and employees—Biography.   5. Arab American women—
Biography.   6. Espionage, American.   I. Title.
JK468.I6P78 2011
327.12730092—dc23
[B]
                                                              2011016922

A catalogue record of the book is available from the British Library.

Design by Letra Libre, Inc.

First edition: November 2011
10 9 8 7 6 5 4 3 2 1

Printed in the United States of America.

To my daughters,

Evangelina and Elizabeth Prouty,

I love you both to pieces

CONTENTS

DISCLAIMERS

All statements of fact, opinion, or analysis expressed are those of the author and do not reflect the official position or views of the CIA or any other US government agency. Nothing in the contents should be construed as asserting or implying US Government authentication of information or Agency endorsement of the author's views. This material has been reviewed by the CIA to prevent disclosure of classified information.

*   *   *

All of the incidents in this memoir are true. However, in certain cases, I have changed the names of individuals to protect their privacy.

"DON'T SHOOT— I'M AN AMERICAN" 1

Looking down the barrel of the M16 shoved in my face, I did what any patriotic American would do: I proclaimed my allegiance to the USA. "I'M AN AMERICAN; I'M AN AMERICAN!" I screamed. I wanted to believe that the young Marine would be curious enough about my Arabic accent to ask questions before pulling his gun's trigger.

An hour earlier, I had been thanking God for my Arab features. I relied on them to help me move, without raising alarms, through Baghdad's spiderweb of streets in search of contacts. Now I was praying for this Marine to believe what I was telling him. Despite my accent and my Arab garb, I was most assuredly on his side. I was CIA, an agent on the hunt for intelligence about Al Qaeda in Mesopotamia in the fall of 2003. He was a young Marine serving his country. *What could go right here?* I asked myself.

He had noticed my vehicle, which had stopped at the entrance to the Green Zone some time before. Impatient Iraqi drivers had lined up behind me, beeping their horns and yelling at me to move. One by one they were ushered forward and allowed entrance. Sweat ran down my back and trickled down my face as I sat in my non–air-conditioned car, breathing fumes from the decrepit jalopies that passed slowly around me.

When the line thinned, the Marine looked my way suspiciously. He began walking toward my vehicle, pointing his weapon, trigger finger resting and ready on the frame of the gun. He ordered me to step out of my car immediately. I wanted to follow his directions, but I feared exposing the Colt machine gun nestled under my flowing *abaya*. That would only escalate the situation. I waited for him to get closer so I could explain to him that I was a government employee returning from a mission outside the Green Zone.

The Marine cautiously approached the unmoving car that, even by my own assessment, appeared to be a prototypical suicide vehicle-borne improvised explosive device (SBVIED). I could see a mix of fear and hesitation in his piercing blue eyes. My attempt to alleviate his concern by reaching for my identification badge, tucked deep inside my disguise, only made things worse. He moved his finger to the trigger. My mouth was dry, and swallowing was painful. My fumblings, as if for a detonator, exposed the machine gun hidden under the *abaya*.

To him, it must have looked like show time. I looked Arab and spoke accented English. I carried a weapon and was inside a suspicious vehicle. He had to make a split-second decision—on which both our lives hinged. Slowly, I raised my hands, palms out, empty. His finger relaxed just enough on the trigger to give me hope. I locked in on those blue American eyes and screamed: "I'm an American; I'm an American!"

"Your ID?"

"Is right here." And, ever so gently, keeping one hand raised, with my free thumb I managed to slide the *abaya* aside enough to reveal the tag hanging around my neck. He looked carefully at the picture and the data there and moved his finger off the trigger. He'd chosen not to engage me with fire. Had I been in his place, I don't know if I would have done the same.

"Good enough, ma'am. Welcome to the Green Zone." He breathed the words hard.

"Thank you, soldier, for going by the book. You have a safe night, now," I managed.

HOURS BEFORE THIS SHOWDOWN, I had received an urgent phone call.

"Sahar, I need to talk to you now. Now!"

My intelligence contact was triggering an emergency meeting. I hoped that he was not in danger or asking to see me for the wrong reasons. Informants sometimes wished to talk to me about their marital problems when what I really needed was to gather intelligence about possible violent attacks. I could help direct people to safe areas if I caught wind of an impending attack, but I had a hard time calming angry spouses.

"OK, Ali," I answered. "I will meet you at one of our agreed-upon locations—location three to be precise—at 4:00 P.M."

"I'll see you there, Miss Sahar."

"*Inshallah,*" I assured him.

Ali was supposed to add two hours to the time I gave him. I hoped he would remember that detail.

I began to prepare for our appointment. First, I went to my supervisor, Ken, to let him know that I would be conducting a meeting that evening. I told him the pickup location, the timing, and the rally and rescue location in case things got out of hand. Next, I started working on my gear. I tested my GPS system with a current reading of my location and confirmed that the reading was accurate. I also made sure the GPS battery was fully charged.

Then, on my handheld radio—also ready for action—I contacted base.

"This is Assassin calling to let you know that I will be making a move tonight, departing the Green Zone at about 4 P.M. and returning at about 8 P.M. The meeting location is Hay Al Sha'b."

"Copy, Assassin," came the answer from base.

I reviewed my map for the possible routes to my pickup location. I mused on how odd it was that I knew my way around Baghdad better than I knew the streets of my neighborhood in Northern Virginia. I tested my cell phone for a signal and battery power; both were fine. I picked up my backpack and made sure I had replenished my supply of water and PowerBars. In the 100-degree heat, the PowerBars had melted to liquid in their plastic pouches. Being pregnant, a fact I had discovered only a few weeks earlier, I had not kept any food down all day, but I wanted to be on the safe side and try to eat later if I could. Also in my backpack was the black *abaya,* my head scarf, and the rest of my disguise. The *abaya* helped me blend in and hide my gear.

At the firearms check location, I loaded my 9mm Glock, putting an extra round in the chamber. More rounds mean more fight. I also made sure I had plenty of extra fully loaded magazines. Finally, I grabbed my Colt Commando—a smart and dangerous weapon I had dubbed "Buba." Buba and I had a fine relationship. He was my silent partner who protected me. In return, I kept him clean and out of sight. And, when no one was looking, I spoke to him.

"I hope that I don't have to use you today, Buba, but if I do I know that you will be there for me," I told him.

Almost ready, I went to the bathroom and threw up again. This was a good thing. There was absolutely nothing left in my stomach, so I wasn't worried about throwing up again anytime soon. Still, just in case, I packed a couple of plastic bags. I knew Ali would have additional bags, as the last time we met I had had a continuous spell of vomiting.

Weeks earlier, I had learned that I was pregnant with my daughter Evangelina. The first time I tried to learn the reason behind my symptoms, I was not successful. I had missed my monthly cycle and was pretty sure I was pregnant, so I decided to visit the American military hospital in the Green Zone to confirm my suspicions. I did not know where to go, so I roamed around looking for a doctor. When I located one, he told me that because he was not equipped with a lab able to verify pregnancy with a simple blood test, the best he could do was to give me an ultrasound. The doctor was busy, so I told him I would wait in the waiting room. A couple of soldiers arrived and I started to talk to them. One was waiting for a prescription, while the other wanted the doctor to check on his recovering wound. I told them that they could both see the doctor ahead of me, since my exam was not urgent. In truth, I was very anxious and could not contain my excitement. My thoughts were racing ahead to all the cute baby clothes and shoes and the smell of baby shampoo when I heard the door to the hospital's main entrance burst open. A soldier was rushed through on a gurney, unconscious and bleeding heavily. Thoughts of babies and nurseries fled. I suddenly felt selfish and inconsiderate. How could I take time away from the doctor? My question was trivial in comparison to the life-and-death struggles of our men and women in uniform. I went back to my room and cried. I don't cry easily, so I blamed the war and my wayward hormones.

Now ready to leave the firearms check station, I headed to the carpool and checked out a vehicle to drive to another location inside the Green Zone, where I checked out one of the junkers. I put on my bulletproof vest and then draped my *abaya* over myself, hiding Buba. Finally, I took a deep breath and said my prayer.

"Hail Mary, full of grace, the Lord is with thee; blessed art thou amongst women, and blessed is the fruit of thy womb, Jesus. Holy Mary, Mother of God, pray for us sinners, now and at the hour of our death. Amen."

My conversion to the Catholic faith had begun shortly before my assignment in Baghdad. I had been attending Mass regularly with my husband, Gordon, after we were married in 2001 at our local Catholic church. One busy and stressful day, when I was readying to depart for Baghdad, I visited the church for some sanity and composure. As I sat in the quiet and stared at the crucifix, I felt the presence of a spirit. I felt calm and at peace within myself. I had no doubt in my mind that I wanted the Lord in my life. I wanted it immediately. However, because the Catholic conversion course was a long process that I could not attend at the time, I promised myself that I would complete the course when I returned.

To me, the strongest pillar of faith has always been one's individual relationship with the Lord. I had grown up a Druze in Lebanon. There is no nutshell description of the Druze religion, which is an amalgam of Muslim, Christian, Sufi, and Pentateuch teachings and beliefs—in other words, a sort of Lebanese condition. There is a definite mysticism to it, and the Druze strongly believe in a supreme being. I had never practiced this religion in Lebanon, but its mysteries and otherworldliness intrigued me at times. I suppose I was similarly susceptible to the mysteries of Roman Catholicism. But most importantly, my marriage to Gordon made me want to share his faith, so I had talked with him about converting. Although official conversion would be months away, I considered myself Catholic on the day I sought the sanctuary of the church.

My prayer finished, I covered my hair with a head scarf before exiting the safety of the Green Zone to drive along the ruined streets of Baghdad. Because one never knows who might be hanging around the Green Zone checkpoint, I wanted to make sure that I was not being followed. Driving always reminded me of the status of the many neighborhoods that made up the city. I learned which streets had recently been barricaded and whether the closures were temporary or permanent, noting the changes on my map, and I'd share my findings with my colleagues at the end of the day.

My route to meet Ali took me along streets where buildings had totally disappeared. Open shops sat next to lots piled with rubble. I saw a little girl holding her mother's hand as they walked through the wreckage of someone's once-grand, elaborate home. I could see myself in that little girl. Twenty years earlier, I had walked through eerily similar destruction in Beirut. War is very efficient at creating chaos. Certainly my life—and no doubt the life of the young girl I had passed—had been traumatized by war. As resilient as children can be, adapting to war can take its toll; I had friends who processed the trauma-related stresses into such behaviors as bedwetting and stuttering. I wondered about the impact of the war in Iraq on this little girl, hoping that she had a strong family or some other support structure to help her get through these difficult times.

These trying circumstances illustrate the context in which my fellow CIA operations officers and I served in Baghdad in 2003. Admittedly, my colleagues' European features prevented all but a small number of them from passing as locals. And among those who could pass, none of them had the language and training to operate independently on the city's streets in the way I could. My duties in Baghdad were always very intense, but I welcomed this daily struggle, knowing that I was contributing directly to saving the lives of both American soldiers and Iraqi civilians. As a covert CIA officer, I conducted an average of two to three high-risk meetings a day when I was serving in Baghdad. Moving across the enormous and chaos-strewn landscape of Iraq meant inviting violence and deception from many quarters. We all got very little sleep and could never be sure who might be friend and who might be foe.

WHERE I'M COMING FROM 2

My parents were Druze, a minority religious faction amounting to approximately 7 percent of the Lebanese population. The Druze religion started as a religious-philosophical movement in Egypt in the tenth century. The Druze consider their faith a blend of Judaism, Christianity, and Islam and believe that their spiritual message was inherent in the prophetic voices of Moses, Jesus, and Mohammad.

Although they recognize the ethical and spiritual practices of these monotheistic religions as wholesome, the Druze argue that individuals who continue to commit transgressions can still be forgiven by God if they fast and pray. Because of this belief, strongly held by Druze in modern Beirut and in the secluded mountains east of the city, the Druze eliminated all elements of ritual and ceremony, leaving no fixed daily liturgy, no defined holy days, and no pilgrimage obligations. Instead, because the Druze perform their spiritual reckoning directly with God, the certainty of their belief requires no special days of fasting or atonement. The Druze religion is also secretive and closed to converts.

Lebanon has two major religious groups: Christians and Muslims. The Druze, though generally despised by these majority groups, have allied themselves, at various times, with either or both to ensure Druze survival.

The Druze inheritance in me ebbs and flows as the need arises. These elastic abilities are what make me both a "world traveler" (a euphemism, apparently, for "traitor," according to the *New York Post*) and a good officer. But there are those who don't believe I am who I say I am: a patriotic American who has consistently put her life on the line to gain justice for American citizens and who, while at the CIA, went up against some of the most dangerous terrorists on the planet.

These people have little idea of what goes into being a good CIA officer. The truth is you have to be a little slippery sometimes. You have to play a role, and it helps to be a part of the world your enemy is coming from. I'll tell you this: the Druze are respected in the Middle East. They are not wild-eyed mystics; they are not moles; they are not slipping-in-behind-the-flower-cart bomb bearers. Instead, they work in sensitive offices of several Middle Eastern governments, or they emigrate and become decorated US Marines, or they line up with their Jewish colleagues in the Israeli Defense Forces. Their long history of serving the people who make history—and this often means picking the strongest dog in the fight—is a matter of public record. The Druze are very international; they get around. And I am lucky to have some of this blood flowing in my veins.

Naturally, my detractors declined to consider the complexity of my background, favoring caricature over truth. Too bad—they might have learned, from my life's struggles, a thing or two about the ethnic divisions in the Middle East, about the nature of assimilation and true patriotism, or simply about how to combat terrorism by recognizing the best tools America has for effective intelligence gathering. But they chose to avoid any serious examination of all of this.

My Druze background is not necessarily a bad thing. Being born Druze is a little like being from the projects: because you live that reality, you're aware that you know more than the talking heads. And if that point of origin makes you more versatile than the average Joe, that's good. And you don't lose that identification easily; it's always a part of you. It makes you work hard, makes you prove yourself at every challenge. A Druze in Lebanon is always a bit of an outsider.

As a Druze, you might be seen by others as a member of an odd cult or group, but this group has a historical reputation for being good ministers and confidantes and advisors to the power brokers. A loyal Druze makes a good ally.

Is there anything wrong with that? Well, no. Unless, of course, your allegiance is to Hizballah, or Hamas, or Al Qaeda. But my heart is here, and, believe it or not, it has been since I was a teenager growing up in war-torn Lebanon. I gave my heart to the Marines who came to help my country; to America when I immigrated; then to the FBI; and then to the CIA. Yes, I was a Druze, a wandering Druze and a woman of my own making, someone who wanted to serve a greater good joyfully. So, I accepted a position in the army of intelligence operatives of the greatest country on earth, the United States of America. Never mind the wondrous sound bite, the power of money being spent to read about "Jihad Jane," my *nomme de mole* according to the *Post*. The anti–Nada Prouty propaganda was and is all about selling the fear that makes careers. None of the media knew the truth about the Druze in me. None of them knew, or seemed to care, where I had come from.

TWO IS TOO MANY

On a cold January day in 1970, my paternal grandmother, Mohsina, paced the unheated waiting room of a primitive hospital in the suburbs of Beirut. She was mumbling to herself, "Please, God, let it be a boy," again and again, loud enough for others around her to hear. My mother, Nabila, had been married off to my father, twenty years her senior, at fourteen. Such arranged marriages of young girls were common in the Druze society.

"I will be so embarrassed if your daughter has another girl," Mohsina told my maternal grandmother, Nabiha. "Two in a row is just too much."

Although women are allowed to attain positions of religious significance, the Druze, like many cultures around the world, prefer sons to daughters. Firstborn sons are particularly prized, but a traditional

Druze family will continue to have children until a son is born. Elfat, my older sister by three years, was present for my birth and understood what Mohsina's sharp words meant. Teta—colloquial Arabic for Grandmother—was mean, Elfat would tell me later, when I was old enough to understand the story of the day I was born. "Don't worry, mother, I have a feeling this one will be a boy," my father, Nadim, had reportedly said. Elfat told me that our father too was upset when I turned out to be a girl. In addition to bringing shame to our family, another girl would be a financial burden.

The actual birth had all the makings of a bad joke. When I entered the world with loud screams, Mohsina gushed, "These are the cries of a boy; I just know it!"

My father, Elfat reported, readily agreed with his mother.

"Finally, God, you have given me my heir," our father exclaimed.

But, of course, it was just me.

Crushed by disappointment, my father and his mother left the hospital, heads down, not wanting to see or hold me. My mother, herself saddened, did not want to hold me either, so Nabiha jumped in and took care of me until my mother checked out of the hospital and came back to our home in Kournayel, a small village twenty-five miles east of Beirut.

Sixteen months later, in April 1971, Mohsina and both my parents would once again be let down at the birth of my sister Rula.

Everyone was still anticipating that male heir when Mohsina passed away, never having known the joys of a grandson. My parents' wishes for an heir were finally realized in 1973 with the birth of my brother, Fadi. The circumstances of Mohsina's death strangely echoed her distaste for baby girls: Mohsina, who suffered from type 2 diabetes, was holding my younger sister, Rula, when she fell unconscious and slumped over Rula's tiny body, cutting off her oxygen supply. My mother, finding Mohsina unresponsive and Rula turning blue, freed Rula from Mohsina's arms and revived her. Hearing this, I suspected that when Mohsina realized she felt faint, she purposefully fell onto Rula. Later in life, I wondered why my mother would leave Rula in Mohsina's care when Grandmother did not take proper medication for her condition and, as a result, often passed out.

With four kids by the age of twenty, my mother needed all the domestic help she could get, so she settled into the same apartment building in eastern Beirut where my Aunt Salma, my father's sister, lived. My father, an engineer who was working as the Middle East representative for a German construction equipment company, often traveled internationally. Teta Nabiha and Aunt Salma helped my mother care for us during his long and frequent absences.

One of my fondest memories of the East Beirut apartment was my sister Elfat, who we all called Lola, taking me to the candy shop for birthday treats. My parents did not celebrate my sisters' or my birthday—though they held elaborate bashes for our brother, Fadi, of course—so we girls had to do our own celebrating. Once, Lola asked my mother for candy money, but my mother refused. Not wanting to face my certain disappointment, Lola took matters into her own hands. Mother had a jacket with buttons that looked like coins, so Lola grabbed a pair of scissors and went to Mother's closet.

"Hold the jacket this way," she instructed me as she cut the buttons out—along with, of course, a large part of the fabric. Determined to celebrate my birthday properly, she held my hand and walked me to the store. We selected some candy together and walked to the owner's desk.

"Here you go, mister," Lola beamed, handing him the buttons. He looked at the fake coins and then at us.

"It is my sister's birthday," Lola said proudly.

"Oh, well, in that case you don't need these lovely . . . coins," he said kindly.

We sat outside the shop eating our candy, and Lola sang "Happy Birthday" to me. We talked, at length, about all the imaginary gifts that I would be getting. As we walked back home, I hugged her.

"This is the best birthday ever. Thanks, Lola!"

Waiting at the door was my fuming mother.

"This does not look good," I whispered to Lola.

"Don't worry about it. This is your special day, and I will handle this," Lola said as she walked defiantly toward Mother.

"I got a call from the shop owner. You two are in big trouble," she shot at us.

"This was an emergency, and I had to take action," Lola challenged.

Without hesitating, Mother delivered one quick, hard slap to Lola's face, and Lola fell to the ground.

I ran to her, just missing another punch from Mother.

"To your room!" she screamed at us.

I knew Lola must be in pain, but she did not cry. We ran to the relative safety of our room and celebrated both our victory over Mother and the generosity of the candy-shop owner. Lola smiled from ear to ear for the rest of the evening. It was a rare day, one I fondly remember.

In these early childhood years, I was not conscious of the larger war brewing around us. We girls waged our own war against our parents, and later our brother, who all insisted on their superiority and domination. The strife was minimized only by the bond I formed with my sisters and the comfort I found there.

LEAVING HOME—1975

My father, holding Fadi in his arms, yelled at my mother, "Hurry up. Pack essentials and some clothes. We need to leave immediately. Any unnecessary delays could result in all our deaths."

I wanted to ask my parents to explain what was going on and who wanted to kill us, but I knew better than to ask any questions, especially when Father was visibly angry. The stress of the country's instability, combined with having to raise three girls, was too much for him. His interactions with me and my sisters consisted only of yelling at, belittling, or shaming us. I rationalized and excused most of his behavior as anxiety about the war.

"Baba loves us," I would often tell my sisters. ("Baba" is the Arabic word for "Daddy.") "He is just nervous and worried from all the danger in Lebanon."

Mother began stuffing suitcases with clothes, running between rooms and screaming at us to move out of her way. We held hands and followed directions. I wanted to get my stuffed camel because I did not want to leave him behind, but I was too scared to ask or to drop my sisters' hands. My mother placed the suitcases at the apartment door, and my father, while holding Fadi, brought them to our car.

"Is that all?" asked Father, after having transported all the suitcases in the entryway.

"Yes. Just essentials, as you asked," Mother replied.

"What are you three looking at? Run down to the car now," Father screamed at us.

In the car, my parents tucked my brother in the front seat between them for extra safety, while my sisters and I sat in the back. We headed to our village, Kournayel, in the mountains east of the city.

"We need to be in a Druze area. East Beirut is now a Christian area. We may never see this house again," Baba explained to our mother. I panicked silently, not wanting to leave our home, my toys, and my belongings. Home was all I knew.

Why do the Christians want to kill us? I wondered. What have the Druze done? Why would anyone want to kill anyone else because of their religion? Sensing that my sisters were also distraught, I told myself that I would have to figure that out later. I didn't know then that it would be much, much later. We eventually reached the village and settled into a rental house there for some time.

Even though I was born in a time of peace, relatively speaking— the Lebanese civil war did not begin until 1975—almost all my childhood memories are of being an unwelcome girl in the midst of the war with chaos, destruction, and lawlessness swirling around us year after year.

TWENTY-SEVEN YEARS BEFORE MY BIRTH, in 1943, Lebanon had become an independent state. French troops, who had invaded the country in the early 1920s, finally left Lebanon in 1946. A constitution was formed and a parliament was created with a number of stipulations, the most famous being the requirement that the president be Christian, the prime minister a Sunni Muslim, and the speaker of the parliament a Shi'a Muslim. Imagine our Constitution requiring the president to be Jewish, members of the House to be Catholic, and members of the Senate to be Buddhist. Needless to say, such an arrangement is a recipe for segregation, dissociation, and isolation.

After the 1948 Arab-Israeli War, Lebanon hosted an influx of Palestinian refugees who had been expelled from their homes or had fled the conflict. Between 1968 and 1975, the Palestine Liberation Organization (PLO) relocated most of its combat forces to Jordan and then to Lebanon, eventually asserting its right to fight Israel from southern Lebanon, causing tremendous instability in that part of the country. The PLO buildup erupted into total civil war when the Palestinian fighters clashed with the weaker Christian-led national government, which was trying to cater to its constituents and, at the same time, maintain order. From this cauldron of instability, a number of religious-based factions, each sprouting well-armed militias, emerged.

In 1976, conflict among these militias, the Palestinians, and the Christian leadership induced the government to call for Syrian intervention. The nation was now strongly divided, with southern Lebanon and the western half of Beirut becoming bases for the PLO and other Muslim-based militias, and with the Christians in control of East Beirut and the Christian areas of Mount Lebanon. The main confrontation line in Beirut was known as the Green Line. It was our proximity to this warring divide that had led my family to leave our apartment building in Christian-controlled East Beirut, and we eventually spent several years in our rented mountain home while tensions remained high in the city.

WITHIN MONTHS OF SETTLING IN OUR VILLAGE HOME, I began to hear my parents talk about returning to our apartment building in Beirut. I was very excited; I thought we were moving back. I missed my home, my friends, and my stuffed camel, and I was ecstatic to learn that we were going to live in Beirut once again. I didn't mind the village rental house we were currently occupying, but it simply was not home. I imagined that moving back meant Druze and Christians had made up and everything was back to normal. I would soon discover how wrong I was.

One of my father's employees, a Christian man named Asa'ad, was going to help us with the transition. Since my father had repeatedly said that the Christians were our enemies, I was confused about how Asa'ad would assist us, but I just wanted to go home and I figured Asa'ad was part of the deal. I assumed it was Asa'ad's Christian friends who would allow us to live there. After all, most of our neighbors had always been Christians. We had all gotten along very well, so I was sure that with Asa'ad's help, they would give us the benefit of the doubt upon our return.

The drive back to the city seemed to take an eternity. We had to pass many checkpoints, something we never had to do in the past, but we finally got there. The neighborhood did not look the same as when we had left. As we parked on our street, I wanted to jump out of the car and run upstairs. However, sensing my father's agitation, I did nothing. I had become quite good at reading my father. He was angry all the time, and he sometimes took his anger out on us verbally and, at other times, physically. My ability to judge when he was close to delivering a beating saved me a lot of bruises, but I worried about my sisters, for they were not as attuned to his moods as I was.

I had gradually learned how to manage his verbal abuse. Initially, I resorted to kneejerk reactions to his taunting, but that never worked. In fact, it provoked him. So I tried to control my emotions and not react to his hateful words. This was very difficult and, of course, took an emotional toll on me, but it surely was better than receiving violent beatings. I've always hated the saying "Sticks and stones may break my bones, but words will never hurt me." Words do hurt—we internalize their impact, and it manifests in long-term psychological impairment.

As soon as we exited the car, I saw a number of family photographs scattered on the street. I knew right then that something was wrong. As we walked toward the building, we realized that the big glass front door had been shattered and glass was lying all over the building's foyer. Walking around the broken glass and up the stairs, I saw graffiti covering the walls of our perennially clean apartment building. It wasn't until I walked through the open door of our apartment that I finally saw the worst of it. The furniture had been slashed with some sharp instrument and turned upside down. All the wall hangings were slashed as well and thrown on the floor. The refrigerator door was lying on the kitchen floor, next to all our broken dishes. I was afraid to go into my bedroom because I did not want to see what destruction awaited me there. It wasn't until I saw my beloved camel cut to pieces that I started to cry. Who would do something like that? Why? I had thought that we would be returning to a place of refuge, to what was comfortable and familiar.

My father immediately ordered us to look for anything unbroken to take with us. *So we are running away again,* I thought. I realized I was about to lose what little control I had over my emotions. As my mother grabbed a bed sheet to use as a bag, I entered a plea for restoring sanity to our lives.

"Let's stay here and fix everything," I sobbed to my mother.

"I don't need more drama," she shot back at me. "Get your ridiculous camel. We are leaving."

"My camel is dead!" I screamed back at her, as loud as I could.

My sisters, both crying, ran up to me and held my hand. I was letting them down. They always looked to me for strength, and now I was falling to pieces. I stopped crying instantly and told my sisters that I would be fine.

"Home is wherever we three are, and I will find another camel," I whispered in their ears.

They beamed at me, and we set about rummaging through the wreckage of what used to be our home. We packed up our unmolested treasures and stuffed them in our and in Asa'ad's car; then we all got ready to depart. I felt an ache in my heart because I knew that this would be the last time I would see my home. I remembered my friends, our easy playing in the streets below, the generous candy-store owner, and, of course, my magical camel. When I finally accepted what was happening, I bid my home farewell. As we drove away, I turned back for a last look. I could not help but shed more tears.

The situation in Lebanon was growing progressively worse. In 1977, Palestinian forces continuously harassed Israeli troops. As a result, Israel advanced into southern Lebanon in 1978 but withdrew that same year. To protect its citizens from further attacks, Israel installed a Christian and Shi'a militia as a buffer along the border. Although they were supplied with arms and resources, the militias sustained continued attacks from the PLO and proved ineffective. The PLO continued to fire rockets into northern Israel. In 1981 and 1982, Israeli warplanes bombed multistory apartment buildings containing PLO offices in Beirut, killing not only many PLO fighters but hundreds of Lebanese civilians as well.

Between 1983 and 1985, various multinational efforts at reconciliation failed and violence worsened. During this time period, sectarian militias clashed continuously. Shi'a militias fought against each other, against Druze factions, and against the PLO.

OUR FAMILY HAD SETTLED INTO ANOTHER apartment building, located in West Beirut, in the early 1980s, and my parents enrolled me, Lola, and Rula in the Lebanese Evangelical School for Girls (LESG). Now older, I was more aware of the destructive nature of Lebanese factionalism. I came to a stunning conclusion: the national factionalism extended right down to the family level, where I saw the inequality my parents instituted between their female children and their sole male heir.

One day in our new apartment, I woke up early after a disturbing dream. Not wanting to burden my sisters, I walked silently to the kitchen to get something from the refrigerator.

"Good morning," I said softly to the maid.

Startled, she jumped up from the table where she was packing our school lunches.

"Miss Nada, you know I just do what I am told. I don't think it is right, but I do it anyways," she said rapidly.

I didn't know what she was talking about at first, but when I looked behind her, I figured it out. She had two sets of food: for my brother's lunch, she had packed sandwiches with expensive lunch meat and chocolate; for us girls, she was packing cheap, homemade *labne* (strained yogurt) sandwiches.

"We have different food for our school lunches. Is that all? What about breakfasts and dinners?" I asked her.

"Please, Miss Nada, don't ask me this question. I don't want to get in trouble. You and your sisters are not supposed to know about these things," she admitted.

The maid, I realized, was truly scandalized over this unfairness, but what could she do? I knew that my father had beaten her on several occasions and that my brother often verbally abused her. I did not want to cause her additional agony, so I promised that I would not utter a word to anyone about my discovery.

As if to make me feel better, she proceeded to confide that when my brother ordered her to bring him a cup of water, she served it to him with an additional ingredient: her spit. Given the way he treated her, I thought him deserving of her special water, and I kept her secret. I considered telling my sisters, but I didn't wish to add to their worries. I would later learn that both my sisters knew about the food management issues at home and had decided not to disclose their discoveries to me (or each other) for the same reason. It seemed the whole world was nothing but a stage for misunderstandings and unfairness. No one was living anything like an ordinary existence.

ENCOUNTER WITH AMERICA

"Medical care for the girls, in case they are injured in a bombing, could cost me a fortune," my father was explaining to my mother. "And, if they were maimed, we are stuck with them for the rest of our lives. Who is going to marry a handicapped girl? We need to relocate elsewhere, for some time at least, until the situation is relatively safe. Perhaps we can relocate to America, where your brother lives, and wait out the war. I will go to the American embassy and inquire about the process."

A week later, in March 1983, I went with my father to the American embassy. I was curious to see what these Americans looked like, whether all the negative press in Lebanon about Americans was accurate. Father parked our vehicle in the embassy parking lot, and we walked into the impressive horseshoe-shaped building. When I saw them—American soldiers—I could not help but stare. When one of them smiled and waved at me, I turned beet red. When I finally managed to stop staring at him, I looked around the room and saw the American flag. It had stars and red in it, two of my favorite things. I loved the order of the place, with people waiting patiently in line and taking turns receiving help from embassy staffers. I was not used to this sort of calm. My norm was chaos. There were no lines or turns taken anywhere in Lebanon—not government buildings or grocery stores. After Father finished his business, I locked eyes with the soldier who had greeted us and summoned the courage to wave back at him. When I told my sisters about my experience, we all talked about what the land of America must look like to have such friendly and helpful citizens. I told Rula and Lola that, after my encounter with the friendly embassy guard, I knew one thing for sure: Americans are not the monsters described on our TV.

In the weeks that followed, my father started getting the required documents for our move to America. I was very excited. America meant hope, a place of refuge far from all the chaos, war, and unfairness surrounding us in Beirut. I envisioned America as peace and calm.

Then, on April 18, a suicide bomber detonated a concealed bomb in the American embassy and killed sixty-three people, seventeen of whom were Americans. When my father drove us by the wreckage, I wondered whether my soldier friend had died. I remember hoping that he had survived this barbaric attack, but of course I couldn't know that for sure. All I knew was that I felt sick and fearful about the violence that never ended, the violence that seemed destined to erase us all at some unknown time in the future.

My father managed to secure the necessary documents required for our journey to America, and on September 19, 1983, we were given a five-year visa that would not expire until September 1988. However, after hearing promises of an imminent ceasefire, my father abruptly changed our plans. My dreams of escaping to a better world had vanished overnight. The militias had decided to take a break from the war, and the PLO was on its way out, headed to Tunis, but Lebanon remained a soldiers' haven.

SNIPERS BE GONE

The fragile ceasefire didn't last long. As another wave of sectarian violence ratcheted up, I realized it did not matter to me which religious factions were involved. What did affect me was the ongoing confinement at home. When factions clashed with machine guns in Beirut's narrow alleys and streets, we stayed inside and kept away from windows to avoid ricocheting bullets.

All this was a far cry from the freedom that would have greeted us in America. I really felt my father had misread the situation. For weeks, we were basically confined to one room in our home. Between the rationed electricity and my brother's continued badgering, I became restless and agitated. Our only sense of community was our fragile and limited interaction with the neighbors in the makeshift shelter of our isolated building.

The doorman, who lived on the underground floor between the twin six-story apartment buildings of our complex, had opened his home as a communal area, with numerous gaming tables where folks played cards and backgammon while enjoying strong Lebanese coffee or tea. Most interesting to me was what I came to call the "Legends of War" corner. The mythical stories spun in this small room, about the war and the sophisticated weapons the combatants used, entertained me. Whether it was the missile that knew its targets' names and chased them before it killed them or the bombs that exploded when the target said certain words, these stories only got better with time. In personifying bombs and missiles by giving them a sense of will and personality, the stories represented a sort of gallows humor that allowed us a measure of oppositional cynicism about the complete encroachment of the war on all our lives. The stories were especially fascinating when the real bombs and missiles were exploding in the background.

One of my favorite stories was about snipers. Snipers were professional shooters whose job it was to kill anyone—civilian, combatant, or other target—who happened to come into the crosshairs of their weapon's sights. In this way, a random—invisible, as it were—killing would create the chaos and fear necessary to empty the streets, ensuring that street-fighting militias could battle it out without having to shoot around pesky civilians. Most disturbing to me was the fact that snipers were allegedly paid a hundred dollars per kill, an unimaginably large sum of money to me then.

After hearing these sniper fables, I had a vivid dream. I dreamed that I was at a "sniper station," watching them report to work. They were all numbered, dressed in black with masks covering their faces, and their weapons had matching numbers. There also was a banker who stood next to them as they took their positions on rooftops. The banker held wads of hundred-dollar bills, ready to hand them one for each murdered civilian. I then dreamed that I was following an individual sniper. I watched closely as he climbed to the rooftop of a building adjacent to our own. When he reached his destination, he lay prone with his rifle, assuming his killing position. Moments later, he fired his gun. I got one, he screamed. The banker walked up to the sniper and asked him who he had killed, and the sniper responded that it was my sister Lola. Satisfied, the banker handed the assassin his pay.

I woke up terrified. I checked and saw that Lola was still alive. But, for days after my dream, I nursed a growing terror of snipers. I thought they were watching us, waiting to kill us when we weren't looking. My fear escalated to the point where I had to finally face it or be controlled by it. So, in an act of youthful defiance, I decided to do something.

It was a relatively calm afternoon. The sounds of a continued engagement were fading, and only occasional bursts of machine-gun fire were audible. Because in my dream, the snipers wore black with black face masks, I was curious to see what real snipers looked like, how they dressed, and if they might chose as a victim a young girl on an otherwise empty balcony. I walked to the door leading to our balcony, took a deep breath, knelt down, and opened it. On my belly, I crawled to the edge of the balcony. I waited a few minutes, then popped my head up for a second and immediately put it back down. Nothing happened. I repeated my actions a couple of times, each time staying up a bit longer. Still, nothing happened. I tried to see if I could identify anyone on any of the surrounding buildings' rooftops, but I couldn't. Finally, I decided to just sit up and concentrate on finding the well-paid snipers. After sitting for some time and not being able to see anyone, I decided to stand up. Perhaps that would give me a better angle.

I finally relaxed. *Snipers are not real,* I said to myself, and I placed my hands on my waist in a dismissive attitude.

"You don't scare me anymore," I said out loud.

Just as I was getting comfortable there, I heard a loud pop right above me and felt something drop on my head. I realized small chips of cement were raining down on me. I looked at the balcony wall and saw the bullet hole. I hadn't heard the originating shot because of the noise from the street fighters. I ran inside and hid in the kitchen. When I was finally able to breathe normally, I came out of my hiding spot and shared the story with my wide-eyed sisters. For some reason, although I initially had been scared and chastened by those shooting at my home, the experience removed my fear of snipers. *After all,* I thought, *what are my chances of being fired on again?*

UNDER PRESSURE

In 1982, a massacre had taken place in the Palestinian refugee camps Sabra and Shatila in Beirut. Hundreds of Palestinian refugees and Lebanese civilians were murdered by Lebanese Christian Phalangist Party members. These actions occurred at night in retaliation for the assassination of the Christian president-elect, Bachir Gemayel. It was reported that Israeli forces assisted the Phalangists in this operation by transporting them and firing illumination flares over the two camps to help direct the artillery fire. What I recall of the tragic incident was the photos of dead women and children continuously displayed on local television. Even more frightening was that politicians used this calamity to manipulate the Lebanese people. Israel was declared the enemy and blamed for everything wrong in Lebanon. While I didn't agree with Israel's involvement in the massacre, I remember finding it deplorable that the Lebanese leadership exploited the tragedy for its own propaganda purposes. They spread the rumor that Israel planned to commit another massacre against the Lebanese, arguing that anyone expressing a different opinion should be denounced as a traitor who was putting the country in danger.

In my experience, people seek to protect themselves from what they fear, and, as expected, the Lebanese people, fearing invasion by Israel, promptly gave up their voice in the debate over the future of the country. In their understandable desire to feel safe, they conceded absolute power to the politicians, a power the government wielded for any crackdown on dissent or negotiation they deemed appropriate. Of course, it also led to personal gain for both unscrupulous politicians and corrupted elements of the populace. Much of this private corruption was little short of brigandry: if you were in a dispute with a neighbor, one who had bravely challenged the government line, and you decided to murder that person, say in order to steal their belongings, you could claim to everyone that the neighbor was an Israeli agent who deserved to be eliminated.

A bunker mentality took hold in our house. My father's abusive behavior began to extend from us to my mother. Upon returning from one of his trips overseas, my father was visibly agitated. I was not sure whether it was a business-related issue or something else, but he accused my mother of cheating on him during his absence. When she denied it, he told her that he had a special way of knowing whether she was lying or telling the truth. He walked over to our large safe, which had a combination he alone knew and in which he kept valuables and money. He opened the safe with a few quick turns of the dial and retrieved his revolver. He walked over to his wife and put the gun to her temple.

"Now, tell me one more time, did you cheat on me?" he demanded.

Tears rolled down my mother's face as she told him that, no, she had not cheated on him. Father walked back to the safe, chuckling, and told her that he would be using the "truth detector" from now on, unannounced, to check on whether my mother was still faithful.

I felt sorry for my mother, but I did not understand why she treated her daughters so harshly, given the mistreatments she suffered herself. And I wondered why my father did not keep his heir in the safe with all his other valuables. My brother, too, thought the "truth detector" was a fun game. I thought about how much easier life would be for me, my sisters, and my mother if the men of our family could be permanently tucked away behind a foot of solid steel and only we had the combination.

EARLY MYSTERIES

For as long as I can remember, I have been inquisitive. An adult telling me "You will not understand" only made me more curious. Sometimes my youthful curiosity got me in trouble, as happened one day when I was nine or ten.

Druze traditional garb worn by males includes the *shirwal:* Aladdin-style baggy pants that are gathered at the waist with a drawstring and tight around the ankle. The extra baggy leg material is tied internally to form a hidden knot that sways when the person wearing the *shirwal* walks. The knot gives the impression of something hidden beneath the garment. I asked my mother what was hiding in the swaying material, and, in her usual dismissive attitude, she told me it was nothing. In fact, the *shirwal* is quite something. I convinced myself it was, most definitely, a secret hiding place. So, I was determined to solve the mystery of the strange lump. I had often seen a young boy, the son of a prominent sheikh in our Druze village, wearing the *shirwal* as he passed my grandfather's house after playing with one of his friends in our neighborhood. Who better to tell me about these strange pants than someone who wore them every day? So I recruited my Aunt Rima to help me in my sartorial investigation. Although she was my aunt (my mother's sister), Rima was a few months younger than I was.

"I'll bet you he stores chocolate or candy in there," I told Rima.

"Perhaps, if we guess right, we get to share some," Rima added.

She was eager to participate in the adventure. We waited on the balcony for the sheikh's son to pass, and when we saw him, we ran down to the street, stopped him in his tracks, and told him that we had a very important question.

"What do you girls want to know?" He sounded bored before we even began.

This attitude bothered me and bolstered my resolve to complete my mission. "We want to know what you keep in that ball," I said, pointing at the lump. He ignored the question and kept walking. I was now furious. I repeated my question, shouting this time. He kept walking away from us.

I looked at Rima and said, "Let's find out for ourselves." I charged toward him, and he began to run. Running was my specialty, and I knew he would not outrun me. I caught up to him, our feet got tangled, and he tripped as I was reaching for him. He tumbled to the ground and rolled upright, looking beyond shocked.

"Yes, I am a fast runner and I am a girl," I explained to him, breathing lightly. I noticed his breathing was quite labored as he got to his feet.

"Now, please, answer our question."

Rima caught up to us and stood next to him with her arms crossed. I decided to take further action. I pulled the drawstring and then the *shirwal* down and reached for the now revealed knot, hoping to find some candy.

"It's a knot of clothing," I revealed to Rima.

"Are you sure? Look some more," she said eagerly.

"I'm positive," I said, disappointedly.

"You girls are crazy," our quarry complained as he restored his *shirwal* to its proper position.

"Crazy maybe, but at least we have our answer," I replied, laughing.

We walked back home feeling let down by our lackluster discovery. "At least we know now," I told Rima.

Having satisfied my curiosity, I put the incident out of my mind until I saw the boy and his father in the living room of my grandfather's house days later. *Should I run away or face the music?* I wondered. I thought really hard and finally decided to stay and tell my side of the story. The sheikh asked his son to recount the event to my family members, all of whom were assembled in the living room.

"I was on my way home when two girls ran down from this house and started asking me questions," the boy began. "I did not want to talk to them, so they chased me and pushed me to the ground." He began to cry.

"Your girls were very rude to my son," the sheikh added, red-faced with anger. One of my aunts saw me peering in from an adjacent room and walked over to me. She wanted the whole story, so I told her.

In the meantime, my grandfather did not quite understand the story behind the story. After all, it was normal for boys to push, shove, and strike girls, and sometimes girls were permitted to defend themselves against this abusive behavior. It was unheard of for girls to start a fight as the sheikh was suggesting. Grandfather told our distinguished visitor that he, Grandfather, would get to the bottom of this and punish whoever was the culprit.

After I told my aunt what had happened, she tried to conceal her amusement as she went back to the living room to whisper to the other women. The sheikh, who was apparently too embarrassed to explain to my grandfather what had really happened, insisted on being allowed to severely punish Rima and me himself. My grandfather, who did not want to let the sheikh have the upper hand, agreed that punishment was necessary but promised to carry it out himself. With that, Grandfather saw the embarrassed sheikh and his less-than-fleet-of-foot son to the door, assuring the sheikh that he would soon hear reports of the great punishment.

All the women in the living room were snickering by now, covering their faces with their scarves and hands. When my grandfather called for me, I was a little nervous, but I figured, as long as he didn't tell my parents, who would most definitely beat me, I was fine. Grandfather's face was serious, and I suddenly feared some harsh accounting. But then, with just the hint of a smile curling at the edges of his thin lips, Grandfather told me that my punishment would be to help him in his vegetable garden.

I was quite happy to do that. The work in the vegetable garden was hard, but it was good, honest work. My grandfather knew that I loved spending time with him in one of his favorite spots. Standing in his garden, we talked about the incident, and at that point I realized that what I had done to the boy was wrong. I promised Grandfather I'd never again let my temper prompt me to bad behavior. But I also felt a little bit proud that the story made him laugh for the rest of the afternoon. I wondered what he would do when it came time for him to report my punishment to the sheikh.

SOME TIME AFTER THE *SHIRWAL* INCIDENT, a fresh round of sectarian violence erupted between the Druze and Shi'a Muslims in the early 1980s. During these types of skirmishes, civilians like us were confined to our homes. My sisters and I tried to entertain ourselves with drawing, reading, or playing games.

Lola and I were arguing about a Monopoly move when we heard a loud explosion.

"Oh no, here we go. Now we have to go to the shelter and we will not finish the game," I said. "I am winning, by the way."

After the ringing in our ears subsided, Lola challenged me: "You think you are winning, but I am planning a big comeback."

"You two, I have the most real estate, so I am declaring myself the winner," Rula, who we called "Roro," declared.

Father, holding Fadi, yelled for everyone to head to the shelter. As my parents and Fadi left, I told Roro to go with them.

"We will be right there. Don't worry, Roro," I assured her.

Asking Roro to trust my parents was not easy, but I wanted to grab some extra clothes before leaving the house. God only knew when we would be able to come back.

As I was rummaging in my closet for some clean clothes, I heard the loud shrieks I had come to know too well. Most likely a mother mourning the death of a child or a loved one, I thought to myself. The bombings were not part of typical street fighting, but perhaps the Druze were shelling Beirut from their strategic mountain hideout. If that was the case, I was upset at their audacity, shelling innocent civilians. I knew these practices were not limited to Druze militia, but I was equally disgusted with all the militias' agendas: to destroy Lebanon for their own personal gain.

Lola and I got what we needed, then left for the shelter. Because of the continuous machine gun exchanges, the street outside our house was a particularly dangerous area. Bullets were flying everywhere, and to get to the safety of the shelter, we had to expose ourselves briefly to the street.

The exchanges died down a bit when the fighters were loading their guns, so I took a deep breath and sprinted through the area facing the street. I waited for Lola for a few minutes, but when she did not come, I began to worry. I called out to her a couple of times, but she did not respond. My heart started to beat faster. I knew I had no choice but to go back to the dangerous spot. Was Lola injured? Had someone taken her? I was getting anxious and continued to call her in an even louder voice. Finally, I ran back and took cover behind a wall from where I could see Lola. She was frozen in place, staring at a body lying in a pool of blood. I shouted at her to run. Over the sound of bullets whizzing by, I begged her to come to me. Transfixed, Lola did not appear to hear a word I was saying. Finally, I ran to her, grabbed her hand, and pulled her to safety.

Not until we were close to the shelter did Lola come out of her hypnotic state.

"It is Kamal," she burst out crying.

Kamal was a boy who we used to see running around in our neighborhood. Like many boys in Lebanon, Kamal had joined the Druze militia. I think some of those kids viewed the militias as some kind of an exciting club where they could socialize with other bored teenagers. Of course, the militias took advantage of those kids, arming them and sending them out to fight. As a child myself, I wondered how these militias operated. Who armed and financed them? Who decided what the militia's objectives were? I often heard adults discuss politics, and although I did not understand all the details, one thing I did take away was that none of the political factions or politicians cared for the Lebanese citizens. It seemed clear that politicians were getting rich by selling out their people.

One of my favorite theories for the cause of the Lebanese civil war came from an elderly neighbor who was relatively well educated. He preached to anyone who would listen that the two big powers, America and Russia, both wanted to take over Lebanon owing to its strategic location and would not allow peace until one of them had control over the country. I had heard virtually every theory imaginable about my country's troubles, so this didn't seem like a stretch. Blaming outsiders for Lebanon's trouble was an easy way to shift blame, so many citizens eagerly latched on to this geopolitical theory.

CHARADE 3

We were all in the car heading for a visit with relatives. Although still in my teens, I was old enough to know that these visits were all about showcasing marriageable girls to the Druze community.

"Put your best outfits on," my father had ordered me and my sisters. Although wealthy by any standard, my father "invested" in his daughters only to enhance our chances of attracting an acceptable suitor. It did not bother me when my parents bought the most expensive clothes from Europe for my brother while dressing us in secondhand clothing. I was a bit of a tomboy, and clothes were well down on my list of important things in life. However, it did bother me when my father bought each of us girls one nice outfit for the express purpose of parading us in front of much older Druze men. I resented being auctioned off like a prize.

This cultural tradition is incredibly derogatory to young women, and it disgusted me. Going with my sisters made the situation more tolerable because we could devise certain ruses to throw off our leering husbands-to-be. We conspired to pick our noses when suitors stared and discussed the best way to feign a lazy eye or a limp.

That day my father was over-the-top angry—about what, we had no idea. His moods were like that—one never knew if something particular had set him off or if he was simply giving vent to his loathing of the world in general. Anyway, his black mood did not bode well for us. It meant that there was a good chance he would pawn one of us off on the family we were to visit.

On the drive to the auction, he asked us whether one of us had some Chapstick for his severely chapped lips. My sisters and I had been discussing what ailment we should fake when a plan occurred to me.

"Father will be the one to nix any arrangement this time," I whispered to my sisters.

"I found some," I announced to my father as I handed him my "Chapstick."

Both Lola and Roro looked at me in bewilderment.

"What on God's earth are you doing?" Lola whispered.

I had given my father a tube of my Magic Lipstick, which goes on colorless at first but eventually turns the wearer's lips bright pink. Father temporarily adjusted the car's rearview mirror, applied the "Chapstick," and handed it back to me.

I could not help but burst out laughing when I saw the expressions on the family members' faces as they opened the door to us and looked at Father. Needless to say, he was mortified—and extremely angry. While I got an earful from him on what a disrespectful little gimp I was, my prank succeeded in warding off any wedding engagements that day. My sisters and I were still free, and we hadn't even had to dip into our bag of tricks for the wandering eye or the rickety limp.

WHEN HELP IS DANGEROUS

One day in the mid-1980s, a young man stood in our doorway begging for water, food, and any kind of help we were willing to provide. He was bleeding from wounds to his ear and foot. His ear injury was not as serious as his foot injury, which was bleeding heavily. I watched, from just inside the door to our apartment, as he leaned heavily against the wall outside. A small pool of blood was gathering beneath him. Without food or water, and losing blood so quickly, his fate was all too predictable.

"No, we will not help him," screamed my father from behind me. "If we did, we would be picking sides, and that would mean we could be in danger ourselves."

I retrieved a cool, damp washcloth from our kitchen and took it out to our visitor, ignoring my father's screams. I could see pain flooding his eyes. His brow was deeply furrowed. I did not know which of the two currently battling coalitions, Hizballah or Amal, he belonged to, and it did not matter to me. He clearly didn't understand why or what he was fighting anyway; both Amal and Hizballah were Shi'a groups. They were fighting to gain power and control over Beirut's future. By controlling territory, their leaders could quickly become wealthy for life. But they needed fodder for the battleground, and disaffected kids like the young man bleeding on our doorstep were easy pickings. Somehow, despite his badly damaged foot, he had made it to our doorstep and away from the killing.

Our last name, which was displayed on the doorbell, was clearly a Druze last name, and this teenager probably determined that, as Druze, we would aid him. After all, the Druze had withdrawn from this round of the conflict. Knocking on the door of a Shi'a family who supported the group he was fighting could mean his death, and I'm sure that he must have been apprehensive about asking for any kind of help from complete strangers. When my mother, also screaming from inside the apartment, started to complain about having to clean up the mess he was making, I stuck my head back into the living room and told both my parents that I would tell him, privately, that our family could not help him. Having him stand there while we argued about what to do struck me as grossly unfeeling, even cruel.

My parents finally quieted down, and I remained outside in the entryway. I told the young man I was going to go back inside and shut the door, but that I would be back after a few minutes.

"I'll get you some water and food," I whispered, "but please be quiet. I don't want my parents to find out I am helping you."

"Thank you," he moaned.

I closed the door and immediately rounded up my sisters. I needed their help.

"We are going to help this boy," I said adamantly. "Roro, you are in charge of watching our parents and alerting us if they come to the kitchen."

"Lola, you go to the kitchen and prepare a package with food and water; I will find some antibiotic solution and some gauze for his wound."

Tasks delegated, we all dispersed. It took some maneuvering around our parents, but we were successful in rounding up the needed supplies. When I had everything in hand, I made my way to the front door while Lola joined Roro on watch duty.

By this time, the pool of blood had grown much bigger, and the kid looked white as a ghost. I handed him the package, but he was too weak to hold it. I helped him drink some water and eat a slice of cheese. He had taken off his busted-up shoes and socks and was trying to tie his sock around his wound, so I splashed some alcohol on the open wound and wrapped it with some of the gauze. He was still hemorrhaging, and the white gauze turned red immediately. I used the rest of the gauze, but the blood soaked right through. I did not know what to do, so I sat with him, telling him that he would feel better soon and that he would be with his family in no time. I heard a quiet knock, the signal that my parents were nearby. I stood up and told him that I had to go back inside.

"Thank you so much," he smiled.

I ran inside and met up with Lola and Roro. I did not want to tell them what I really thought would happen to the boy: that it was going to take a miracle for him to survive. Instead, I told them that he looked good and was in good spirits, and they were both pleased that taking a chance to help someone had resulted in a good outcome. Later, I looked through the peephole to find him gone. There was a lot of blood in the entryway, and I offered to clean it. While cleaning his blood, I wondered why he had been shot and if he had also shot someone else. I thought about his family and whether his parents were aware of his involvement with militias. They probably had no idea that he was injured. I prayed that he would live and would learn from this experience that militia leaders used people like him to achieve personal goals and would abandon fighters like him in a heartbeat. Looking back, I don't regret helping that kid regardless of the potential danger to which I exposed myself. Sometimes, doing the right thing means taking a chance.

THE CONSEQUENCES OF BEING CHILDREN

When I peeked out the window and saw the soldiers walking in front of our house toward higher elevations in the east, I silently blamed them for my home incarceration. I was about thirteen years old then; I felt that I should have been playing outside with my siblings instead of being stuck in the house. They were armed with machine guns, dressed in green military fatigues, and looked tired and beaten down. They would stop to eat figs from the tree across the road from our home or steal apples from the orchards about a hundred yards east, up a slight hill. They were ragged Palestinian soldiers escaping their strongholds in the Maten Mountains, which Israeli planes were bombarding.

"Don't even think about it." My father looked at me, knowing what was on my mind. I wanted to go outside and talk to them, and I knew it would drive him crazy. *So*, I thought, *there is reason number two to speak my piece to the Palestinians.*

The soldiers appeared to be in their teens, and their soft, boyish faces bore the slack look of hopelessness. I decided that while I might not get an audience with them, I could at least let my pitifully apolitical father know what I was thinking. So I asked Father which of Lebanon's many depraved and immoral leaders were using these misguided teens to do their dirty work. I used just those words, and Father flew into a rage, accusing me of being too dense to ever be a good, silent wife to some important man.

Yes, the discussion always seemed to come back to my suitability for marriage. It was a subject that continued to raise my ire. I asked the question again and again, but my father, tired of yelling, just walked away, leaving me to figure out what I could learn from the troops in the streets below. But our meeting never came to pass. Another round of shelling had suddenly driven everyone off the streets.

The air assaults continued for days. Sighing against the glass door to our balcony, watching the window fog up, I knew that soon we would go to the basement for protection and would only come back up to street level when the bombs stopped falling. We had already been cooped up at home for weeks now. The PLO was leaving Beirut, and skirmishes were popping up at all times and in all places. We were all on edge and, oddly, bored.

I managed to persuade my father to let me and my sisters play in the playground area near our mountain home. This area was the parking lot of what had once been a hotel. The hotel had been converted into a textile factory sometime after the civil war started. My father usually parked our burgundy Oldsmobile right next to the house, but this time he parked it next to the entrance to the factory, thinking that the manufacturer would be relatively safe from aerial bombardment.

As my sisters and I grabbed our ball and headed out, my father told us that we had to include our brother in the game. Grumbling, we consented. We dragged Fadi down to the street, where we decided on dodgeball and started marking out boundaries for the game.

We noticed a large group of Palestinian soldiers walk by. The Israeli planes that had been flying overhead during most of the day began to swoop closer to the ground. I was a bit concerned, but I reasoned that the Israeli pilots would not bomb the soldiers. The pilots, flying so low, must have been able to see that the soldiers were not carrying surface-to-air weapons.

We were totally absorbed in the dodgeball game when the first cluster bomb exploded in the apple orchard. I stood still for a moment, trying to figure out what to do next, surrounded by the relentless popping from the bomblets. I screamed to my siblings to run and hide behind our father's car, which was parked about a hundred feet away from our dodgeball court.

While we were running for cover, a second cluster bomb went off. Judging by its sound, it was much closer to us than the first. I was momentarily afraid that it might have hit our home, but all I could focus on was finding a safe place to hide.

"Faster!" I hollered at my siblings.

"Get behind the car."

When we all got behind the car, I told everyone to hide behind the wheels, thinking rubber would protect us better than the car's metal. As we huddled between the rear wheels and the factory wall, the third bomb exploded right where we had been playing.

"Heads down, everyone," I yelled.

I don't know why, but I instinctively jumped on top of my siblings. The percussive blasts of the cluster bomb continued, and one of the bomb's fragments blew out the window above us and broke a box of metal snaps that fell on my back. Adrenalin started rushing through my body, as I assumed that I had been hit by the shrapnel. The cold snaps running down my back felt like blood. An eerie silence followed, during which I realized that I was uninjured.

Then, out of the terrible silence, we heard our father's voice calling. I was still in shock, but I thought, *Our father is genuinely concerned for us. I could have died just now.* All of us had been right there, playing a stupid game of dodgeball in the middle of a stupid war. But Father was looking for us. I knew it! *Father loves us girls; he just has a funny way of showing it sometimes,* I told myself proudly.

Then I was checking Fadi, and Roro, and Lola. They were all fine. Suddenly, our father's voice was right on top of us.

"Is Fadi all right?" Father's voice shook a bit, and he looked at me, expecting an answer. His only concern seemed to be my brother's welfare.

Suddenly furious, I screamed back at him.

"We are *all* OK! *All* of us are OK! Fadi is OK!"

Father carried Fadi back to the house, and we all ran behind him. No matter how hard I tried to please my father, it seemed to me that my efforts were always futile. Not even the threat of my death could change the way he thought of me.

LOSING A SISTER

The fall of 1988 found Rula and me, crying loudly, bidding our sister Lola goodbye. Lola, unbeknownst to us, had secretly started dating a Muslim man, Tariq, and had fallen in love with him. In her new-found state of mind, she knew that if she and her lover were to have a future together, it would not be a future in Lebanon. Tariq had persuaded Lola to travel to America, where they could spend time together and give their relationship a chance to develop without the fear of death hanging over them. Lola, using the visitor's visa my father had acquired, was leaving with Tariq for America. She had found a way out of our family nightmare.

As the eldest sister, Lola had always tried to shelter Rula and me by taking the brunt of the abuse from my parents and brother. During the preceding two years, I had noticed a change in her personality. She had become more withdrawn, quiet, and compliant. The years of belittling, shaming, and humiliation had finally worn down her spirit. One day, while searching for an item of clothing, I found a letter written by Lola and addressed to "my real parents." In the letter, Lola created imaginary "real" parents and told them that it was time for them to come back and retrieve us girls from the "man and woman" who were currently playing the role of our parents. Lola wrote that she had completely forgiven the man and woman playing the role of our parents, but she wanted these other parents to immediately come and change our living conditions. Lola had always internalized her feelings, which often led me to believe that she was fine. The letter made me realize just how much pain and suffering she had been carrying around. I knew that leaving our home and Lebanon would be better for her than trying to make a go of a relationship in the face of all our difficulties. But losing my sister, who had tried her best to protect me and Rula from the abuse, was difficult. My life at home would now have a huge hole in it; I would now have to occupy the places where Lola had stood tall against my father's brutish behavior. I knew now that my responsibility was to protect Rula the way Lola had protected both of us.

Along with my parents' abuse, I also had to weather beatings from my brother, which my parents encouraged in response to any real or imagined offense I might commit. As a male, he was in training to dominate and control females. Because we were older than he was and could physically defend ourselves from his violence, my parents would often hold us girls down and cheer Fadi on to beat us harder. This was the sort of education that my brother grew up with.

As any child unfortunate enough to experience this type of abuse can tell you, sibling abuse is often the cruelest and most damaging form of abuse. Feeling betrayed by a loved brother or sister, victims usually turn to their parents for help; in my case, my parents condoned and encouraged my brother's extreme behavior. Arab culture, like many other cultures worldwide, favored boys over girls, but my parents took this favoritism to an extreme. Perhaps my parents were unaware of any point of view different from their own Druze background. The Druze, in part, believed in cosmic rulers who embodied the most ethical aspects of mind and soul. The good was important. But Druze doctrine also included evil anti-beings who created a cosmic battleground of good versus evil. Perhaps, I thought, my parents were emanations of these evil anti-beings. It was hard for me to understand where my parents' bad behavior came from. To this day, I am still trying to figure out an answer to that question.

THE LAST STRAW

I woke up bruised and lying in a pool of blood. I realized that I had been unconscious and bleeding for some time. My entire body ached as I stood up and tried to exit the bathroom, but the door had been locked from the outside. I was a prisoner.

I sat on the floor and recalled what had happened. My father normally did not need an excuse to beat his daughters, but this time he'd come up with one: I had changed the channel on a television show that, unbeknownst to me, my brother had been watching. This oversight upset my brother and incurred my father's wrath. By then, my father required little provocation to assert his dominance. His anger had grown into a hardened habit. This time, after he beat me severely with his fists, he threw me in the bathroom and locked the door.

My sister Rula sat outside the bathroom door, whispering how terrified she was and asking repeatedly whether I was all right. When the coast was clear, it was Rula who let me out.

With Lola no longer around to protect us as best she could, Rula and I supported each other in dealing with my parents. Just a week before the television-related beating, I had held Rula's hands during her root canal. To save money, my parents had told the dentist not to use anesthesia. Given their wealth, this was unfathomable to me, and it led me to conclude that my parents' issues with us girls, particularly my father's issues, were really not all about money. There also seemed to be a sadistic element in the pleasure he derived from our pain. These were the sick, elitist, woman-fearing actions of a man who was completely out of touch with anything remotely spiritual.

I left my bathroom prison physically battered, but I knew, deep down, that I had the will to survive. As a result of my maltreatment, I had learned unique ways of dealing with agony and hardship. I was always prepared for the worst and ready to roll, both literally and figuratively, with the punches. This toughness would prove useful to me in the future when I found myself being bullied by others intent on smearing my good name. And the battles with my brother and my parents also instilled in me another part of who I am. My childhood, beset as it was with war and family abuse, certainly elicited in me a desire for normalcy. And whatever anyone has to say about normalcy—that it may be a myth or a state of mind that excuses the oppression of the have-nots at the expense of those who have—I sought after that normal existence.

BOMBING AT THE IC

After graduating from secondary school in 1989, I applied to and was accepted at the American University of Beirut (AUB). Before learning of my acceptance, my father visited the AUB dean and in true Lebanese fashion claimed to know a number of Lebanese politicians who were anxious to learn of my acceptance. Connections to powerful people, also known as "vitamin W," or *wasta,* was a way of life. Lebanese love to drop names and claim connections to important, connected people—sometimes movie stars and other celebrities—whether they have them or not. To me, a college degree meant not only postponement of an arranged marriage but also potential independence from my parents. Like Scheherazade of old, I wanted to do what I could, in a creative fashion of course, to postpone my fate. To my parents, it was an investment in my chances of marrying rich. A college-educated girl would attract suitors from the upper echelon of Lebanese society.

In early 1989, we were in chemistry class when we heard the first bomb explode. It had landed squarely on the American University of Beirut's track field. My immediate concern was to wonder if anyone had been injured, but I also realized that even in the best-case scenario, one of my favorite places to exercise might not be available to me in the future. Once an area was bombed, it became "registered" among the locals as a potential target in the exchange of fire.

As usual when a round of bombing hit, chaos ensued. Everyone rushed to a safe location, such as a shelter or the basement floor of a building. I packed my book bag and headed to the basement floor of our school, the International College (IC), debating whether I should run home or wait out the shelling in the basement. Sometimes the bombings would subside after a few minutes and everything would return to normal, so I decided to hang out in the shelter and talk to the students who were waiting for their parents to pick them up. These situations of extreme stress made students close to one another, and, although I did not like being bombed, I did enjoy the times when shared danger made everyone pull together. Living in a war environment, you really have to sometimes force yourself to look at the glass as being half full; otherwise, you allow the war to take over your life.

As I sat with my fellow students and chatted, the second wave of bombing began. Although many children would be happy that school would likely be closed the following day because of the bombings, I dreaded being home more than I dreaded the actual bombing attacks. The situation at home, in so many ways, was worse than the war itself. Our new home in West Beirut was now within walking distance from my school, but I routinely lingered around the campus until all of my friends had departed before I trudged toward our unhappy home.

On this day, with the bombing over and my good friends gone, I was preparing to leave our basement refuge when I heard the terrified screams of a young child coming closer. Students were ushering her to the basement floor, where the remaining students were all located. She looked to be about eleven or twelve years old, and she was obviously feeling lost and frightened, so I rushed to her and attempted to calm her down. When I discovered she did not understand Arabic, I quickly switched to English and asked her whether she was being picked up. She told me no, there was no ride coming, adding that she had run from her school, the American Community School (ACS), to fetch her sister here at IC.

"I didn't know what I was supposed to do, so I came for my sister. I have only been in Lebanon for a few months," she sobbed. "I am American," she added.

Some students heard her declaration and gave her a suspicious glance. I felt awful for this child who, I assumed, had been plucked from a stable environment in her native country and brought to Lebanon to live under horrible conditions. We looked for her sister among the remaining students, but we were not able to find her.

"Your sister was probably already picked up and your parents are probably on their way to get you at ACS," I told her. The ACS catered to international students or children of Lebanese immigrants who were not educated in the Arabic language. The ACS and the IC were within walking distance of each other, both overlooking the Mediterranean Sea. I was hoping what I had told her was true—that there had been a simple mix-up in picking her up.

"I am too scared to walk back to my school," she confessed.

"We can walk back together," I told her.

Although walking back would expose us to some danger, I reasoned that it would put her family in greater danger to walk around trying to figure out where she was. Besides, no bombs had fallen for the last half-hour or so. I left my book bag in the basement and held her hand while we headed up to the street to begin our trip to her school. I explained to her that we might hear some loud noises, and if we did, we needed to focus on one thing only: running to the shelters at the ACS.

"All right, ma'am," she answered politely.

I could see the unsure look in her eyes, so I held her hand firmly, and we raced out of the building. I hoped that the halt in the bombing would last while we made our dash to her school.

Halfway to our destination, we heard an explosion so loud that the sound alone almost knocked us down. My new companion screamed loudly and pointed at her ears.

"Your ears will ring for a while, but you will be fine," I explained, but I instantly realized that the ringing in her ears would prevent her from hearing my words.

"Stay focused and keep running. We are halfway there," I shouted, as much to myself as to her. She held my hand tighter, and we kept running. I was surprised by her determination; I had been worried I would have to carry her at least part of the way.

When we arrived at the ACS, both out of breath, she spotted her family's car in the adjacent lot.

"There they are," she shouted. I could barely hear her now and realized the ringing in my ears was quite loud. Over the ringing in our ears, she pointed at the vehicle.

"Run. Go, now!" I shouted at her. She let go of my hand and ran to her family's car. I waited for her to get in the car and for the door to close. As the driver pulled away fast, I saw her in the rear window, waving happily to me. I caught my breath, ran back to the IC, picked up my bag, and went home. I did not tell my parents about this as I was sure that they would criticize me for exposing myself to the bombing. I never saw the girl again, and I wondered whether she and her parents returned to America. I also wondered why someone would leave America to come to a war. What strange or scary events must have happened to drive them to return to a place torn apart by conflict?

PLAN B

All of our plans for my future were disrupted in 1989 by a major dissolution of the Lebanese government. AUB shut down after weeks of heavy bombing, and I knew this would change things for me at home: I was a depreciating investment that needed to be liquidated sooner rather than later. After my older sister, Lola, rejected a rich suitor chosen by our father and left Lebanon for America, I became the oldest "available" daughter. My father expected me to step up and accept a proposal that would enhance our family's business portfolio. In his reasoning, Lola's refusal to carry out his plans had tarnished the family's reputation, and only I could recover our marred honor.

Despite the peril to our family's honor and my father's pocketbook, I did not want to sacrifice my life to a loveless marriage. Arranged marriages were the norm in Lebanon and are still common today, but they are becoming less prevalent as Lebanese society slowly modernizes. My knowledge of romantic relationships was solely based on the Harlequin novels I read without my parents' knowledge. I imagined marriage as an adventure in which two people love each other unconditionally and treat each other as equals. I fantasized about meeting my knight in shining armor, a man who would sweep me off my feet and carry me to a loving home where I would be a contributing partner in our future.

In Druze culture, dating was prohibited, even punishable by death under certain circumstances. Yet I refused to be a pawn in my father's game. I knew what I had to do. I needed to follow in Lola's footsteps and continue my education in America.

I called Lola to inform her of the situation. Lola had left without my parents' financial support, and although I did not realize it at the time, she was struggling to make ends meet in America. Despite her difficulties, Lola knew I would be better off struggling in America than acquiescing to my parents' wishes. She sent me applications to a number of colleges in Michigan, where she was living, and I filled them out. Two months later, I was accepted at Detroit College of

Business. I was getting closer and closer to escaping my father's plan. But escape was not my only motive: I was determined to make a success of my life.

In June 1989, I was in a taxi with Samar, Lola's best friend from school, and her mother heading to Damascus, Syria, to apply for a student visa. The American embassy in Lebanon was closed because of the political and security situation. Samar also was facing some tough family matters: Samar, who adored her father, had learned that he had a second wife and a child whom he had kept secret from her. (Multiple wives are not illegal in Muslim society, though men are limited to four wives.) Devastated, Samar stopped eating, and her weight had dropped to a mere fifty pounds. Her mother, fearing for Samar's life, thought that leaving Lebanon to continue her education elsewhere would give Samar a chance at survival. Samar, too, had filled out the applications that Lola sent and had been accepted at Detroit College of Business.

We arrived in Damascus and spent the night at the home of Samar's relatives. They were gracious and hospitable. Samar and I needed to be up very early to line up for entry into the embassy. Worried that I would oversleep and miss my opportunity, I barely got any sleep. Samar's mother woke early and prepared breakfast for us. Although Samar had not eaten a proper meal in weeks, her mother always prepared food for her in the hope that she would change her mind.

Samar's food went untouched, and her relative dropped us off at the embassy. As we waited in line, I reviewed my documents again to make sure I had not forgotten anything. I had my passport, my acceptance letter from Detroit College of Business, and a few of my father's bank statements, among other necessities. After processing through security and entering the embassy, we were given numbers and asked to wait our turn. When my number was called, I headed to the booth where a consular officer waited behind a glass window.

"Good morning," he said with a smile.

I was nervous and could barely hear myself reply. I handed him the envelope, and he opened it and examined my documents.

"Your five-year multi-entry visa expired a few months ago," he told me.

"Yes. We did not travel to America after all," I explained.

"Why do you want to get your college degree from America?" he asked.

I wanted to tell him how dim my future looked if I stayed in Lebanon to endure my parents' abuse and capitulate to an arranged marriage, but I was too embarrassed.

"Well, the American University of Beirut is closed because of the war," I answered him.

"Good enough," he said, and waved me back to the waiting room. I wasn't sure whether my interview had gone well, but I followed his instruction and waited. A few minutes later—though it felt like an eternity—I was called back and handed my passport with a student visa stamp. I looked at it in disbelief. Then I realized that the visa would expire in one year. I told the officer that I was planning to attend a four-year program and did not understand why I had gotten a one-year visa.

"They will adjust it when you get to the States," he clarified.

I waited anxiously for Samar, praying for her to pass through, too. Unfortunately, she did not. She and her mother were extremely disappointed. Out of respect for their feelings, I did not celebrate or show my excitement. I hoped that in the future she would find a way to come join me.

We traveled back to Lebanon by taxi. On the way I started pondering ways to approach my parents, for I wanted to leave as quickly as possible. I gazed at the passing Beqaa Valley. Its rich fields, peppered with sun-washed buildings, contrasted with the deep green of the trees. Looking upon this beautiful Lebanese landscape, it occurred to me that I would need my parents to perceive my trip as an investment in my brother and the family's future. My brother had performed poorly academically and had behavioral problems that had gotten him expelled from a number of schools. At this rate, college in Lebanon would be a stretch for him. Having both sisters in America could open up different doors for him.

At home, I told Rula my news. She was genuinely happy for me but, understandably, a bit anxious about being left behind with my parents. In an attempt to prepare me for bad news, she told me that she seriously doubted my parents would pay for my ticket or spend any money on the college tuition. I told her my idea about our brother, and she thought it was genius.

As I had hoped, my approach struck a chord with my parents. Securing my brother's future was their sole priority. I explained to them how I planned to find a college in America for my brother and how I would cost them less money if I left Lebanon. Running down some numbers aloud, my father agreed that my departure meant big savings for him. They reluctantly said they'd pay for a one-way ticket to America and the tuition for one semester.

"Imagine the suitor she would attract if she graduated from a college in America," I heard my father bragging to my mother as I left the room. I assured myself that when I returned to Lebanon, there would be no suitor. I would find a job, become totally independent of my parents, and move to my own place.

All of the following week, I worked on getting my ticket and readying myself. I found an old torn-up suitcase and piled all my clothes and shoes in it. I did not have a lot of clothes, so it only took a few minutes. I made sure to leave behind all the expensive European clothes whose purpose had been to auction me off to suitors. I was leaving that life, and if I accomplished what I dreamed, I would never need clothes like that again.

I was one step closer to freedom and I could taste it. *Don't count your chickens until they have hatched,* I reminded myself. But, in my mind's eye, I already saw chickens roaming freely all over the place.

My flight was booked for June 23, 1989, my bags were packed, and I was counting down the days. I spent time with friends and said goodbye to neighbors and relatives. I caught myself daydreaming and staring into space, euphoric and overwhelmed.

Just days before my departure, my father called me into the kitchen. My heart was racing; I did not want anything to get in the way of my future. Apparently, news of my departure had traveled, and my parents had received an "inquiry" from a wealthy family about my "availability." My father knew that with the ticket already purchased and the cash in my hand, he was not in the driver's seat, so he softened his usual bullying approach and asked me to rethink my "America plan."

"You will have maids, clothes, jewelry, a fancy car, a driver, a big, beautiful home, and whatever you need," he explained.

I wanted to tell him that none of these material things meant anything to me; I longed to tell him that I wanted someone to love me and not buy me, but mostly, I wanted to tell him that I hoped to be as far away from him and his kind as possible. Instead, in a rare instance of good sense, I reminded him of my brother's future. "You need me to go to America because Lola alone isn't enough to help Brother," I told him.

"I know we have not been in good contact with Lola, but I am sure we can get hold of her and she could look into colleges for your brother," he answered.

I saw my dream slipping away. Father wanted to put Fadi in my place. Suddenly, I feared my "value" was too liquid.

"I need a few days to think about this," I quickly offered.

There was no point in arguing with him every day until my departure, so I figured I would wait until the last possible moment to tell him that I'd rather die than sell myself. Two days before my scheduled flight, I broke this news to him. Irate and bitter, he finally gave up and accepted my decision.

America, here I come!

COMING TO AMERICA 4

"Go ahead and fail in America!"

My father, still angry with me for refusing the marriage he had arranged, shouted these words at me as I passed through my last security checkpoint at Damascus International Airport. I was nineteen and on my way to the land of freedom. June 23, 1989, the day of my flight, marked nearly fourteen years of bitter civil war in Lebanon. I desperately needed to get away from the violence.

As I sank into my seat on the plane, I was overwhelmed by the thought of all the uncertainty ahead. I soon dropped off into a deep sleep. Waking once in the twinkling darkness of the nighttime cabin, I heard my father's words again: "Go ahead and fail in America." Was my plan all wrong? I didn't dwell on that possibility. My sister would know how to help, I thought, and with that I dozed off, waking only when the plane began its descent into New York City's LaGuardia Airport.

At that time, America was an unknown land for me. The anti-Western propaganda in Lebanon did not help ease my fears. A majority of Beirut's newspapers, radio broadcasts, and political parties claimed that Americans hated Arabs, would never welcome them as equals, and would certainly never accept Arab traditions in American communities. My experience with Americans indicated otherwise. The calm, strong demeanor of the American peacemakers who had come to Beirut when I was just entering my teens had contrasted starkly with the violent hatred between rival militia groups in the civil war. This led me to imagine America as a place where problems were addressed reasonably and solved more often than not. America, I believed, would reveal her true character to me through the personal laboratory of my own experiences.

My chances for a better future would increase greatly once I secured an American college education. My future in Lebanon without that degree would be to compromise, obey, and slowly erase myself. I wanted something different. I wanted to break the cycle of dependency on men and become self-sufficient, free to pursue my own hopes and dreams. I knew, without question, that my choice to pursue education in America was right: I had escaped a miserable life sentence. I was young when I stepped off that plane in New York. Youth was on my side, and youth is a powerful force when freedom is a goal. The moment I touched American soil, I embraced a new motto: to always ally myself with the promise and the hope that I believed existed in America.

The immigration official looked at my passport and asked me for my name. Thinking this was a test of my heritage, I took a deep breath and blurted: "Nada Nadim Nassib Muhammad Mahmoud Kassem Abbas Faour Al-Aouar."

He glanced at me from under his thick glasses before looking at my passport again. He smiled thinly. "What is your abbreviated name?" he inquired.

"Nada Nadim Al-Aouar," I replied bashfully. He then asked me whether I would be attending Detroit College of Business for a four-year bachelor's program, and I said yes. He stamped my passport and attached a form to it.

"Is this my permission to study in Detroit?" I asked him eagerly. "For all four years?"

"Yes, look at the form, please," he said. "You are all set to go."

The officer at the American embassy in Damascus had been correct, I thought. An American official did adjust my one-year visa to a four-year stay, and he did it immediately upon my entry to the States.

When the official saw the anxious look on my face, he relaxed, smiled, and said, "Welcome to America."

After passing through immigration, I asked, in my heavily accented English, about my luggage. I was informed, in the most rapid English I had ever heard, that I needed to pick it up at the international arrivals terminal. Although able to communicate, I was very nervous. I had a hard time understanding English spoken at that speed, but people were generally nice about slowing down a little if asked.

Three Arab women who had apparently heard me speaking English approached to ask in Arabic about the next step on our journey to Detroit. Before I knew it, I had a trail of elderly Arab men and women following me to the domestic terminal. I liked helping people and enjoyed leading the pack.

After boarding the Detroit-bound flight, my anxiety returned. I had a window seat, and, to distract myself, I glanced below, where I saw a sea of lights. I was so amazed that I had to share it with the man sitting next to me.

"You have a lot of lights in America!" I said. Because of the war in Lebanon, electricity was constantly being rationed, and only citizens who could afford generators and fuel had lights on in their homes after dark.

My seatmate was less than excited about my discovery. He said, rather condescendingly, "Of course we have lights. We need them to see at night."

I thought that perhaps he did not know that electricity was a privilege in other countries, but given his hostile tone, I did not explain further. Lola greeted me at the airport. I was so glad to see her beautiful smiling face. My big sister was caring and loving, more like a mother to me than my actual mother. I gave her a big bear hug, and we held hands tightly as we walked to the baggage claim. We picked up my luggage, got her car, and drove to an apartment she had rented in Melvindale. I was amazed by everything. There were driving rules to obey, traffic lights, and signs everywhere. And there was no military presence to be seen. While she gave me a tour, I caught her up on events since her departure.

It was so exciting to see her, but I was also exhausted and needed to sleep. When we got home, I took off the pantyhose wrapped around my waist with all the tuition money my father had given me. He told me that this was the safest way for me not to lose it. Although I was still nervous about being in this new country and wanted to chat with Lola all night, I went to bed. I slept well that night and woke up feeling rested.

My first full day in the States was a beautiful, sunny Sunday. Lola was full of energy. She wanted to show me around and teach me everything she had learned. I was hungry, but there was no food in the refrigerator. We took a walk in her apartment complex, and I was amazed by how clean it was. I did not see a single piece of trash on the street. Instead, I saw more signs: PARKING, SPEED LIMIT, CHILDREN AT PLAY. The complex also had a fenced-in swimming pool with even more rules and regulations. I thought to myself that the States had many rules, and it appeared that people actually followed them.

Later in the day, Lola took me to a restaurant with a wonderful salad bar. I was not familiar with the concept of self-service, but I followed along. I had taken a $20 bill from the pantyhose pack and offered to pay for lunch, but Lola refused.

Lola had millions of questions about friends and family members, and I had millions of stories to tell her. We talked for a long time. She too had left Lebanon to start a new life. Her face seemed younger. I also noticed that she had developed good self-esteem and self-confidence. The toll that war and abuse had taken on us seemed to have faded from her features. I thought about the same happening to me. I imagined that I, too, would learn to radiate contentment.

The hot and humid weather that day made swimming a must, so I asked Lola if we could swim at the pool. I did not have a bathing suit, having left my old, worn-out bikini in Lebanon. I asked if I could borrow a suit from Lola.

When she looked inside my modest piece of luggage, she said, "Oh boy, you are going to need more than that for the winter." My clothing consisted of three pairs of jeans and a variety of T-shirts. I had a few pairs of shoes, mostly sandals. She laughed about traveling light and then found a one-piece suit she had used for distance swimming. It fit perfectly.

Lola and I enjoyed our time at the pool, but the visit grew somber when we talked about what Rula might be doing without either of us by her side. We prayed that she would be all right, and that we would be reunited with her, in Lebanon, before any harm could come to her. It was our plan to learn and return, to bring a little piece of American freedom and openness back to our father's house in Beirut.

IMMIGRANT LIFE

The next day, Lola and I drove to Detroit College of Business in Dearborn. Lola dropped off Tariq, her Muslim boyfriend from Lebanon, at his job since they shared a car. I registered for summer and fall classes and paid the tuition, depleting all the money my father had given me. I knew Lola would support me, but having no money in my pocket in a new country felt frightening.

Over lunch, I asked Lola about finding a job so I could start earning money for school and living expenses. Several months earlier, Lola had switched her visitor's visa to a student visa. To save money for college and to help herself and Tariq make ends meet, she was waiting tables. She told me that I could do the same.

I was overjoyed to start working. I had never been an employee anywhere, and the thought of earning a wage and meeting new people excited me. Lola worked in Dearborn. Dubbed "Little Beirut," it was a city with a large immigrant Arab community. I was a bit surprised to see store signs in Arabic, people dressed in traditional garb walking along Warren Avenue, and scores of Arabic stores and merchandise. I felt, momentarily, as if I were still in Lebanon. But when a car backfired and I jumped what felt like ten feet in the air, I caught myself laughing. Lola smiled, and we said simultaneously, "Beirut, Beirut."

I interviewed at the restaurant on Warren Avenue where Lola was working and got the job on the spot as a waitress, dishwasher, and cleaning lady, all at the same time. I was paid $2.50 an hour and shared my tips with the cook. Despite wages well below the minimum, I was excited to be working. I found out later that foreign students and immigrants can't be choosers—wages were suppressed because we were a desperate labor pool.

It took me some time to learn how to wait tables. My initial difficulties were mostly to do with language, which I had studied in secondary school and was picking up faster every day, but I also had some trouble with coin values. These problems were unavoidable but eventually surmountable. I enjoyed the job because it helped me learn English fast, but more than that, I loved the interaction with people. Socializing was a new skill for me, but to my surprise it energized me and made me feel like part of a group. According to my father, no one was interested in talking to me, but now I had proved him wrong.

My first American summer was one of learning, personal growth, and adventure. It took a few weeks to adjust to peaceful living. Whenever I heard a loud noise, whether it was a door slamming or a vehicle backfiring, I would automatically ready myself to head to the shelter. Just before sunset, I found myself making preparations for losing electricity by setting up a candle and matches or checking the flashlight I kept next to my bed. I had never understood the full impact of war on my daily activities until I was away from it. But, with time, I shed these deeply ingrained practices and started enjoying a secure lifestyle. With every passing day, I was more thankful for this opportunity.

A few weeks after my arrival, Samar, who had secured a student visa from the embassy in Cyprus following her disappointing trip to Damascus, joined Lola and me. Samar was also registered for the summer session at DCB, and we had one class in common. Samar, Lola, and I were all waiting tables and saving money for school. We joked that we were the Three Musketeers, telling each other tall tales about the hardships and dangers of our American adventures.

I was consciously changing my daily routine in the hope of transforming my destiny. Independence and self-sufficiency were my goals.

One of the most thrilling feelings was the power to make decisions for myself, no matter how insignificant. I could come and go as I pleased and eat and wear whatever I wanted. Because of the restrictions under which I had lived in Lebanon, my decision-making skills were in some ways those of a child. My individual identity had not developed. Really, my only peer group had been my family. And now, as a young woman, I didn't even know what I liked. But I found the journey exhilarating.

On the rare occasion when all of us had a day off from work, we went out driving. We would get lost for hours in the rolling countryside west of Dearborn. Every drive, every outing was an adventure for us. We enjoyed each other's company, laughed hysterically, and explored new areas. Although we did not discuss it or analyze it, each of us was shedding difficult experiences and healing from our painful pasts. Work and leisure created an unprecedented rhythm to our lives. We were rebuilding and repairing the damage caused by war and our families, and our feelings of worthlessness and rejection were slowly changing into feelings of dignity and worth. I was maturing fast. I was finally making all my own decisions, wrong or right.

Sharing hardships made us all very close, but when it came time to solve the myriad problems immigrants face, it was often a case of the blind leading the blind. In the absence of more appropriate guidance, we resorted to Dearborn's Arab-American community. We all used Lola and Tariq's car as our sole mode of transportation: we had been told that public transportation was not safe, especially late at night, and that Arabs were not welcome on buses. When our schedules became too complex, Samar decided to buy a car. She asked around and was told the best deals were found at auto actions. Following that advice, Samar went to an auction with a coworker and bought a white Ford Mustang with darkly tinted windows. The car cost less than a thousand dollars. The tinted windows hid the fact that the car was completely gutted on the inside. But the engine was functional, so we placed discarded beach chairs inside the car and drove it around. The driver's "seat" was held in place by blankets and bags stuffed behind it. The seatbelt served to secure it in front. Yes, we were in Michigan, home to the country's auto industry. We didn't realize it then, but we were at the forefront of creaky auto recycling.

SURVIVAL SKILLS

With our International Driving Permits (IDPs) about to expire, we needed to apply for our American licenses. We had been driving for some time on our IDPs and could easily pass the driving portion, but the written section gave us pause. Again, we asked members of the immigrant community for help and were directed to a person who sold us a "study guide" that turned out to be a copy of the test. With the "guide" in hand, we memorized the answers and got our Michigan driver permits.

I was amazed at all the recommendations the locals had to offer. We were told that when reporting to an emergency room, we should immediately claim to the physician—no matter what real ailment might have brought us there—that we had heart trouble. It was the only way to receive rapid treatment and cut the line in front of the other patients. This may sound juvenile, and I suppose it was. Still, we were neophyte Americans who were learning just how much time, daily, was spent standing in lines. *It's part of the American way,* I thought. All those services—and all that waiting.

By the end of the summer, I had settled into a routine of school and work. In both endeavors, I was learning more and more about American society. I had many misconceptions to remedy, but I was making small discoveries daily. As it turned out, not all Americans were on drugs or in a constant state of drunkenness. And apparently, not all Americans hated Arabs. In fact, by the end of summer, I had determined that Americans were friendly people who worked hard and loved life. I could not wait to share this discovery with my friends in Lebanon when I returned.

As the weather changed, I needed to buy some new clothes and shoes, so we all went to Kmart to shop for winter. After checking the prices of even the cheapest socks, jackets, and shoes, I was aghast to learn that I would have to spend all the savings my meager salary had permitted. From my first day in America I had been very conservative about my spending, and now I knew that I had to sit down and make a plan. I needed to save a certain amount over the next four months. Otherwise, I would lose my student visa status. My dreams of getting a college degree and returning to Lebanon a success would vanish otherwise. I would fail, just as my father had predicted—just as he wanted.

Failure was not an option for me. I went home and worked out a budget. My expenses were easy to figure out: college tuition, my portion of the rent and bills, and basic clothing. I was already saving money on my food bill by setting aside the scraps from customers' plates at the restaurant. On my days off, I walked to the nearest grocery store and bought a soda and a bag of corn chips, which would last me all day. I brainstormed different ways to reduce my expenses, determined to eliminate every penny of spending in my control. Perhaps keeping the heat turned off would help. I talked to the girls about it, and we decided to keep the thermostat down, and I budgeted some money for thicker socks.

Because my income all came from one source, my options for increasing my earnings were severely limited. I asked to work every available hour when I was not in school, and I did get some extra time. But it wasn't enough. I had zero time for anything but school and work. I found myself studying until the early morning hours. I had to learn completely new words—not just new terms—in what was still, for me, a foreign language. Technical English was dense and challenging. It did not take me long to figure out that at this rate, even working every possible hour and studying deep into the night, I would never be able to save enough money for my tuition. I was devastated and depressed. I did not know what to do.

I mentioned my financial dilemma to some coworkers and asked them for ideas about making more money. I was maxed out in terms of hours, so they suggested I change jobs. One suggested I work as a topless dancer at a local night club, but I knew that was not for me.

I was desperate, but not that desperate. Another commented that people who sell drugs seemed to make a lot of money. I was not interested in anything related to drugs, I told him. The war in Lebanon was, in part, a war over the opium fields of the Beqaa Valley. I thought a similar kind of war might be the norm in metro Detroit, and I was right. Murders were reported daily, ascribed to gangs and drug territory. That was not the America I wanted anything to do with. Finally, someone noted that I could lower my tuition by becoming a resident alien. I asked how to become one. My coworker simply said that if I married an American citizen, my status—my student visa—would change into a resident visa. I told him that I was not ready to get married. God knows, I had escaped an arranged marriage in Lebanon only months ago. He pressed his point, explaining that I did not need to be truly married. "You can just be married on paper," he argued.

He saw the worried look on my face. I knew this shortcut was wrong. He went on to assure me that nothing would come of it. It was a simple, near-invisible process. "Don't worry. This is normal. I know many immigrants who have done this. The American government knows about these sorts of marriages, and you will be fine as long as you contribute back to the government by paying your taxes."

The idea made sense in some ways, but it also seemed crazy. Where would I find someone who would agree to marry me under these conditions? I shared the thought with Lola and Samar, and we burst out laughing. We started to pick husbands for each other. But beneath our hysteria, I think we were all a bit panicked about the impossible odds we were facing.

My fears of not doing well in college because of the limits on my study time disappeared when I got my report card for 1989: all As. Apparently, I was a pretty good student. My ability to read English had improved markedly, and the goal of graduation was within reach. I had saved enough money for the 1990 winter quarter, and, thanks to unexpected Christmas gifts from customers, I had a good start on savings for the spring quarter too. With my new source of income—shoveling snow from neighbors' driveways—spring would be fine. It was the fall quarter I was worried about. I had asked about taking only one class, but I was told that in order to preserve my student visa status I had to be enrolled on a full-time basis. The other girls were in a similar position. We all prayed for a miracle.

Detroit had several snowfalls that winter. I rejoiced when I saw the white stuff, but on one occasion, after waiting an hour at work for Lola to pick me up, I finally gave up and started the long walk home in my inadequate, dollar-store cloth shoes. I had barely served anyone because of the snow, and no customers meant no table scraps and no dinner. Something must have happened. I was used to waiting hours given all of our competing schedules, but Lola had told me she was going to be on time today. When I got home, I took my soggy shoes off and stared at my chilled and reddened toes. I was hungry, tired, and cold. The real Michigan winter was far worse than the descriptions I had heard from Lola. Huddled on the living room couch with a cup of warm tea, I could see my breath; I wanted to turn up the thermostat, but I couldn't. More heat meant fewer dollars for tuition.

SURPRISE PACKAGE

Despite the depressing weather and my relative poverty, my first eight months in America had been the happiest time of my life. I might not have had much money, new clothes, real shoes, good food, or proper shelter, but I did have something I had never before experienced: hope. I was especially hopeful this week. Relatives of ours who lived in the Detroit area and had recently returned from a trip to Lebanon had contacted us to say that they had a package for us from our parents. Frankly, I was surprised to hear it. They had not been in touch for months—not even a simple phone call to see whether I had arrived safely in America. I told myself they had misplaced Lola's number, or perhaps international calls from Lebanon were not getting through, but I knew those were lies to make myself feel better. When I heard they had sent a package, I reproached myself somewhat for thinking badly of them. They were, no doubt, under an enormous amount of stress owing to the war, and I should have been more understanding. A better daughter, I told myself, would empathize. I assumed my parents were sending me the money I needed. All my worries over tuition would dissipate. I could not wait to pick up the package.

Lola and I drove for over an hour to our relatives' home. When we got there, conversation was stilted. I kept eyeing the package; my obvious anticipation must have made our relatives anxious. I was sure it was filled with money, and if I opened it in their presence, the relief they would see on my face would expose the shameful doubts I'd had about my parents supporting me.

As soon as we got out of their driveway, I tore into the package. I was aghast to discover that it contained lists of items my father wanted us to send him: medicines, vitamins, even car parts. The shock of my parents' indifference shook me to my core, but I shed no tears over their "care package." I crumpled my father's handwritten list in anger. His selfishness hurt, but I stiffened. He couldn't reach out and hurt me from 8,000 miles away. His betrayal reignited my determination to succeed at any cost.

Later, I was surprised by a phone call from my brother. I did not understand the purpose of the call until after he had hung up. Failing to find a school in Lebanon that would accept him with his poor academic performance and his behavioral issues, my parents had paid dearly to send him to a private school in Cyprus. The school was a known diploma mill, and it suited him. He told me that he did not have to study and that he bought all the tests. He explained that he was having the time of his life, an extended vacation. He owned two motorcycles, one for everyday driving and the other for recreational driving. In addition to having all his school expenses paid, he received $500 weekly from home. (To put this in perspective, a normal professional salary in Lebanon at that time was about $100 per month.) My brother boasted to me about the expensive watches he had started to collect. He never asked me about how I was doing or how I was making ends meet. At the end of this galling exchange, he told me that he had to run because he was going parasailing with his friends.

I was not a bit surprised at this point. It was clear that I would have no help from my family. That night I decided to go through with the arranged marriage. It was my only remaining option. I had fought my way this far, I told myself, and I wasn't going to let anyone take my dreams away.

PAPER PARTNERS

Samar, who was in a similar situation, had been introduced to a man who agreed to, as he put it, "do her a favor." He explained to Samar that he had a number of unpaid traffic tickets and needed money fast. He suggested that it was a fair trade—paid parking tickets for lower tuition and a probable green card. At the very least, Samar was going to enjoy her tuition reduction. So Samar started the process of "getting married." I then approached her husband-to-be with a request: Could he find someone willing to help me as well? Sometime later, he introduced me to his brother and told me that the brother would be willing to earn some money in return.

In April 1990, Samar was married. With that one piece of paper, the threat of being forced to drop out of school and return to Lebanon—now in the throes of a new round of sectarian violence—dissipated. I would soon follow in her footsteps.

On a typically humid August day in 1990, I took a step that, for most women, is magical: I got married. For me, the occasion was devoid of meaning. And I never considered that it might *negatively* alter the course of my life. At the Detroit courthouse, in a short, civil ceremony, I married an American man I barely knew. I acknowledged the irony of arranging my own marriage to a man I did not love in order to solve my financial problems. But to me this was not a marriage in the true sense. It was a simple piece of paper that allowed me to breathe freely and to work toward a promising future.

At the time, apparently, one could request asylum because of the war in Lebanon. I would have easily qualified for this asylum, but I was ignorant of its existence. Certainly, had I known, I would have done things differently. But I had learned that in America, pieces of paper didn't have to define your life the way they did in the petty bureaucracies I knew from my youth. In America, you are judged on what you do with your life: your caring, your service, and your sacrifice. I simply needed a little more time in America to build the kind of life that would live up to that ideal. My pseudo-marriage would make that possible.

Following the pro forma civil ceremony, the next steps in the marriage were impersonal, consisting for the most part of exchanging paperwork with faceless government offices. I would receive a list of request items or a form to fill out and I'd do it. I paid my "husband" with the money I had saved for fall classes, so I was not able to attend school that quarter. Obviously, I was not happy about that, but I assured myself that I could take a heavier class load the next semester and still graduate on time. *Postponing my dream of a college degree is a necessary step toward a brighter future,* I thought.

Samar's "husband" contacted me on a number of occasions to say that my husband needed money for bail or other pressing expenses. I was not sure whether it was a ploy to get more money. Nonetheless, I helped him out as my finances permitted. At one point, when I needed him to sign a form, I had a hard time getting in touch with him and worried that I would not be able to meet the INS's paperwork requirements on time. When I finally reached him, he gave me permission to sign on his behalf in the future when in a pinch. At least in that sense we were really married, he joked. His gentle humor alleviated some of my stress, but his repeated calls, pressing for money, were difficult to handle. I found myself wishing that I had found another way around my financial dilemma. My new resident alien status reduced my tuition expenses considerably, but now I had to support a spouse on the same income.

DRIVING, DANCING, AND DATING

In mid-1990, Lola, Samar, and I moved to a three-bedroom townhouse in Taylor. Calculating the time I wasted waiting for rides, I discovered that it made sense for me to invest in a cheap car. Like Samar, I bought a car at an auction. It fit my budget, and I made sure it had seats. Because I wasn't in school, I worked more and was able to save enough money to return to school for the 1991 winter quarter.

Around this time, I summoned the courage to venture into American society. The distance from our home in Taylor to the immigrant Arab community in Dearborn forced me to frequent nearby American stores and interact more often with Americans. I made a friend, Tammy, who loved to show me around and teach me new things. One of our favorite activities was to drive around in an area frequented by other teenagers. One reason I enjoyed spending my rare free time with Tammy was that we both loved to dance. I did not drink alcohol, and I had no interest in drinking, but I really wanted to go to a nightclub and dance. I was still under twenty-one, so I borrowed Samar's license and explored an American nightclub with Tammy. Right away, I discovered my passion for dancing. I got on the dance floor and went for hours. I did not care how I looked, who was watching, or what song was playing. My problems seemed to drop away, and I danced until the club closed. I paid dearly the next day at work, but it was well worth it. I realized that I liked and accepted the person I had become. To my surprise, I was finding this American journey enjoyable. I was a hardworking, goal-oriented individual who loved her freedom. I enjoyed the respect I received in America. I could no longer hear the harsh words of my father. I saw his lips moving, but nothing came out. I felt as if I had crossed over to a place where he couldn't hurt me.

One night at the club, a young man came up to me and introduced himself as Neil. He gave me his phone number and asked me to call. Dating someone outside the Arab-American community was frowned upon, but that did not stop me from being curious. I had never dated in Lebanon and did not know what to expect. Nonetheless, I did not want my fear to make the choice for me, so I called Neil. After we talked for some time, I felt comfortable enough to go out with him. He was a friendly, slightly bashful, kind man. I wasn't quite ready for dinner and a movie, so I chose a public park as the venue.

When we met and started talking, I realized that I was more nervous than I had anticipated—so much so that on our walk, I decided to climb a tree. Neil was very patient, and we carried on a pleasant conversation as if he chatted with young women in trees every day. I only came down when I felt a bit calmer.

Neil and I dated for a little less than two years, and we had lots of fun adventures together. Once Neil knew of my financial troubles and my arranged marriage, he expressed his understanding of my decision. In fact, Neil agreed to write a character reference, one of the requirements of the immigration process. Neil's attitude confirmed my views of the arranged marriage. It was legally wrong and punishable—up to five years in prison and up to $250,000 in fines—but socially and culturally accepted. Although this does not excuse my wrong decision, I did not understand the gravity or the implications of what I had done.

While I welcomed Neil's attention and advice about the new world I was experiencing, I retained some of my Middle Eastern values. Neil respected my decision to not be physically intimate during the time we dated. Eventually, and maybe because of such boundaries, Neil and I grew apart. We went our separate ways.

Lola and Tariq also split a short time after we moved to Taylor. and Tariq took his car when he left. Without access to a car, Lola took a job waiting tables at a restaurant called La Shish, located across the street from the college. The convenient location streamlined our always complicated carpool operations. Sometime after she started working there, Lola and the restaurant owner, a young Lebanese man named Talal, started dating. Thinking they were dating exclusively, and still on the rebound from her breakup with Tariq, Lola was devastated when a statuesque blonde walked into La Shish while Lola was working and announced that she was meeting Talal for a late-night date. Lola was depressed for weeks.

I was still waiting tables at the restaurant on Warren Avenue. The next time I waited on a certain regular customer, who was a travel agent, it occurred to me to ask her about affordable beach getaways. I was surprised when she told me that she knew of a great promotional special to Cancun, Mexico. Later, after talking with her about the details and reviewing my meager budget, I decided I could make it work. I would be able to take Lola on the trip as well. We were between quarters, so the timing was just right for a small break.

In Cancun, I had the opportunity to relax and bond with Lola. Although she remained too reserved to join me at the resort's night club for dancing, we talked about our dreams, about men, about where we saw ourselves in five years. She was still bummed about Talal. Though he was not a good match for my sister, I was not in a position at the time to tell her that. I wanted her to come to that conclusion for herself. It turned out that Talal was far worse for any of us that we knew—and we didn't find out until it was too late.

YOU REALLY CAN'T GO HOME AGAIN

After finishing the 1991 spring quarter, I was ready to return to Lebanon and explore my future there once I graduated college. Finding a job in Lebanon is a lengthy process for females because of our limited job options, but I expected that my future American degree would open doors for me. Finding a place to live would be a much bigger challenge. Unmarried women in Lebanon live with their parents, period. Those who live outside of their family's home are thought to have loose morals and are rejected by Lebanese society. This is especially true in the Druze culture. I hoped to challenge these restrictive beliefs successfully.

To maximize my chances, I needed to prepare for my return as soon as possible. I planned to look for a job at the bank in my hometown because I knew the bank's owner and thought that he could help me. As for living quarters, I would need to consider them upon arrival. Lebanon was moving, in fits and starts, from warring chaos to a burned-out peace. Things were still unclear politically, so any transition was bound to be difficult. Lola would accompany me.

Seeing my sister Rula and my friends was wonderful. The reunion with my parents, however, was demoralizing. I was reminded, within seconds, of the daunting process that stretched before me.

Instead of hugging us or saying hello, my father greeted us with complaints about the long wait he had endured because of the plane's delayed arrival. Then he greedily questioned us about how many items we had purchased for him from the seemingly endless lists he had mailed to us. Reproaching us for not getting everything on the lists, he told us how disappointed he was with us. Within minutes of our arrival, he made it abundantly clear that he considered our two years in America a failure. Of course, this verdict validated his parting judgment two years earlier.

We drove away from modern Beirut to our secluded village in the Maten Mountains. Rula had been ordered to wait for us back in the village. She felt that Lola and I had left her behind, but she'd built a network of friends to help her deal with the stress of living with my parents and brother. Still, her damaged spirit was apparent. I hoped that Fadi's upcoming departure, for his second year at his prep school in Cyprus, would alleviate some of Rula's stress. I felt guilty for having abandoned Rula, but I assured myself that my sojourn abroad was nearly over. I would soon be returning, and I would make amends to my younger sister. I would take care of her.

Since my departure two years before, the political situation in Lebanon had undergone some intriguing changes. Christians and Muslims now held an equal number of ruling seats in the government, in compliance with the National Reconciliation Accord of 1989. Many viewed this step as the beginning of the end of the war, and a period of rebuilding was apparent. Considerable construction had occurred during my absence. I reasoned that the next two years would usher in a booming job market where my newly acquired accounting skills would be in great demand.

When Lola and I arrived in our village, the neighbors came to welcome us back. In the tradition of visiting returned family members, my father boasted to the locals about the amount of money he claimed to be spending on our education and living expenses in America. Clearly, he was making the point to potential suitors that he had a considerable amount invested in his daughters. I found the boldness of his lies disgusting. He had given us next to nothing. With newfound courage from my experiences in America, I finally decided to confront him.

I paced back and forth in my room, waiting for the guests to leave. When they did, I walked right up to my father and looked him straight in the eye.

"You never sent us a single penny. You are lying to these people. You have not even paid for our food since we got here, and you should be ashamed of yourself."

He was surprised at my defiance and chuckled in amusement. He had refused to pay for the extra groceries, forcing me to use my meek savings to feed the large number of visitors who had gathered, even though in the Arab culture, a father's honor is irrevocably tied to providing generously for his children. If the villagers had known how flagrantly my father had snubbed his guests and daughters, it would have brought unmitigated shame to our family.

I briefly considered trying to expose his hypocrisy, but I knew no one would believe me—not because I am female, but because no one who knew us would have been able to imagine the true cruelty and stinginess of my father.

"Do you know that I had to marry an American man in order to survive in America? You gave me nothing, nothing to help me." Upset by his contempt for the truth, I grabbed at the only scrap of information I knew would get his attention.

"If you are not a virgin on the day of your wedding, I will kill you myself!" he threatened.

Pleased to see a reaction, I told him, "Don't worry, I am still pure. It was all fake, simply so I could afford college."

I walked away, fuming at his disrespect for me and for the truth. I wanted to be as far away from him as possible, but I had no place to go to in our isolated village.

After a week of trying to adjust to living with my parents, I was struck with a strange feeling. I missed America; I missed Dearborn and my silly job. I missed the struggle I'd engaged in on my own. I missed the freedom to do as I pleased without being criticized or judged by others. I missed making my own choices, creating my own destiny, and growing into the person I was becoming. I missed my ability to believe in what I wanted to believe in without any fear of retribution. I missed the respect people in America had shown me. America had welcomed me with open arms; America had not judged me for my religion, my gender, or my family status. I had been respected and given opportunities that I had never been given before. In just two years of living, working, and studying in the greatest country in the world, I had developed powerful feelings for it. I knew why I had fallen in love with America and why I had no similar feelings for the country of my birth. America had become my home. Although I was not yet a citizen, I felt I was becoming part of something greater than myself. I loved America like I loved my sisters.

I was confused and overwhelmed by these new feelings. How would they impact my future? I was not afraid, but I knew my future plans would have to change. I had never thought that I was going to be an immigrant. I had never doubted that I would return to my native country. Now I knew better.

In America I would pursue my American dream. It was attainable, I told myself, and I would work hard to achieve it. I had already set things in motion: my degree and my "marriage" had allowed me to choose between Lebanon and America. I realized, as I sat in the sunshine outside our family's mountain home, that I had not married a stranger illegally. No, I had married America. When I left Lebanon shortly thereafter, it would be for good.

My remaining days in Lebanon solidified this decision. Those around me considered my clothes too Western. They warned me that expressing my opinion of Lebanese politicians was dangerous. Any time I made a choice or decision, someone was there to restrict or criticize it.

On my last day in the village, yearning to escape, I sat with my father. I listened to him enumerate the tasks I should complete and requests I should fulfill in support of his future plans for my brother. My father reminded me several times that he had allowed me to go to America on that very condition. It was my duty to serve my family, he told me. He knew full well, given the way I stared right through him, that I was not listening. He became visibly frustrated, but he did not scold or strike me. I suddenly realized he needed me.

Later, he approached me carrying an envelope. When I opened it, there was a familiar sight: a bundle of new requests.

Topping the list was, "Secure your brother's future at any cost."

This sealed the deal for me. All my father could think about was my brother's welfare. His daughters were a mere afterthought. I looked over the hastily scribbled note. I folded it several times and left it lying on the table there between us and walked away. My brother would have to deal with his own demons. I was putting mine behind me.

Lola and I returned to America and resumed classes for the fall quarter. Because of the trip to Lebanon, I needed to put in some extra hours. The restaurant where Lola worked, La Shish, was growing in popularity. After comparing my tips with Lola's, I decided to wait tables with her. La Shish was closer to school, offered better money, and was easier on me when I needed to transport Lola to work.

I started to rethink my plans for my life after college. For the first time, I was not feeling pressure. I learned that my married status meant I didn't have to leave America immediately after completing college. I was not sure what I would do, or where I would settle, but now I had two years to figure that out. I was a real immigrant, and my future would be up to me.

REUNION

I completed the 1992 winter and spring quarters and was now eligible to graduate with an associate degree in accounting. When I called Rula to tell her, I was surprised to learn that my father had declared that she would travel with him and my mother to Michigan to attend my graduation in June. Suddenly, I felt a strong desire to share this moment with my parents and show them how much I had accomplished on my own. In the classic flawed logic of an abuse victim, I thought perhaps my parents would be proud of me and grow to love me for my significant achievement. Of course, things didn't turn out that way. My father simply sought to use my moment of joy to leverage a better future for Fadi. With the graduation announcement in hand, he obtained visitor visas for himself, Fadi, my mother, and Rula.

Within days of their arrival, my parents announced that they would be taking us to attend the American Druze Society (ADS) Convention, which is held annually around the Fourth of July. The 1992 convention would take place in New Jersey. Never having attended an ADS convention, I wasn't sure what to expect. I soon realized that it was essentially an opportunity for American Druze families to introduce their children to potential suitors. Displeased with my father's renewed agenda to marry off his daughters, I spent most of my time exploring New York City with a friend.

My parents had all but moved themselves into our rented townhouse in Taylor. When it got too crowded, we all moved into a house in Dearborn. The bigger house meant that Lola and I saw our rent increase proportionally. Rula, wanting to contribute to the burden, also started waiting tables at La Shish.

One day, after early morning classes and a busy shift at the restaurant, my father asked me to take him and Fadi to a Toyota dealership because Fadi had seen a sports car that he liked. I drove them to the dealership, and Fadi pointed at a car. My father wrote a check for the entire purchase price. Once again, my father was able to get in his digs at me. It stung, even though it had happened so many times before.

When my father announced a plan for a family vacation, I was immediately dubious. When he asked me and my sisters to start a fund that he would manage for this vacation, I was angry, but for my sisters' sakes, I started giving him all my extra savings. I often wondered where he planned to take us. One night I overheard him telling my mother how well his trick to collect money from us was working.

"They don't suspect a thing," he told her, adding that he was using the money for Fadi's weekly allowance. Needless to say, I stopped giving him any of my extra savings after that night. And I began formulating a plan to get out of the house permanently. I couldn't let my father turn my American dream into a nightmare.

Having extended their visitors' visas, my parents had now been in America for months. In their presence, I had regressed to the insecure, dependent, and restrained child I had been in Lebanon. The timing of their arrival, combined with my foolish, last-ditch effort to resurrect their love and acceptance, was the final straw. At last I fully understood that their influence stunted my growth and development. Although I was still vulnerable and could have used the guidance and the support of loving parents, I knew I was alone.

Looking back, I do not find it amazing that despite all their mal-treatment, I loved my parents and I wanted them to love me back. What else can a child do? I would create rationalizations and excuses for their behavior and tell myself that if I accomplished something better or followed their instructions more closely, they would have to love me. Time after time, my love was rejected, and, despite continued achievements, I never heard those three words I was so desperate for.

To be honest, I sometimes wondered whether my parents were really interested in my brother's welfare either. I think they saw him as a business project. He was to be the molded image of my father, the one to carry the patriarchal torch. He would prove to my father's friends and family that my father was successful in business. But this warped sense of love did not serve Fadi well either. His later prob-lems—and even the problems he would eventually cause me—were based on the weak foundations my parents instilled in him. Eventu-ally, his life spiraled out of control—there was no love or remedy for him from my father in the end, either.

For so long, I believed that I was at fault and that I deserved the unhappiness I was dealt. Their message was loud and clear: I would never be good enough.

In early 1993, exhausted, I moved to Arizona. I had always dreamed of moving to California, but a friend suggested that there was a better job market in Arizona. My parents were still in the Dearborn house when I left for Phoenix, and they seemed as glad to see me go as I was to leave. I did not know when—even if—I would see them again.

Arizona might not be the "Golden State," I reasoned, but at least I was heading west. While I was living and working there, Lola called me to let me know that she had met a man of Druze decent, Andrew, who she thought had a lot in common with me. When Andrew and I first spoke on the phone, it was obvious that she was right. We talked over the phone for months.

Eventually, Andrew visited me in Arizona, and we went on our first date. Soon after, I visited him at his home in Berwick, Pennsylvania. I grew to know Andrew well and found myself strongly attracted to his impeccable character. Andrew was a respectful, honest, hard-working, loving, and trustworthy man. One trait I admired a great deal in him was his service to and love of America. Andrew was an active-duty captain in the Marine Corps and had led men in battle during the Persian Gulf War. His distinguished service had earned him a Bronze Star. Andrew's selfless service to America inspired me to seek out a similar way to serve. Although he did not live in the Middle East or speak Arabic, Andrew had a good understanding of Arab culture. His worldliness was important to me. Andrew and I dated for several months before getting engaged in September 1994. I was truly happy with Andrew, but I had unfinished business in Michigan. For one thing, I had a marriage I needed to end.

BELONGING

I decided to go back to Michigan so my sisters could support me in preparing for my wedding. Against my better judgment, I moved in with my parents, reasoning that it was only temporary and thinking that my engagement to a Druze man might please them. While I looked for work in the accounting field, I waited tables at La Shish for a couple of months to make ends meet.

My parents expressed their satisfaction with my choice to marry a man from our culture and suggested we go shopping for a wedding dress together. Surprised at their eagerness to help, I went with them to a bridal store. After I had tried on a few dresses, the clerk told my father that even the cheapest dresses could cost more than $400. I was crushed when I saw my father's demeanor change. We immediately left the store. In the car he started to complain about my "excessive" spending. Having reached my humiliation threshold for the day, I informed him that I would buy my own dress.

A short time later, during one of Andrew's visits to Dearborn, my father pulled him aside and informed him that we were a traditional Druze family. Using our culture as an excuse, he told Andrew that in Lebanon the groom's family is responsible for the wedding. Capitalizing on Andrew's generous spirit, my father extracted from him a promise to handle the financial arrangement as my father wished. Then he rolled out his list of demands. The wedding required at least three hundred guests and an exceptionally luxurious venue.

Embarrassed beyond words, I quietly encouraged Andrew to think about the kind of ceremony *he* wanted. But Andrew just laughed good-naturedly at my father's demands and noted that they sounded like just the kind of party he wanted for our special day. I was relieved by his kindness, and later I sarcastically thanked my father for his generous "offer" to Andrew, adding that I realized his "sacrifice" meant I would not expect a wedding gift. There was another issue I needed to handle prior to my wedding: my former marriage. I got in touch with my husband and told him that we needed to get a divorce. I had called an attorney who prepared the necessary paperwork, and we met at his office to sign the divorce decree. With a handshake and an exchange of appreciation for helping each other out of difficult circumstances, we went our separate ways. I would never see or hear from him again after that day. That risky chapter was now behind me, I thought.

In September 1995, Andrew and I were married in a lavish ceremony at the Hotel Hershey in Hershey, Pennsylvania. I moved from Michigan to Pennsylvania to be with Andrew. I was still undecided about my future, contemplating different careers, and thought that it would be advantageous for me to work on a master's degree in the meantime. Building on my 1994 bachelor of accounting degree, I enrolled in a master's in accounting program at Bloomsburg University and started preparation for the Certified Public Accountant examination. I also started working full time at Andrew's family medical practice office and volunteered with a number of local charitable organizations.

In June 1997, while walking across the stage to receive my high honors diploma, I was overcome with thoughts of the six years since I had arrived in America and how quickly they had gone by. I was caught up in the heady feeling of being one of the fortunate immigrants who had realized the American Dream. I had grown accustomed to American traditions and to a productive, work-oriented way of life with Andrew; more importantly, I had come to appreciate and understand the value of democracy, freedom, and fairness. By this time, I thought I could not be entirely naïve in my feelings about my new country. My time in America had made me an American.

I took pride in learning American history. One book that turned my head a good deal was Malcom X's *Autobiography*. Malcolm X's words on the importance of living as an American reverberated within me:

> Sitting at the table doesn't make you a diner, unless you eat some of what's on that plate. Being here in America doesn't make you an American. Being born here in America doesn't make you an American. Yes, one only truly becomes an American through a kind of conversion, and that conversion arises out of a desire to join in a common hunger for the rule of law, for equality for all, and for the benefits of cultural heterogeneity.

These words rang so true for me. Being Lebanese meant that I was aware of Lebanon's failure to let bygones be bygones. Cultural heterogeneity was the norm in my native country. But unlike class and ethnic differences in America, which could be managed, even celebrated, it seemed that cultural differences in Lebanon meant only political strife and open warfare. I sensed that Americans believed differences were less important than shared responsibilities. And that's when I knew my "conversion" was in full swing. Part of that conversion was realizing that it was time to do something for my new homeland. I had eaten abundantly of the fruits of freedom. Now, I felt, it was time to make returns on that precious gift.

Prior to graduation in 1997 and during a break in one of my accounting classes, I had walked to the back of the class and done some push-ups. Sitting constantly during these late hour-long classes sapped my energy, and I had to move to keep myself focused and awake. I probably looked silly, but at least one person in the room thought otherwise. The instructor, Dr. Baker, approached me and asked me whether I had ever thought about working for the FBI. He explained that the FBI often sought candidates with an accounting background. I was surprised to hear that, since up to that time the only thing I knew about the FBI was that they investigated high-profile crimes. I had great respect for Dr. Baker, and when I told him that I would certainly consider it, I meant it.

Sometime later, I called the FBI recruiting office nearest to me, the Philadelphia field office, and asked them to send me a package of information. I received it within a week and started reading. I was fascinated by the possibilities therein. Beyond my desire to follow Andrew's example and serve my country, I got a little thrill from the title I might someday hold: special agent. With such a position, I could finally be someone worthy, someone special doing special work.

JOINING THE FOLD 5

already held the titles of bachelor of science and master of science, and I was on my way to a CPA. I even had a real, loving husband. But these honors were still not enough to fill the hole that war and abuse had carved in my self-esteem. Among the reasons I applied to the FBI was the desire to belong to an extended family. Special agents, I read, were part of an important network in which people functioned as a team and supported each other. I knew I could work very hard, and I believed the team could accept me for who I was, without bias as to my gender or ethnicity. I knew that if the only requirement was a strong work ethic and a commitment to justice, I had finally found the right place for me.

The FBI's hiring process consisted of two phases. Phase one was a written application. If accepted, a more comprehensive application process followed, with more in-depth questions, a medical exam, and a physical fitness test.

After my written application was accepted, I contacted my parents for the required background information because they kept most of my records, but I did not share my specific aspirations with them at that point. After numerous discussions with the applicant coordinator in Philadelphia, I finally mailed my completed application in July 1997.

When filling out the application, I was not sure how to handle disclosure of my former marriage, so I sought Andrew's counsel. We agreed that I needed to list my complete biographical information, and that I should follow up with a phone call to explain the circumstances of the marriage in detail. Therefore, on the first page of the application, I listed my ex-husband's name, the date of our marriage, and the date of our divorce. I copied verbatim from the divorce decree the reasons for the divorce. After receiving confirmation that the FBI had my application, I contacted the coordinator, Ruby, to discuss my former marriage. I was nervous. I recognized that my impetuous teenage decision to find a way to study in America could mean the end of my dream of serving in the FBI.

Andrew could sense my concern and hovered near me while I was on the phone. He heard me telling the coordinator that I needed to discuss the circumstances of my former marriage. I referred her to the front page of my application, but before I could say anything else, she interrupted me and said, "Don't worry about it."

Andrew, who had overheard, clearly shared my surprise. I looked at him for guidance, and he shrugged. I figured the FBI knew what they were doing and wanted to evaluate my application in their own way. I thanked Ruby for her help and told her I looked forward to hearing back from her.

When I was off the phone, I asked Andrew what he thought, and he advised me to take her at her word. Having held a security clearance in the Marine Corps, he explained that background investigations weren't necessarily designed to make sure that a person had never made a mistake. Their purpose was to look at the individual's life in a broad context and to determine if there was any behavior that fell outside of a reasonable—sometimes even forgiving—set of norms. To wit, he referenced the FBI's drug policy for new hires. The guidelines stated that FBI employment is forbidden to anyone who had used marijuana more than fifteen times in their lives or had used illegal narcotics—cocaine, heroin, or speed—more than five times.

"If there is a tolerance for felony drug use," Andrew said, "I can't imagine that a rather innocent, harmless marriage would be grounds for an application's further review. A marriage designed to keep you from returning to the war in Lebanon shouldn't be a big deal, especially with the skills you bring to the mission."

He noted that I had documented the marriage in black and white on the first page of my application. At this point, he said, I needed to let the FBI do their job. They would contact me if they required additional information relating to the marriage. Andrew assured me that the FBI would most definitely talk to my former spouse, and if they thought it was relevant to the job, they would certainly raise it in the myriad interviews I still faced prior to obtaining employment. I thought about Andrew's words. They made sense to me, and I concluded that he was right.

During my background investigation, which took two years to complete, I was prepared to answer questions relating to any aspect of my application. However, I never heard a word about my first marriage even after I was selected for the next step in the hiring process.

This phase required a trip to New York for an interview and a written examination. I arrived at the FBI's New York field office early, eager, and ready to go.

While in the lobby waiting to be called, I looked at the candidates around me and noticed that the majority were white males. I would be an anomaly in this crowd, to say the least. When I saw that one man was reviewing the names of state representatives, I started to get nervous: I must have missed something! I remembered reading that the interviews were about specific life experiences and their outcomes. Had I overlooked the requirement for extensive political knowledge? *I will find out soon enough*, I thought to myself.

We were all called into a large room and divided into two groups. The first group would be interviewed while the second group would take the written examination, and vice versa. I really wanted to be interviewed before taking the exam so as not to exhaust all my energy there, but naturally, my name was called for the examination-first group. The exam was easy overall, but it required attention to detail and good documentation skills, two of my strengths, given my accounting background. After finishing the exam, I was directed into a small room for the interview phase. Across from me sat a panel consisting of a man and two women. They sat at a table with files scattered all over it; they had my application open and were examining it intently. When the interview began, my heart started racing. Intuitively, as if she could hear my thumping heart, one of the women looked at me and smiled. I relaxed a bit and regained my focus.

The panel took turns asking questions, each of which required me to describe a problematic situation, how I sought to resolve the problem, and the outcome. Most involved my handling of stressful situations. Initially, I was not sure what situations to choose; they had clearly read every page of my application and knew I wasn't a typical FBI candidate. For instance, I had no experience in law enforcement. Yet my life up to that point had been one stressful event after another, from dodging murderous militias and parental abuse in Lebanon to sorting out the myriad difficulties of being an immigrant.

I decided against abuse stories, as I knew my discomfort with the topic might shade my answers. I also decided against hard-luck immigrant stories. The last thing I wanted my interviewers to think was that I had not assimilated into American society. Instead, I told my Lebanese war stories and recounted the current stress I was facing in managing time to study for the CPA exam, work full time, and volunteer with charitable organizations.

While describing a story of being shelled in my village and running for cover, I briefly noticed that the panel members were listening intently. They had set aside the files in front of them. After my story, one of the interviewers asked me what skills I thought I had that could assist the FBI mission. This was a question that I had prepared for.

"I am hardworking, dedicated, and work well with others. I never give up," I said emphatically as I looked each of them in the eye. Because of my noticeable accent, one of the women asked me if I spoke any other languages. Until then, I was convinced that the FBI's interest in me was due to my accounting degrees, so I had not thought to highlight my native Arabic or my French reading, writing, and comprehension skills. But when I mentioned these abilities, the interviewers seemed obviously interested and jotted down a lot of notes. I left the interview feeling confident.

As I waited to hear from the FBI, a friend who knew about my efforts sent me an article about FBI hiring statistics. He noted that out of about 800,000 applicants for the special agent position, the FBI was hiring only 800. The odds were against me at a thousand to one, but I knew I had done well so far, and I was hopeful.

A few weeks later, my application coordinator contacted me and told me that I had passed phase two and been selected for the last part of this long process: the polygraph examination.

When I arrived at the Philadelphia field office, I was escorted to a small room and introduced to an examiner. Prior to the test itself, the examiner went through my application line by line and explained to me the types of questions he was going to ask and how the machine operated. He stated that we would do two sessions, a morning session and an afternoon session, with a break for lunch in between.

The questions were straightforward for the most part. Then, suddenly, I was asked whether I had been sent by the Lebanese government to infiltrate the US government. I tried unsuccessfully to suppress a smile at the preposterous idea of a teenage Druze girl being sent on a secret mission by the men who ruled Lebanon. The examiner patiently reminded me to give a "Yes" or "No" answer without displaying any emotion. I apologized, realized it was an important question to ask any immigrant applicant, and simply said, "No."

After completing the first round, I was asked to go to lunch and return for the afternoon session. When I came back, I was told that I had passed and that no additional testing was necessary.

I drove back to Berwick elated, even though I knew that I had to wait for the paperwork to be processed. The glacial pace at which the government operated surprised me, and I wondered why everything took what seemed like an eternity to get done. I would later learn about the FBI's long-entrenched and often frustrating bureaucracy, but for the moment I was on pins and needles.

I also wondered why my former marriage was never brought up. Neither the coordinator, in our many phone calls, nor the interviewers in New York, nor the polygraph administrator had asked anything about why nor how I had engaged in my first marriage. Naturally, I had prepared myself to explain the circumstances. At one point, late in the application process, I even brought it up again with Andrew. He explained that the FBI had likely adjudicated the potential concern and decided in my favor. Satisfied, I never gave the matter another thought.

BECOMING SPECIAL

In early 1999, I received my offer of employment as a special agent for the FBI and was asked to report to the FBI Academy on April 25, 1999. I was ready to start serving my country.

But I was in no mood to celebrate. The happiness of a promising future was overshadowed by the painful decision I was facing in my marriage to Andrew. Both of us had been keeping increasingly busy schedules as a way to avoid dealing with the fact that we had grown apart romantically. We had become more like roommates than husband and wife. Neither of us wanted to admit that, much less do anything about it. Andrew was my role model, my support network, my confidante, and, most importantly, my best friend. We both knew that our relationship would have to end, but neither of us was ready to face the painful process of divorce. In some strange way, we both used the FBI Academy as a way to buffer the pain of our imminent separation. My ongoing application consumed nearly all of my attention, and Andrew made a point of helping me with the finer points of the process. It was like we were feeling out a new way of relating that didn't require the passion of marriage.

I often wondered why this happened. I was a virgin when we married. Yes, I had managed to fulfill my father's dictates on that matter, though not as consciously as he probably wished. But I was still rather inexperienced in this thing called love. Maybe my Druze background—where marriages are often arranged—coupled with the complete absence of romance between my mother and father had left me lacking in models to learn from. My mother and father were quite unromantic, at least where we could see. And I was still young enough, and still very naïve in some ways, despite my years in America, that I thought all you needed to make a marriage work was respect and friendship. I know now that although these feelings are important parts of any lasting relationship, they are not the entirety of what a marriage partnership is based on. I did want a more complete romantic feeling, and Andrew and I simply had not achieved it. So, we did the best we could. We knew the relationship was ending, but we helped each other avoid any lasting hurt by being as respectful as we could toward one another.

On April 24, 1999, Andrew dropped me off at the FBI Academy in Quantico, Virginia. On the drive from Berwick, Pennsylvania, we were both quiet. We understood that we were getting ready to say goodbye forever. I was about to embark on a new journey, and I wanted my best friend by my side, but I knew that contacting Andrew regularly for support would not be fair to him. I loved my friend, and I wanted to make our separation as easy as possible for him.

As I looked out the car window at the green fields of Northern Virginia, my thoughts wandered. A few thousand years ago, the Greek philosopher Heraclitus observed that, "If not for injustice, man would not know justice." I had been the victim of an unfair culture in which I was treated as a second-class citizen based purely on my sex; I had suffered physical and mental abuse at the hands of my parents and brother, and I had grown up in the dark shadows and ruined cityscapes that were my birth country's lot as a result of the seemingly endless Lebanese civil war. But I had also experienced justice in America. As I prepared to enter honorable service to my adopted country, I knew what I needed to do. I declared my own personal war against injustice and vowed that I would use the survival skills I had acquired along the way to succeed in my mission. I felt I was in a good place now, a safe place from which I could finally challenge the violent elements of human nature I knew so well.

These thoughts fluttered on the wind through the car window and wafted out into the greater world. Fog-shrouded mountains obscured the horizon. I realized what a great swath of unknown territory surrounded me. I thought achingly of Andrew's love for me, and

I said a short prayer for him. Becoming special was already turning out to be damned difficult.

TRAINING

When we arrived at Quantico, I carried my luggage in, checked in at the front desk, and turned around to say goodbye to Andrew. I did not want to cry; I needed to be strong for both of us. Andrew had a long drive ahead of him. I gave him a big hug, slung my bag over my shoulder, and walked halfway down the hallway, where I turned around to see Andrew walking away, his figure disappearing suddenly into the intense glare of the sunlight reflected off the building's glass facade. That's when tears started to roll down my cheeks.

I checked into a temporary room in one of the three Academy dormitories with the rest of the recruits while we waited for our permanent rooms. I shared a suite, consisting of two rooms and one bathroom, with three other women, including Christina, my roommate, and Lori and Kim We were instructed to stencil our last names on the back of our FBI-provided gym shirts. I did not know what the word "stencil" meant, and I had never stenciled anything prior to that day. Embarrassed to ask, I watched what others were doing and followed suit. I met my class, the class of 99–10 (this number signified that we were the tenth class trained that year), that night. Of the forty students, most were white males, similar to the candidates I had seen in New York. Although there was not a single African-American, Hispanic, or Asian candidate in my class, I was told that we did have an exceptionally large number of female candidates—eight. Among the women, I was the only minority. I was a bit surprised to see how poorly this group reflected the America I knew, a country of great diversity. We all gathered in the lobby and stenciled together, then headed to the dining hall for dinner. There I enjoyed listening to my classmates talk about their "former lives," as we called them, and realized that many of them had military or law-enforcement backgrounds. We also had a good number of former attorneys. I was the only candidate with language and foreign-born cultural experience.

On the first day of the administrative lectures, we were introduced to our counselors—two experienced field agents, Mark and Jane, who had volunteered to shepherd us to agenthood. We were told that Mark and Jane would live on the same floor of our dormitory and would be available to answer questions after class hours. Mark was an extremely helpful individual who went out of his way to assist us by offering his valuable advice. He often reached out to candidates before small issues became bigger problems. Judging by the number of students who were in and out of his room daily, he was a good listener. I thought that it was especially honorable of him to volunteer for this assignment, as he would be away from his family for the four-month period.

Jane, on the other hand, was much more reserved. We barely saw her, and when she was in her room, the door was closed. Clearly, she did not want to be interrupted or bothered. I was told that she had volunteered for the assignment because she wanted to be away from home after a bad breakup in a relationship. Given my own situation, I empathized with her and thought it best not to reach out to her with any issues or concerns. In addition to Mark and Jane, we were introduced to our class coordinator, Lorraine. She was a no-nonsense, hard-core, authoritative agent. I never figured out, in my interactions with her, whether she was putting on an act or was actually straight drill-sergeant material. The only time I saw a soft side of her was when she discussed her daughter.

The administrative sessions eventually ended. After much debate among the instructors, Lorraine, and Mark about our group's title, it was decided that we would be referred to as new agent trainees (NATs), rather than special agent trainees (SATs). It was interesting for me to see how the group dynamic generated a democratic election process on what I viewed as a rather trivial issue.

We took our physical fitness test the second day, and although I was not pleased with my score, I was happy just to pass. Seven candidates failed by a few points and were put on probation; had their scores been lower, they would have been sent home. The test was challenging, but given the weeks we all had to prepare for it while the background investigation was being completed, I felt there was no excuse for failure. I continued working on the exercise regimen I had developed in the months leading up to camp, hoping to beat my score next time.

KILLING MACHINES

On the first day of firearms training, I was a bit apprehensive. The variety of weapons on the table in front of our primary firearms instructor (PFI) recalled earlier, distressing scenes for me, militiamen shooting innocent civilians, the snipers firing at me, and my father placing a revolver to mother's temple. I had never cared much for guns, and I was terrified at the thought of handling a weapon. I knew that the FBI required its special agents to carry weapons, but I was not aware of how often, where, and when I would be required to be armed. I associated weapons with revenge, treason, and murder. Now, in order to do my job as a special agent for the FBI, I would need to carry a gun every day and be ready to use it if necessary. It was only when I saw the weapons display in front of me that I realized my apprehension regarding weapons. This was the first significant challenge I faced in training, and I knew that I had to get over my fears quickly.

The second challenge was learning American law relating to the use of deadly force. Unlike those of my classmates who were former police officers, attorneys, or military, I had no solid basis for understanding the legal system and its complex terminology. My knowledge of law came from what I had experienced in Lebanon, where it was set by whoever had the most guns or troops: survival of the fittest. The consequences of misunderstanding this law meant death. Clearly, I had some mental obstacles to overcome and a lot to learn, but I was committed to doing whatever it took to get the job done.

One thing was apparent from the earliest days of the course: when you join the FBI, you become part of a family. This family loves you, looks after you, and gives you all kinds of support. My legal instructor told us the story of an agent who stayed at the hospital by his dying wife's side. While the agent grieved, his officemates all pitched in by cooking, taking his children to school, and, in an inspiring if somewhat fraudulent move, filling in his timecard as if he had been on duty.

My thoughts about teamwork were interrupted when the PFI racked the shotgun. I listened intently as he spoke about safety when handling firearms and the basics of the weapons we were going to train with. On the table in front of him were a .40 Smith & Wesson Glock 23 pistol, a 9mm MP5 submachine gun, and, what would come to be my favorite, a 12-gauge Remington 870 pump-action shotgun. After viewing a number of PowerPoint slides on each of the weapons, the PFI told us that by the time we graduated from the Academy, we would have fired around 10,000 rounds of ammunition. Sitting back in my chair in the classroom, I wondered why we needed so many rounds and PowerPoints to perfect the skills that young men in Lebanon had mastered pretty well with only the most informal instructions. Perhaps they practiced more than I was aware. When we finally got on the range, I grew to appreciate the importance of mastering firearm skills in an environment where agents are accountable for every round fired. The instructions were precise, clear, and comprehensible, and I relied on them as I might rely on a map to reach an important destination.

Some of the firearms instructors, however, did not live up to the trust I automatically placed in them. I'll never forget one incident at the shooting range when one of these marginal instructors, thinking our earmuffs prevented all of us from hearing him, screamed into the ear of a trainee, "You're shooting like a girl." I heard the charge accidently as I was adjusting my own hearing protection. I also noticed a drop in my scores when he was on the firing line—at least until I learned to ignore him. I gained some degree of satisfaction in dubbing him a "range pest."

Unfortunately, it wouldn't be the last time I experienced unprofessional behavior on the firing range during my time with the FBI.

Once, after graduating from the Academy, owing to my excellent shooting scores, I was chosen along with a handful of other agents to represent the FBI at a "tour shoot," at which elite shooters demonstrate the many weapons used by the FBI under various conditions, such as complete darkness, police lights, and so forth. In advance of the demonstration, which was held at the FBI headquarters, a number of fellow firearms instructors used the range for their quarterly qualification, and the primary instructor, Burt, asked me if I also wanted to qualify. Although I was wearing a business suit, required dress for the tour shoot, I decided to take the opportunity to fulfill my quarterly qualification because it would save me a day of traveling to the Academy range in Quantico. As I completed my shooting, I noticed a number of the instructors laughing. I later learned from the female range assistant that one of the instructors, Rick, had zoomed the camera used for the tour shoot on my behind for the benefit of his fellow instructors, who joined in with hearty laughter and rude comments. When I heard the story from the range assistant, all I could say was that I could outshoot all of them any day, even in heels.

Firearms weren't a joke for me. I didn't come from the macho "gun culture" encouraged in the FBI. I was one of the statistically small number of agents who actually used weapons as tools to accomplish the FBI's real missions. As an example, in 2000, the FBI reported six incidents where special agents fired their weapons. Just a week before Rick's offensive cinematography, I had been on the street of a hostile foreign country with a concealed machine gun providing security for a fellow agent, who was going to meet a potentially hostile individual. The agent believed he would likely be murdered instantly should the situation turn bad. If things got out of hand, my instructions were to kill the responsible individual and any accomplices, seize control of a vehicle, and "escape and evade" (E&E) out of the location. I was ready for whatever happened. And yet I was so easily thrown off by Rick's juvenile joke or the range pest's "you shoot like a girl" comment. My career would eventually teach me that while the FBI has good firearms instructors and excellent facilities, it also has, unfortunately, some marginal employees who hide out on the range performing a pretty basic set of tasks while enjoying the full pay and benefits of agents working real cases.

Once they realized there was an independent witness to Rick's behavior, Burt, his supervisor, terrified, contacted me to offer a written apology. I hesitated just long enough to make him squirm, and then I told him that I was not interested in making a big deal out of the incident. It was a distraction from accomplishing the government's mission, I told him. Having grown up in a society that oppressed females, I was very sensitive to this sort of harassment, but at the same time I had developed reasons not to deal with it and to focus on more constructive issues.

I now regret not standing up for myself. I loved the FBI, and, at that time, I thought any reaction would be interpreted as betraying the organization. Of course, I was not the only female agent who had such experiences with the FBI's male-dominated culture. In fact, the endemic gender bias of the FBI was also reflected in who was given certain assignments. It was not uncommon for women to threaten or even file law suits just to receive assignments for which they were well qualified. The range pest's petty comment was annoying—I just did not realize that it was a sign of things to come.

We were issued holsters and asked to wear our solid plastic training guns, also known as "red handles" because of their brightly painted handles, at all times while at the Academy, in order to get used to carrying our sidearm every day on the job. We also used them to practice. Boy, did we ever practice. Not a day went by when we weren't improving our skills with one of our many weapons. Because of my inexperience, I felt I needed to practice on every possible occasion if I wanted to reach the level of my colleagues. Many nights, my suitemate, Lori, and I would head to the firing range and work on our qualification drills for hours. I was glad to have Lori around. We built a strong friendship at the Academy and became expert marksmen in the process.

On one occasion, our PFI offered an extended shooting session for NATs who felt like they needed extra help. Lori and I readily volunteered, but it wasn't until the end of the session that we realized we had made a mistake. During the training exercise, the PFI insisted we lie down on searing hot blacktop for part of the class. When we tried to tell him that our skin was burning, he told us that we had to learn how to shoot "under various conditions" and that our complaints would only lead to flimsy shooting skills. I thought a better lesson would have been on how to avoid being burned by the blacktop when shooting. In the end, the only lesson we got was in treating the first- and second-degree burns inflicted during the exercise.

Despite these challenges, I was quite pleased to prove the range pests wrong when my scores, in our first firearms exam, qualified me as one of the top five shooters in our class.

FUTURE ASSIGNMENTS

The seventh week in the Academy was a milestone. Not only did we complete our midterm examination, but also we learned where we would be assigned once we graduated. After successfully passing policy tests, firearms drills, defensive driving tactics, the TEVOC (Tactical and Emergency Vehicle Operations Center) course, and other requirements, we gathered in our classrooms and were called upon one by one to open an envelope containing our office field assignment. I did not have a strong preference as to where I would like to serve, but I was happy to learn that Washington, D.C., was to be my new home.

The remaining weeks of the curriculum were pretty much instruction in the same disciplines with the addition of some computer classes, instruction in classified information handling, and the dreaded "mace" exercise. The computer classes entailed very basic familiarization with ACS (Automated Case Support), the outdated DOS-based FBI computer system. I had learned by now that a lot of the Academy classes were more or less introductory. Instructors often reassured us that we would learn and understand the details of a subject on the job. For example, our name-trace computer class, which is basically an electronic records check, took only a few minutes as the instructor walked us through an example of a check on a standard

American name. More complex search techniques would follow in the context of actual cases.

I eagerly awaited the two-day classified information lecture and wondered whether we would learn about classified programs such as Area 51. Having never been exposed to classified information, I did not know what to expect. The day we were to be lectured, we walked to the classroom and found that the classroom door was locked. When our instructors opened the door for us, I noticed a sealed envelope lying on each desk. After almost thirty minutes, when the tension and curiosity in the room couldn't get any higher, the class coordinator walked in and told us that, owing to a scheduling conflict, the lecture had to be canceled. I had to content myself with imagined encounters with aliens and secret military bases on the moon. Eventually, when we did undergo this training, the classified material was far less exotic than my dreams.

BURNING UP

The much-anticipated pepper-spraying exercise was finally here. Our defensive tactics (DT) instructor explained to us that after he sprayed us, we needed to perform a noncompliant arrest scenario. Basically, after being liberally sprayed in the face with a powerful capsicum-based irritant, we were required to wrestle with a subject, draw our weapon, and order the subject to the floor, after which we would apply handcuffs to the subject. The waiting was getting to me, so I asked the instructor if he would allow me to go first. He was surprised, but said that if I really wanted to, he would oblige. He paired me up with my roommate, Christina, then, called my name. He asked me if I was ready, and I could barely hear myself say "yes" over the sound of my heart beating. We had been given some training in how to deal with a fear that can slow or even paralyze reaction time. What I didn't know was that the first blast from a new container of pepper spray was the most powerful. Needless to say, I got a good dose of the spray, took it in, found my center, and completed the exercise successfully by handcuffing Christina while avoiding injury to myself. At the end, Christina and Lorraine held my hands and walked me over to the shower area where I was to be doused with cold water. I had the burning sensation in my eyes under control, but when Lorraine accidently turned on the hot water tap and forced my face under the shower, I started to scream.

"I'm burning, I'm burning," I shouted.

"That's normal," Lorraine explained with some impatience.

"No, my face is burning; it's the hot water, not the spray," I spluttered.

"Oops," said Lorraine, quickly turning the cold water on. I nicknamed Lorraine "the Mistress of Pain" on that day. This was the last of my combat training; I had successfully completed the FBI Academy with high marks and was scheduled to graduate on time with my well-trained and newly confident family of "specials."

SELF-DISCOVERY

I had learned a lot of techniques, strategies, and tactics during the sixteen-week information dump at the Academy. Now, when I reflect on all the material I was exposed to, I can say with certainty that one of the biggest areas of learning was personal. After a few weeks at the Academy, I was discovering things about myself that I'd never known. My lingering lack of self-esteem didn't stop me from enjoying competition and interaction with others. I realized I was a problem-solver, energized by the challenge to fix things. I was particularly adept at breaking a problem down quickly, be it practical or conceptual, identifying its core components and contributing factors, and suggesting solutions. I look back at my training as a set of challenges to be overcome, and I see how fully I enjoyed conquering them.

I had replaced the void created by my Lebanese family with my new family—the FBI. Whatever the FBI needed me to do, I was always ready and capable. I wanted to fit in and do well for them because I knew that they would respect me in return. Throughout most of my FBI career, this proved true; in fact, for a long time, the more

I gave, the more they asked for and the more recognition I received. The FBI gave me the title Special Agent, and I felt special. Unlike my blood family, this family showed appreciation for the work I did for them.

But at the Academy, I also discovered I had not entirely assimilated into American culture. The immigrant's assimilation process is often complex and gradual and takes place in varying stages. For instance, upon my arrival in America, before I learned to converse directly in English, I mentally translated my sentences from Arabic to English. As time went by, I slowly dropped this process. But in times of stress, I found myself falling back on the translation process. That, in itself, was not an issue; the problem was when it came out skewed. These errors in translation arose from an unusual source, a source I had not previously considered: the condition of war. I had not understood its impact on the way I spoke until a telling incident at the FBI Academy.

During an exercise, I witnessed a subject committing a criminal act. When asked to brief my fellow classmates, I told them, "I think I saw the subject committing the act."

Upset by my indirectness, an instructor sarcastically questioned me.

"Well, Nada, do you 'think' you saw the act or did you actually see it?" His challenge struck a chord. Having translated my thoughts from Arabic words to English ones, I realized that I had retained, in my verbiage, the wiggle room of the Arabic. One needs such wiggle room in a war environment. Committing to, or being positive of, anything in a hostile environment like Lebanon had potentially lethal consequences. To avoid such consequences, certain words are added to give the speaker room to reinterpret words and adjust meaning according to what the person with a weapon wants to hear. For example, if a militiaman stops you at a checkpoint in Lebanon to ask you whether you had seen something, your answer had better be both yes and no because the wrong answer is going to get you killed. As a result, you train yourself to respond in a noncommittal way until you figure out the right answer. This way of speaking becomes deeply ingrained in citizens who live in fear, as my unconscious evasion betrayed to the Academy instructor.

CULTURE SHOCK

As I was adjusting to my new family at the Academy, I realized that some colleagues would benefit from learning about Arab culture. I was sure that agents would be exposed to investigating individuals from Arab or Muslim cultural backgrounds, where familiarity with different cultures could be a key to solving a case. An incident that took place at the Academy in the class following ours solidified my thinking. I was pleased to learn that this class included a male of Palestinian descent, Aaron. Diversity, I believed, would certainly help the FBI accomplish its mission more effectively; after all, deploying an ethnic Italian agent to infiltrate the mafia or using an agent of Asian descent to penetrate a triad gang makes a lot of sense.

A few weeks prior to Aaron's graduation, a classmate grew suspicious of him when he noticed Aaron using his personal laptop. Aaron, it turned out, kept an electronic diary of his experiences at the Academy, so he logged onto his computer when he got the chance. Other trainees had their own personal electronic devices, of course, where they kept in touch with the world. But Aaron was also a private person who kept to himself. Being a Muslim, he did not join his classmates at the after-hours FBI bar.

Misunderstanding his reserved nature and computer use, the classmate reported him to Academy management as "acting suspiciously." Aaron's computer was confiscated, and he was subjected to an intrusive investigation that ultimately cleared him. But the harm had been done. As any agent will tell you, no one needs added stress during training.

When I first heard this story, I wondered why Aaron's classmate could not be objective in his thinking about Aaron. Unfortunately, this was not the only aggressive attack on Aaron's character. He later served with me in the Washington field office and was also wrongfully accused, shortly after 9/11, of sympathizing with terrorists. He was once more investigated and cleared. He was then given a plum assignment overseas, in compensation, I believe, for the repeated and unfounded personal attacks he had faced from his fellow agents.

One may wonder what happens to agents who make such accusations. The answer is shockingly simple: nothing. This lack of accountability no doubt encourages this sort of malicious behavior. More shockingly, this behavior often carries over to investigations. There are no consequences for falsely accusing someone of a crime, and if character assassination is accepted as a form of vigilance, then what prevents overzealous agents from taking advantage of these lapses in institutional oversight? I know from firsthand experience that the answer is one every overzealous prosecutor wants to hear: nothing.

CERTIFIED

On August 13, 1999, I walked across the stage at the Academy auditorium to receive my FBI credentials and badge from then-FBI director Louis Freeh. I had made it. The stress, the hard work, and the late nights had finally paid off. After learning and understanding the laws and regulations of our great nation, I was more certain than ever of my decision to join government service.

After graduation, I rented an apartment in Alexandria that was very close to the Washington field office (WFO). I was informed that I would be working on an international terrorism squad. I was surprised at this assignment, as I had convinced myself, given my accounting background, that I would be assigned to a domestic corruption squad. I thought I would be chasing the money, not the terrorists!

I made arrangements with a moving company used by the FBI to view my apartment in Pennsylvania and quote me the cost of moving to D.C. Their quote was preposterously expensive, and I knew I could save the government thousands of dollars if I made the move myself. I contacted the FBI's administrative office and informed them that I would not be using the services of the moving company and would move myself. I was advised to keep all my receipts and submit them with my accounting voucher. I rented a truck, packed it with my belongings, and, with the help of a friend who drove my car while I drove the moving truck, I moved to D.C. Ironically, the bureau rejected my voucher for submitting toll fees for both the moving truck and my car. I was told, according to regulations, that only one set of toll expenses could be submitted. So much for doing bureaucracy a favor!

Later, when I reported to WFO and shared the details of my moving experience, my supervisor, Joe, gave me one of my first real-world FBI lessons.

"Nada, do not save the government a penny," he counseled.

Having worked in the private sector, I thought of saving as key to business success. It was difficult for me to comprehend such wasteful thinking. More alarming still was the advice given by a squad mate, who I'll call John, about "padding" my voucher. He told me that he routinely added fake expenses, below the amount that required provision of a receipt, to his vouchers. As an example, he would charge the FBI $25 for a taxi even though he did not use one. John justified his accounting fraud by telling me that he was just getting his due. Agents, he claimed, would often spend money out of their pockets for business-related expenses and would not be reimbursed. Confused, and thinking he might be right in his math but wrong in his ethics, I told John that I would ask Joe about this accounting advice. John became visibly irritated and went to Joe for a closed-door discussion. After he came back, he shot at me, clearly annoyed, "Forget what I told you, Nada."

On my first day at WFO, as is customary with all new agents, the supervisor introduced me to the top manager at the field office, the assistant director in charge (ADIC). He welcomed me to WFO and quickly stated that my language skills would be in high demand.

"I will do my best to catch Osama Bin Laden for you," I blurted out in complete sincerity. I wanted to make a good impression on the ADIC, and I thought that since I had been assigned to a terrorism squad, I needed to apprehend the person I believed was the most notorious terrorist in the world. To my discomfort, both Joe and the ADIC burst out laughing. Osama Bin Laden (OBL) was not a concern for WFO, the ADIC explained, adding that I should let the New York office worry about him. I did not understand his comment at the time. Only later did I learn that OBL had been indicted by the Department of Justice, New York office, for his role in the 1998 US embassy bombings in Nairobi, Kenya, and in Dar es Salaam, Tanzania. As a result, according to management, I was to leave any concerns about OBL to our "rival office."

Joe ridiculed me for a week straight, deriving obvious pleasure from informing his buddies on our squad about my OBL promise. These fine agents excelled at one thing for sure: mockery. In fact, the story of my ignominious introduction to the ADIC disappeared only after the 9/11 attacks, one of which was practically in WFO's backyard.

Despite my bumpy first day in the office, I was excited and enthusiastic. But, when Joe told me that my training agent, Karen, would not be in for a week, my sails deflated. I wanted to hit the ground running and get busy clearing my probationary agent requirements. Probationary agents, better known as "new guys," are provided with a two-page list of "Suggested Tasks" to complete over a two-year time frame. This list, with many addenda and notes, eventually grows into a booklet that the new guy submits to a supervisor for review. I did not want to let the absence of my training agent slow me down, so I decided to introduce myself to agents on the criminal squads and offer my help.

Before I knew it, I was busy with all kinds of work. From drug arrests, to serving warrants, to background investigations, to monitoring phone calls, I was engrossed in new and exciting adventures. The WFO agents I met were professional, experienced, and hardworking. WFO's criminal division was well managed, agents were productive, and morale was high. Their stats were great too. Some new agents figure out quickly that it doesn't matter whether you complete these suggestions; there is almost zero accountability for not turning in a complete new-guy book within the allotted two-year time frame. But it remains true that the more one does one's homework, the more one learns about the job. I figured, as with any job, knowing my duties and parameters was important, so I took these requirements very seriously and worked on them around the clock to complete the book in my first year.

While there is scant sanction for not completing a new-guy book, a good book can bring positive attention, even, possibly, a major case assignment. Major case assignments receive special funding direct from FBI headquarters, as compared with field cases where the investigatory budget is much more limited. My focus paid off immediately. Shortly after I submitted it for review, my supervisor, Joe, assigned me the William Buckley assassination case. Although not familiar with the details of the case, I knew Buckley's abduction and murder—he was CIA station chief in Beirut—had major case potential. Most FBI agents never get a chance to work on a major case, so Joe's recognition of my hard work and potential energized me: I vowed to put in as many hours as necessary to bring to justice the criminals responsible for Buckley's tragedy. I thought immediately of the Buckley family, and I committed myself, regardless of the fact that FBI special agents are not paid for overtime work, to put in all hours necessary for a proper and effective investigation.

THE BUCKLEY FILE

From the Bureau's voluminous case file, I learned that Hizballah guerillas were responsible for Buckley's murder. In a strategy that would become a habit, I made a list of "action items" and then sought out Joe to review my ideas and get advice. At the time, he told me that the evidence in the Buckley case was not strong enough to go to trial. The FBI, he said, had a better chance of prosecuting these same terrorists for their role in a separate criminal act, the 1985 hijacking of TWA flight 847. Joe then told me to keep the "intelligence sub-file" on the Buckley case active and up to date. He specifically suggested I review all material on Hizballah and select appropriate items for placement in the file. Having missed the briefing on classified material at the Academy, I did not know what some of the letters preceding paragraphs meant, and I would not figure it out, much to my eventual distress, until much later. As an example, the letters (S), (N/F), or (T/S) meant the information in the paragraph was Secret, No-foreign, or Top Secret.

Joe's accurate observation on the weakness of the Buckley evidence disappointed me; I realized I would be handling the case administratively, which was fine but not particularly exciting. However, as long as justice would eventually be served, I was happy to familiarize myself with Hizballah. Eventually, this group, or its proxies, will be prosecuted, I thought, so I imagined I could help in crafting an interview strategy or interrogating a Hizballah operative, if one were captured. For the rest of my time at the FBI, supported by the intelligence analyst on our squad, I kept myself apprised of the activities and events surrounding Hizballah terrorists. I had no idea at the time that my investigations of Hizballah, an investigation directed by my supervisor and pursuant to the Buckley assassination, would be used down the line by the government to attack me and my family in the vilest manner imaginable. While claiming publicly, through a compliant media, that I never worked on a single Hizballah case, federal prosecutors were secretly constructing their castle-in-the-air theory that I had, all along, been a mole for Hizballah, the very organization I had sworn to bring to justice for its role in murder and mayhem directed against American citizens.

A GOOD NEIGHBOR

Within months at WFO, I was approached by a fellow agent on my squad, Tim, who had a vast knowledge of the FBI's outdated DOS-based Automated Case Support (ACS) system. He told me that, because of my cultural and linguistic knowledge, I would be called upon to help other agents with computer searches. He pulled his chair next to mine and gave me a tutorial on searching for Arabic names in a system never designed to deal with the intricacies of transliterated names. I wrote down the list of the DOS-based commands used to clumsily navigate the name search page and the search commands. Once I learned the commands, I wanted to check my ability to perform a search based on the instructions I had just received. To do so, I needed to use Arabic names of individuals that I knew would be listed in the FBI computer system as well as names that I knew would not. The first names that came to my mind were the names of family members. I knew their names would be in ACS as part of my background investigation, and I used their names for training purposes. I used the name of a long-deceased village elder in Lebanon for training on names that would not be in the system. I kept my cheat sheet next to my computer and referred to it often. The ideas worked. I had been inaugurated into the geek squad, and I loved it.

Tim was right about agents seeking my help on the spelling and tracing of Arabic names. My squad was located on the fourth floor, adjacent to the Hizballah investigation team, and agents on that squad often stopped by with questions. I was happy to help others jump-start their investigations.

MAJOR CASE 6

In June 2000, Joe called me to his office and informed me that Pakistani authorities were set to release from jail in Pakistan Zayed Hassan Safarini, the lead hijacker in the murderous assault on and hijacking of Pan Am Flight 73 in Karachi, Pakistan, in 1986. Joe assigned me co-case agent duties and told me that John would be serving as the case agent.

I was shocked. I had been an agent for less than a year. I had worked hard and had earned the respect of my supervisors, but to be assigned a major case so early in a career was nearly unprecedented. There were several hundred special agents in the Washington field office who had more experience and more time on the job than I had—and most of them had never spent a day working a major case. Although Joe routinely complimented my work, I never imagined it would lead to major case involvement so quickly.

To be clear, I didn't think I was unfit for the assignment. I reasoned that my work record proved my worth. I had earned some early stars on my FBI report card and had logged more than a few miles for the Bureau. Within weeks of my arrival at WFO, my travels had taken me to Atlanta to assist in the interview of a Hizballah operative indicted for the 1996 Khobar Towers bombing in Saudi Arabia, where nineteen American service personnel died; to London, England, a month later, to work with Scotland Yard detectives and MI5 officers on a high-profile 1999 kidnapping in Yemen; and, eventually, to the United Arab Emirates to work on the detail team of then-FBI Director Louis Freeh—a task that Freeh himself insisted I take on and for which he later complimented me. There were operatives in the Bureau who appreciated what I brought to the table, and each of these assignments proved to any of them that I was qualified to handle the Pakistani job. Even so, I was both surprised and proud. I was going to have a chance to bring Safarini to America to face a trial—and, hopefully, justice.

The case agent and the co-case agent on a major case have distinct responsibilities. The case agent needs to assume an executive role and pay close attention to the details of budget, briefings, and marshaling resources. The co-case agent takes the investigatory lead, drilling down into the details of the case and mastering the intricacies of motivations—political, psychological, or simply maniacal—behind complicated crimes. Such investigation can span months or even years.

The investigation of the Pan Am 73 case spanned a period of nearly fifteen years. The boxes of files to go through and mounds of paperwork to review required me to work on the case around the clock. As a new agent, one of my probationary requirements was to listen to hour after hour of tapes of phone taps, wiretaps, and other forms of voice monitoring evidence called "Title III" after the federal code that provides the authority to collect conversations. Because such work often doesn't directly support cases that fall under your supervisor's responsibility, there is pressure to do the work "after hours," when it won't interfere with what your boss perceives to be your "real work." So I hauled the Pan Am 73 case materials to the listening station for my Title III work and spent a grueling night going over the files and learning the details of the hijacking as known to both the FBI and other intelligence agencies, such as the CIA (Central Intelligence Agency) and the DIA (Defense Intelligence Agency). I also scheduled an appointment to visit CIA headquarters at Langley: I wanted to learn what the CIA knew about the involvement of ultraviolent PLO (Palestine Liberation Organization) splinter groups in the hijacking. I wanted to dig into the motive and brutality behind the crime. My goal was to know my opponent. When I approached the soon-to-be-freed hijackers of Flight 73, I wanted to be in the best possible position.

BULLIES

My excitement about the new assignment was tempered a bit because I had to work with John, who had a reputation for creating a hostile work environment and for being degrading to women. Joe suggested that John and I meet him for lunch at a restaurant close to WFO where we three would "talk business." During lunch, John, apparently trying to make light conversation, managed to make offensive comments on a number of subjects. It did not take me long to realize that he did indeed have issues with women. He came off as obnoxious and overbearing.

After Joe, John, and I were seated and had ordered our lunches, John asked me about my religion. I explained to him that I was born to Druze parents, adding that I did not practice the Druze faith.

"Oh, a Druid," he commented. "Do you worship trees? You can't use paper if you do, and you have a lot of 302s to write!"

Was it an attempt at a joke? I really wasn't sure. It is not uncommon for the average American to be unfamiliar with the small, tight-knit communities in the Middle East that practice the Druze faith, but for an FBI agent assigned to the Extraterritorial Terrorism Squad, an agent with numerous cases and subjects located in the Middle East, not to be familiar with a key religious faction would be a shocking admission of not having done one's homework. If John was joking, then his comments were hardly professional, even insulting; if he was serious, then his comments were derelict. Either way, it was troubling.

The luncheon conversation did not improve when John told a joke about two bulls having a conversation over whether they should run or walk down a hill to mate with the cows in the pasture below. I decided to play along and feign amusement. This deferring action on my part—you know, women in the Bureau are treated better when they play the old-boy games—had the unfortunate effect of encouraging Joe to tell stories about his college days. A boorish monologue ensued that culminated with Joe's revelation that he and his roommates used to chant, "We must, we must, we must increase their bust!" about fellow female students whose breasts Joe and his male buddies deemed too small. Joe pledged to me and John that he would be careful not to repeat this chant in front of certain female squad members.

While I am sure that the intent of that qualifier was meant to reassure me that my bust was of acceptable size, I was angered by Joe's thoughtless commentary. This sort of blather was demeaning to *all* women. As the supposed "talk business" luncheon devolved into sophomoric ditties, I found myself repeating the submissive and self-effacing behavior I had so disliked in myself while I lived in Lebanon. Such a response bothered me, but what else could I do? This sort of damned-if-you-do, damned-if-you-don't frustration is a problem for women in top-heavy male organizations, especially in top-heavy male organizations where most people carry guns. I really wanted to tell John and Joe how offended I was. But by this time in my life, I had accepted that the Bureau was my new family. I had decided, sometime prior to this luncheon, that when such encounters sprang up, I would bite my tongue, put up with questionable family members, and hope that all would turn out for the best.

I would later learn from John that he had gone through a bad divorce. I would also learn from an agent who had attended the Academy with John that he had been an unpopular student. He was also a bit of a proselytizer: he thought the FBI needed to follow the same rules as the US military, and he had advocated to his classmates that FBI Academy rules should require a trainee to make his or her bed up so tightly that a quarter would bounce off it. I have the utmost respect for our military, but most agents will agree with me when I say that military training and FBI training are two different animals. The agent who confided this detail to me also told me that during John's Academy training, he was viewed by the other NATs as a teacher's pet, another reason, the agent claimed, that John was kept at an emotional distance by his fellow trainees. While none of this excused anything, over time I came to understand the roots of some aspects of his rudeness.

ULTERIOR MOTIVES

I recognized early on in my career as a law-enforcement officer that having an ulterior goal for an investigation, a goal that went beyond the intricacies of the investigative work, was beneficial for my state of mind. For me, my feelings of empathy with the victim's family became a complement to the painstaking work of realizing a conviction. My empathic feelings were far more than simple post-conviction spin. Empathy with families that had been traumatized by the loss of loved ones was a motivating factor pushing me to work long hours and to take seriously my responsibility for winning a case.

I have often wondered if empathic connection with the families of victims is a common feeling among male agents. My experience with John and Joe at our "boys will be boys" luncheon caused me to question whether other male agents could summon—or cared to summon if capable—empathy for victims' families. In fact, I found myself gravitating to the belief that my empathy was, in good part, a quality entwined with my gender: feminine ideals of nurturing, I reasoned, bring on a high level of empathic concern. And while males can certainly exhibit feelings of empathy, I was beginning to question in what ways the male-dominated culture of the FBI, with its ultra-competitiveness and its all-too-often macho reaction to putting the bad guys down, might push male empathy out of the picture. I wondered, too, if male agents believed that empathy for victims might actually retard progression toward conviction. Is empathy, for them, a feeling detracting from investigative, and ultimately prosecutorial, zeal?

My empathic identification with terrorism's victims was an important part of my *investigative* zeal. That said, in no way does my emotional level of involvement with a crime's victims interfere with my work as an investigator: the conviction is still the prize, of course, and shoddy investigative work, as we well know, has jeopardized many a prosecutor's case. I was, first and foremost, an agent who did her job by the book—first for the Bureau and then for the Agency. I went by the book in order to ensure unsullied convictions of dangerous criminals. But my empathic nature motivated me to go the extra mile, work the extra hour, and put in the extra effort that would, hopefully, pay off in a major-case conviction. By ratcheting up my natural empathy for the living victims of the Pan Am hijacking, I was giving myself another tool to use in my upcoming major-case confrontation with Safarini and company.

SPONTANEOUS CONFESSION

"Let me tell you why I did it!" said Zayed Hassan Safarini, the lead hijacker of Pan Am Flight 73, as he dashed into the interview room at the Adiala Jail in Rawalpindi, Pakistan. He had been waiting in an adjacent cell under armed guard while I questioned his accomplices, and he knew that "the Americans" were interested in talking to him. He was dressed in a light-brown *shalwar khameez,* the traditional Pakistani garb. His outfit was covered with stains, and his body odor was almost suffocating. He wore sandals that exposed filthy and infected toes. I had to fight the instinct to glance away in revulsion.

The interview room had a single scarred table and four flimsy chairs. A Pakistani official sat across from me, while Mike—the FBI assistant legal attaché (ALAT)—and another FBI special agent filled the remaining chairs. As a result, the prisoners were forced to stand when we spoke to them, not the ideal setup. I had just finished interviewing in Arabic two of Safarini's accomplices and had obtained from them "knowing waivers" of the constitutional rights usually accorded to suspects in US custody. I had also obtained inculpatory statements from each suspect. To further strengthen our case against these terrorists, and for the benefit of the two other agents, Khalil, Fahad, and Mansoor—Safarini's three accomplices—had repeated their statements in English.

"I don't hate Americans; I hate America's foreign policy," was the gist of the excuse Safarini offered. As soon as he walked into the room, Safarini had identified me as an Arab and immediately engaged me in Arabic. He was eager, after fourteen years in a Pakistani prison, to explain the hijacking. Because of America's support for Israel, he began, innocent Palestinians, mostly children and women, were killed daily. He then asked me whether the life of a Palestinian had the same worth as the life of an Israeli. Of course, I told him.

Growing up in Lebanon, I was intimately familiar with such arguments, and I knew it would be futile to respond directly to Safarini's justifications or to debate their truth. I wanted to tell Safarini that killing innocent people—many of whom, in the case of Pan Am Flight 73, were young children—furthers no cause. I wanted to show him the gruesome pictures of the deceased and tell him how their deaths would incite more bitterness. But mostly, I wanted to lunge across the narrow table and choke him. I hated what he had done. It took extraordinary effort to restrain myself.

I smiled cautiously and continued to engage him in his native tongue. I was able to retain my composure because I saw the payoff. I recognized, from my legal lectures at the FBI Academy, that his initial statements to me, legally titled "an excited utterance" under the *Federal Rules of Evidence,* constituted a hearsay exception and would be admissible in court as proof of the truth of the statement itself. As I heard the words "let me tell you why I did it," my adrenaline surged: it was the confession we so desperately needed. Without it, prosecution in US courts and justice for the victims of Pam Am 73 would be distant prospects.

To participate in these interviews, I had flown for two straight days in July 2000 from Washington, D.C., to Islamabad International Airport, arriving at dawn. I was met by an American embassy expediter, rushed through immigration and customs, and taken to the embassy well before normal business hours. There, I learned that the interviews were to be conducted immediately and that I had only minutes to prepare for departure to the jail. I pulled my hair back, washed my face, and gathered my notes before climbing into Mike's government-provided SUV.

As we drove, I considered how fortunate I was to have this rare opportunity to interview our subjects. I owed it to the hard work and the outstanding relationships Mike had built with local law-enforcement officers. He filled me in on the details of the planned interviews. We were uncertain of the specific location, duration, and other pertinent details relating to the interview. The situation required us to be extraordinarily flexible and to adapt on the fly to whatever circumstances we might face. I didn't know what to expect, but I was sure I'd be getting a whole new set of debriefing skills.

I thought of the interview training I had received at the FBI Academy eleven months earlier. The relatively brief interview and interrogation of American role-players in a clean, well-lit room at the FBI Academy in no way prepares an agent for working in a foreign jail—the heart-pounding tension and the anticipation of getting a real confession from one of the world's most notorious terrorists.

After all, "flashing the badge" meant nothing to these terrorists, and using the "good cop, bad cop" approach lacks the necessary cultural context when a person comes from a place where many police officers are violent and corrupt. Only a deep understanding of Arab culture and, in this case, Palestinian issues could elicit the statements necessary to further justice.

Unfortunately, the training I received actively devalued the importance of cultural understanding, and the relatively short four-month new agent program does not offer diversity training for the overwhelmingly white male agents. In my experience, new agent trainees (NATs) are taught that "a crime is a crime" and that reducing the inherent complexities in foreign investigations makes the investigation easier. I would have to forge ahead, drawing on my life experience and the example of the few experienced and culturally aware FBI agents I had worked with overseas.

"Nada, we do not know specifically where, under what conditions, or even how long we can talk to these guys—you are going to have to get what we need fast," Mike told me.

So be it, I thought. Although exhausted from the flight, my mind began racing. I had read the case files over and over and knew every detail of their crimes. I read the psychological and sociological descriptions of the hijackers, but knew, given the passage of years, that much would have changed. I wondered if I would even recognize them. When we arrived, I quickly realized the situation was worse than I ever could have imagined. We parked on an area of packed dirt and walked to a low-rise brick building that could easily have been mistaken for a warehouse. After processing through the "official entrance," we entered the inmate area. My only experience with jails thus far had been the maximum-security prison in Atlanta eight months earlier, where I had interviewed Hani Al-Sayegh, a member of Saudi Hizballah, who would eventually be indicted for his role in the Khobar Towers bombing. While American jails are rightly considered violent, even the worst jails in the United States compared favorably to Adiala. Here, it turned out, food must be purchased, running water is nonexistent, and the doctor is called only when a prisoner is literally on his deathbed. On our way to the interview room, an elderly man with nothing but a dirty white cloth thrown over his private area lay on a gurney, shaking in the throes of a seizure. Flies covered his face and body. I wanted to insist someone help this person, but who?

WHEELS OF JUSTICE

The Pan Am hijackers, initially sentenced to death, caught a break when Benazir Bhutto, in one of her first acts as Pakistan's new prime minister, commuted all existing death sentences to twenty-five-years-to-life terms. The Pakistani government eventually oversaw the remission of the Pan Am hijackers' new sentences to fifteen-year terms. They were due to be released in late 2001.

In considering the hijackers' mass murder of twenty-one people and their cold-blooded execution of two US citizens, the American justice system sought a more proportional response. We hoped to bring them all to trial in the United States. Safarini, who had been indicted on hundreds of criminal counts—including murder and air piracy—was scheduled to be released first, so pursuing him was my primary responsibility. If he was cooperative enough to travel to the United States voluntarily following his release, I would, of course, arrest him. But even in this unlikely scenario, a confession would be key.

The task was daunting. Safarini, of course, would likely resist our every effort to bring him to justice in the United States. That meant I would need to bring him on an "extraordinary rendition," a relatively rare and obscure practice at that time, that would later become infamous as the CIA moved individuals around the globe as part of the Bush administration's post-9/11 counterterrorism mission.

The FBI has some experience with ordinary rendition, defined as the transfer of an individual from one jurisdiction to another in accordance with legal process at both ends of the transfer. Rendition is the mechanism used when an extradition treaty isn't in place, but two jurisdictions agree to a transfer via their respective legal systems. The Pakistani legal system wouldn't overtly support a transfer or ordinary rendition. But they would permit us to build a case against Safarini, and that was where we started. With Safarini's confession in hand, I had what I needed to prod the rest of the big legal machine back in Washington into action.

Federal prosecutions are handled by an assistant United States attorney (AUSA) and, for a major case, a Department of Justice (DOJ) attorney. I knew that the DOJ attorney, Gwen Cohn, was a detail-oriented, hardworking woman selflessly committed to the US justice system. Gwen handled most of the terrorism cases that my squad investigated, including the 1986 TWA Flight 840 bombing, the 1990 kidnapping of US citizen Brent Swan, the 1983 bombing of the US embassy and marine barracks in Beirut, and the 1996 Khobar Towers bombing. I knew these cases were complicated. If we brought Safarini to the United States and lost in court, he could possibly be eligible to apply for US citizenship, and if he were successful, we would have set a terrorist free among our citizens. I was confident that with Gwen involved, we couldn't lose.

I returned to Washington and got busy gathering the evidence to complement the confession. I needed to interview witnesses and victims, locate the family members of the deceased, and formulate a plan for the investigation's next steps. Much of the physical evidence associated with the Safarini case was stored in Pakistan, and we needed to find it, examine it, and transfer it—if permitted by the Pakistani authorities—to the United States. I prepared a prioritized list of witnesses for Pakistani officials with a request to locate them and make them available for interviews.

In September 2000, the Pakistani government gave us access to the first batch of witnesses. I wasn't scheduled to make this trip because I was studying for the CPA exam. The FBI greatly valued those qualified to investigate white-collar crimes. But my plans to take the CPA exam changed quickly when a group of terrorists brazenly bombed a US Navy destroyer in Yemen.

DIVERSION TO SEA

Early on the morning of October 10, 2000, Joe called the squad for an emergency meeting. We all piled into one of the conference rooms on the fourth floor of WFO, and Joe briefed us on the bombing of a destroyer, the USS *Cole,* hours earlier in the port of Aden, Yemen. We did not have a lot of information about the perpetrators at the time, but Joe informed us that the US government would be sending a rapid deployment team from a number of agencies, including the FBI, DIA, CIA, NSA, and the Department of State. He chose me to join and asked me to meet him at Andrews Air Force Base in a couple of hours. I rushed home, packed some clothes, and sped off to catch the flight.

Although I was bummed that I was missing the CPA course, the trip took on a new significance when I met the love of my life in "heaven"—the English translation for Aden. Gordon Prouty, who was part of the political section of the Department of State, was dispatched to Aden from Islamabad, Pakistan, where he was assigned at the time. Gordon was a fluent Arabic speaker whose skills were desperately needed in Yemen. I had seen him before, at the cafeteria of the US embassy in Islamabad months ago, when I had obtained the confessions from the Pan Am 73 hijackers, but we had not worked together. Gordon still teases me, saying he fell in love with my dog-tired, worn-out, exhausted look and my "exclusive diesel-scented perfume."

I ended up spending two months in Yemen investigating this infamous Al Qaeda (AQ) attack. It was my first exposure to AQ. I would soon develop a deep understanding of this organization, particularly from working with top cop John O'Neill. He'd been on AQ's trail for some time, and working alongside him, I resolved to cripple and then destroy AQ.

The Cole investigation and the Pan Am 73 case required frequent travel to Islamabad, giving me the opportunity to get to know Gordon better. Our relationship moved slowly from professional courtesies to friendly camaraderie. Finding a bravura Arabic speaker in the form of a tall and handsome anti-terrorism warrior was a new and unexpected thrill for me. We saw each other on and off over the next year or so. My travel schedule in 2001 was incredibly hard to sustain, but after all, when the mission calls, you drop everything and respond.

SKY FEAR

While I found traveling to be one of the most enjoyable aspects of my work for the FBI, this enjoyment was tempered by a deep-seated fear of flying. I worked hard to prevent my fear of flying from interfering with my duties and eventually developed a routine of running more than ten miles prior to getting on a transoceanic flight. The running helped me relax on the plane, which made work easier when I arrived at my destination and invariably discovered that my language and professional skills were needed immediately and that I wouldn't be joining the other agents I had traveled with at a local hotel to rest prior to doing field work.

Fortunately, I have always loved to exercise. Culturally, as a young female in Lebanon, exercise is permitted: however, when a girl reaches the "marriage age," which could be as young as thirteen years old, she is discouraged from exercising, as that activity may be interpreted as the behavior of someone who enjoys "excessive" freedom. A bit of a rebel by nature, I continued to exercise even after I passed the permissible age. Exercise, specifically running, had made me feel free in the female-oppressed society of Lebanon, and I continued to enjoy this freedom as an agent. A lot of stress melted away as the miles piled up.

Running also helped me deal with another issue. I am claustrophobic and often have a hard time letting go of control of my surroundings. But my fear of flying was not entirely the result of this feeling of vulnerability. My fear was also based on an incident I witnessed as a teenager. During the Lebanese civil war in the early 1980s, the Syrian forces occupying Lebanon and the Israeli forces fighting them clashed repeatedly in the sky over Beirut. As a young teenager, I watched Israeli planes strike Syrian targets around my village, Kournayel, in the Maten Mountains, located some fifteen miles east of Beirut. The Israeli targets were, apparently, locations where the Syrians deployed surface-to-air missiles (SAMs) for use against Israeli fighter planes. From the balcony of my home, in an age before satellite television and iPods, these skirmishes were a spectacular, if frightening, show. The Syrians fired the SAMs toward Israeli aircraft, which avoided the missiles by ejecting a dazzlingly bright flare designed to draw the tracking missile away from the aircraft and toward the heat of the flare.

One day, observing this cat-and-mouse game, I was shocked to see that one of the Israeli aircraft was not ejecting its flares. I instantly knew that something was wrong. Shortly thereafter, a missile arced upward and struck the aircraft, which exploded in midair. Fortunately, the pilot had had enough time to eject from the cockpit prior to the missile's impact. Unfortunately, he parachuted down into the hands of Syrian troops on the ground. I knew that if he made it safely to earth, he would likely face harsh treatment at the hands of those Syrian forces the Israelis had been bombing with near impunity.

As I watched his slow, perilous decent, I wondered whether he might be a father and worried about his children. I imagined, too, that he might be a young man who would be missed by a loving family. I also thought a lot about what it would be like to fall out of the sky after a terrible and fiery explosion.

NIGHTMARE: THE TAKEOVER

The more I studied the Pan Am 73 hijackers, the more convinced I was that justice had not been served. While fifteen years in a South Asian prison is no joke, it didn't seem like a fair trade for the hundreds of years the hijackers had taken from their victims. In the summer of 2001, during long runs or while stuck in Washington, D.C.'s gridlock traffic, I found myself replaying the hijacking over and over again in my head. The hijackers' release date was fast approaching, and my thoughts kept racing back to that horrific September day in Karachi.

. . .

On September 5, 1986, four armed men, led by Palestinian nationalist Zayed Hassan Safarini, stormed aboard Pan Am Flight 73 as the aircraft was boarding passengers on the tarmac in Karachi, Pakistan. At the time the hijackers seized control of the enormous Boeing 747, 379 passengers and crew, including 78 US citizens, were on board and moving about the aircraft. Pan Am Flight 73 carried the United States' aircraft registration number N656P on its tail. The flight's international route had originated in Bombay, India, and had stopped in Karachi en route to Frankfurt, West Germany. Following the stop in Germany, the flight was scheduled to fly home, to New York City's Kennedy International Airport. It was due to arrive in New York at 8:30 P.M., and expectant families and friends were no doubt arranging their days to meet and greet their loved ones.

The three accomplices assisting Safarini in taking control of the aircraft were young, uneducated, and highly motivated Pal-

estinian nationalists eager to use media coverage of the hijacking to propagate their message of Palestinian oppression. The three hijackers were Jamal Saeed Abdul Rahim, also known by the alias Fahad Ali Al-Jaseen; Muhammad Abdullah Khalil Hussain Ar-Rahayyal; and Muhammad Ahmed Al-Munawar, also known by the alias Mansoor Al-Rashid. The plan for seizing the aircraft was simple, inexpensive, and proved to be highly effective. Exploiting a thriving black market for weapons in Pakistan at the time of the Afghan-Soviet war just across the border, the four hijackers easily acquired AK-47 assault rifles, pistols, hand grenades, and plastic explosives. They fashioned a significant quantity of the plastic explosives into a suicide belt. At approximately 6:00 A.M. local time, Safarini and his fellow hijackers, dressed as Karachi airport security guards, drove a van modified to look like an airport security vehicle through an airport checkpoint without challenge. None of the hijackers spoke Urdu, so it is not clear what they planned to do if they were stopped by airport security; given the firepower the hijackers carried, however, it is unlikely that airport security could have effectively stopped the van. As the last Karachi passengers boarded the plane, Safarini parked the van next to one of the two mobile stairways being used for boarding. He and one of his fellow hijackers boarded the plane via the forward stairway, while the two other hijackers moved on board the aircraft via the rear stairway.

The hijackers moved quickly to dominate the aircraft and terrorize the passengers into submission. At least one of the hijackers released a burst of automatic weapons fire from his AK-47 while entering the aircraft. The sound ripped through the calm morning air and reverberated inside the tight confines of the aircraft. Safarini grabbed a flight attendant and demanded that other flight attendants close the forward door of the aircraft. Meanwhile, Mansoor ordered a flight attendant to close the rear door of the aircraft. When the stunned flight attendant had trouble locking the door, Mansoor responded by firing several shots in her direction. Eventually, the flight attendants were successful in securing the doors.

*Hundreds of terrified souls were now trapped inside a claustropho-
bic, aluminum time bomb.*

*While Safarini and his fellow hijackers were taking control of
the plane, quick-thinking flight attendants used the plane's intercom
to alert the cockpit crew to the attack. This heroic action allowed
the pilot, co-pilot, and flight engineer to escape through a hatch in
the cockpit before the hijackers could reach them. The hijackers
had made a serious mistake. Not realizing that the cockpit of a Boeing 747 was up a short flight of stairs at the back of the first-class
cabin, Safarini's men had initially looked for the cockpit where one
might naturally think it would be located—at the head of the first-
class cabin. But the cockpit was not there, and this brief delay allowed the cockpit crew time to leave the aircraft. Safarini and his
team were not pilots, so the plane was now effectively grounded.
Unless the authorities took the highly unorthodox step of supply-
ing the hijackers with a replacement flight crew, the cockpit crew's
fateful decision to escape forced Pakistan into the role of playing
the unwilling host to Safarini's murderous intentions. This drama
would end where it had started, but not before changing the lives
of every single person on board.*

・・・

BEFORE 9/11, THE THREAT of hijacking had faded from the memories of
most Americans. Not mine, though. As a special agent for the FBI,
familiar with the history of various Palestinian terrorist organizations, and as a native of Lebanon, I was well aware of the chaotic
and murderous history of airplane hijackings in the 1980s. Sifting
through my consciousness in the aftermath of 9/11—and coming to
grips with the imminent release of the Pan Am hijackers by the Pakistani government—I often thought of the 1985 hijacking of TWA
Flight 847 and of what unfolded at that time in a war-torn Beirut. I
was fifteen years old, and I remember being glued to the news coverage of what was happening just a few short miles from our family's
Beirut apartment. TWA Flight 847 originated as an Athens-to-Rome
flight, but the plane was diverted to Beirut (and eventually to Al-

giers and back to Beirut, twice) by hijackers demanding the release of hundreds of Lebanese Shiites from Israeli jails. Most were there as a result of the Israeli incursion into southern Lebanon during the Israel-PLO War.

The TWA 847 hijacking would prove to be an early operation by newly formed Hizballah. When Flight 847 ended up in Beirut for good, the hijackers led the hostages off the plane and sequestered them in the warren of alleys and lanes around the airport. At that time, there was almost no security cordon around the airport. No local authority in Lebanon could deal with the problem, so the Syrians, the Americans, and the Israelis negotiated with Hizballah and with Amal for two weeks until the ordeal ended.

My sisters and I discussed the event endlessly. I felt horrible, so powerless to do anything. I loved my birth country, but the hijacking revealed the insanity that had consumed it. Lebanon had been torn apart by a war it did not invite. I was ashamed and angry with the terrorists, with their grievances and their angry, fanatical posturing. Lebanon had become a battleground between the PLO and the Israelis, with everybody else in the world standing on the sidelines passing judgment.

But as a fifteen-year-old, what most chilled me was the murder of the one hostage who died, an American. Navy Diver Robert Stethem was young; he had a family, I was sure, that loved him. On the morning after the hijacking, with the plane on the runway, he was savagely beaten and then shot in the temple. Like Rajesh Kumar, the first victim of the Pan Am hijacking, he was pushed out onto the dirty tarmac. And like Rajesh Kumar, Stethem's only crime was being American.

Even at that tender age, I could not accept the political imperative that drove the TWA hijackers. I recognized, when our family discussed the matter and as news coverage of the hijacking reached epic proportions, that ignorance and unquenchable hate can lead men to commit horrific acts—and to then follow these acts with proclamations of their own moral justification. It all came rushing back to me that September in Washington. With images of Safarini's freedom looming, I pored over the Flight 73 file. I needed to focus on getting justice for some families, if not all of them.

NIGHTMARE: CHAOS INSIDE THE TUBE

. . .

The aircraft remained on the ground in Karachi throughout the morning and into the day as negotiations between Safarini, the Pakistani government, and Pan Am personnel continued. Safarini served as spokesman for the hijackers. His initial demand was the return of a flight crew, which would allow him to fly the aircraft to Larnaca, Cyprus, where he sought to secure the release of Palestinian prisoners detained by Cypriot authorities.

During the cockpit-to-tower negotiations, Safarini made it clear that the hijackers were suicide operatives prepared to kill all of the passengers, adding that he possessed enough explosives to destroy the plane instantly. (Throughout the hijacking, Safarini wore a heavy, six-inch-wide belt around his waist that was visible to the passengers and crew. The detonator-studded belt encased a Soviet military-grade plastic explosive, Semtex H. Should Safarini choose to detonate the belt, the shock wave from the blast would massacre the passengers and utterly destroy the aircraft.)

On board the aircraft, Safarini carefully controlled the movements of the passengers and the remaining crew. He insisted that passengers keep their hands up and heads down, a painful position they were forced to maintain for hour after agonizing hour. Throughout the hijacking, Safarini used Fahad to patrol the upper deck and front cabin when Safarini was elsewhere in the aircraft. Fahad kept flight attendants from communicating with one another and treated passengers brutally. He carried a Chinese copy of a Russian AK-47 machine gun. With a collapsible stock, an improvised sling made from strips of torn white cloth, and a curved black magazine containing thirty rounds of ammunition, the weapon measured just over two feet long with the stock folded—ideal for use in the narrow aisles of an aircraft. He menacingly displayed a hand grenade as well, handling it at times with the pin pulled out.

Meanwhile, back in the rear of the aircraft, hijacker Khalil spent the first three hours of the hijacking holding a gun and, at times, a grenade to the head of one of the flight attendants. Khalil and his partner, Mansoor, alternated in guarding the rear sections of the aircraft and intimidating the passengers. Both Mansoor and Khalil were well armed with handguns and grenades, and Khalil flashed a knife with a large blade.

Shortly after seizing control of the aircraft, Safarini ordered the flight attendants to collect passengers' passports. As the flight attendants moved among the passengers to comply with this order, they surreptitiously skipped or hid the US passports from the hijackers. When this collection process was finished, Safarini instructed members of the flight crew to separate the American passports from the others and to deliver the American passports directly to him. He became visibly upset when the only American passports belonged to passengers of South Asian ancestry. He was apparently trying to locate "real" Americans to ensure that they were among the first hostages slaughtered.

After the passport review, Safarini walked through the cabin demanding that passengers state their nationalities. When asked, Rajesh Kumar, a 29-year-old California resident and recently naturalized American citizen, said he was from India. But Safarini didn't believe him and ordered Kumar to the front of the aircraft, where he forced the young American to kneel beside the door while placing his hands behind his head. In this position, Kumar doubled over and started to cry. He sought sympathy from Safarini by telling him that he was traveling with his grandmother, but Safarini only kicked him and told him to shut up. Safarini then ordered the door of the aircraft opened. Discovering that authorities had removed the stairway to the aircraft, Safarini again shouted his demand for a replacement flight crew. The Pan Am representative agreed to relay Safarini's demand to the authorities and warily moved away from the aircraft. An eerie silence hung over the scene as Rajesh Kumar continued to kneel beside the cabin door.

When, several hours later, the Pan Am representative returned to the aircraft and informed Safarini that a replacement cockpit crew was being flown to Karachi, Safarini became enraged by what he saw as a delaying tactic. Roughly seizing Kumar by the shirt collar and dragging him to the threshold of the open door, Safarini threatened the negotiator on the ground, telling him that he would shoot Kumar if something was not done within fifteen minutes. The aircraft door swung shut.

Those fifteen minutes passed all too quickly. Safarini again ordered that the door to the aircraft be opened. Safarini seized Kumar, placed a pistol to his head, and dragged him to the threshold of the opened door. Without missing a beat, he fired a single round into Kumar's head, and then kicked his bleeding body over the threshold of the door, dropping him onto the tarmac thirty feet below. Safarini threw the gore-splattered weapon out the open door, and it smashed into the pavement next to Kumar's body. Pakistani rescue personnel present at the scene would later tell reporters that Kumar was still breathing when he was placed in an ambulance, but he was pronounced dead shortly after arriving at a hospital in Karachi. Four hours into the hijacking, Safarini had changed the rules. There wouldn't be a peaceful resolution to this terrorist act. The question on everyone's mind now was how much blood would flow before the nightmare ended.

· · ·

CHECKMATE POINT

I am no stranger to cold-blooded murder. At age nine, I'd witnessed an execution-style murder at a military checkpoint where our family was stopped during one of our many flights out of war-ravaged Beirut. My father was in Egypt for a business meeting, and my mother, my brother, my sisters, our family's maid, and I were alone in our Beirut home when terror struck. At the time, I was unaware of the details, but I would later learn that the Druze leader Kamal Jumblat had been assassinated, setting off a round of deadly violence in the city. My grandfather, Amin, decided to leave the Chouf Mountains and travel to Beirut to help us when he heard the news. Storming into the apartment, he instructed my mother to pack what we needed: he was taking the family to the relative safety of the mountains, which were heavily populated by our fellow Druze. I knew from my grandfather's panic that something was terribly wrong. I quickly deduced that we were not getting bombed—otherwise we would be heading toward the shelter. No, we were at the mercy of street war. It made perfect sense to leave.

After packing some clothes, emptying all the food from the refrigerator, and switching the power off for the entire apartment—the typical emergency checklist—we rushed down the stairs. We lived on the sixth floor and normally used the building's elevator, but on this day we used the stairs. The elevator wasn't reliable owing to unpredictable and frequent power outages. That was not the day to risk being caught between floors crying for help.

Outside, we piled into Grandfather's orange and brown Pontiac sedan. My sisters, our maid, and I were stuffed in the back seat while my mother and brother occupied the front seat. Amin asked my mother whether she wanted to stay at her parents' home in the Chouf or be taken to our family's country home in the Maten Mountains. My mother nervously deferred to her father as to which location would be safer. He decided on the Chouf.

On our way out of Beirut, we got stuck in unexpected traffic. I soon realized that we were trapped in a line of cars because two armed men were stopping vehicles and asking for identification cards. Lebanese identification cards listed the individual's religious affiliation; therefore, during times of sectarian violence and depending on who passes judgment on the card's information, an ID card can serve as one's death warrant.

One of the armed men checking ID cards was wearing a ski mask, but the other did not cover his face. Both were carrying weapons. While the ski mask and weapons were terrifying, I knew that an individual with an uncovered face was actually more dangerous—he would likely leave no witnesses to any serious act of violence. The unmasked man had an ominous look on his face that made my heart skip a beat. I kept swallowing in fear, trying to keep myself from acting out the anxiety and frustration I felt. As the old Pontiac edged closer to its rendezvous with the two gunmen, I realized that both of these men were actually little more than boys in their early teens. I also realized we were going through a "flyby checkpoint," a hastily erected, informal screening of travelers designed to provide security to an area—or to extract revenge against an opposing sect. I feverishly prayed the Druze were not the target today.

My grandfather, meanwhile, had quickly figured that these militiamen were Druze by a small flag displayed on their Kalashnikovs. In a lightning-quick motion, he ripped down the rosary that was hanging on the rearview mirror and concealed it his pocket. Although my family belonged to the Druze sect, we followed and believed in Christianity; Grandfather realized any confusion on the part of the guards would be trouble. At this point, we were the second vehicle in line. The two armed boys, one on each side of the light blue Peugeot in front of us, started to yell at each other and then at the Peugeot's driver after examining the driver's identification card. They ordered the driver to move his vehicle aside. I saw that his wife was clutching an infant and turning to the children in the back seat, likely telling them that everything would be fine. The armed men continued to argue with each other; suddenly, the unmasked man broke off the argument, walked over to the Peugeot, and shot the driver in the face, point blank. The driver's wife, covered in brain- and blood-splatter, began to scream hysterically. Her wails were so loud that, although the children were crying too, I couldn't hear them over her screams. Grandfather used the confusion and noise to lurch the Pontiac forward and sped away from the horrific scene. I braced myself for a hail of bullets that, fortunately, never arrived. It was not difficult for me to understand how the passengers of Flight 73 must have felt when their passports were being collected. To this day, I know all too well the shock felt by the children on the plane when they were made witnesses to the sudden and horrific act of violence that took Rajesh Kumar's life.

NIGHTMARE: EXECUTION

. . .

Satisfied that he had captured the attention of his negotiators with the murder of Kumar, Safarini threatened to kill another passenger every ten minutes until his demands were met. Safarini selected another passenger to come forward, but when the passenger began to offer Islamic prayers, he was returned to his seat; Safarini called forward another passenger, a UK citizen, and instructed this passenger to kneel at the front of the aircraft. For reasons that remain unclear, Safarini did not carry out this latest threat. Hours passed and nightfall came; roughly sixteen hours into the hijacking, the auxiliary power unit that supplied electricity for the main lights on the plane spluttered and failed. As the fuel ran out, the emergency lights on the plane began to dim and flicker, a development the hijackers misinterpreted as a deliberate cut in power in advance of an assault by security forces. To ensure that their mission did not fail, Safarini instructed Fahad to shoot him if commandos stormed the aircraft, in the mistaken belief that the military-grade explosives he wore around his waist would be detonated by the impact of a bullet. He wasn't seeking to martyr himself; instead, he was demanding that he be turned into a human bomb that would kill as many passengers as possible.

As darkness settled over Karachi, the hijackers stampeded the passengers and flight attendants into the center section of the aircraft. It must have been a horrible scene, with some passengers clawing to get on top of other passengers to distance themselves from what must have appeared to them as the beginning of the end of their lives.

Safarini and Fahad positioned themselves in front of the crowd of passengers and crew in the right and left aisles, while Khalil and Mansoor remained at the rear of the aircraft. The hijackers recited a martyrdom prayer in Arabic, then unleashed their fury on the assembled mass. The attack was horrifyingly methodical, with hijackers interrupting bursts of automatic weapon fire to throw their grenades among the terrified passengers. The interior of the plane lit up with the intermittent explosions and the sheets of fire from the AK-47s. In the mayhem, either by accident or design, Safarini was shot, just as he had asked. The shot missed his explosive belt, and the wound was apparently serious enough to prevent him from firing the detonators in the belt himself. It was a single stroke of luck in a night of bleak despair.

Nineteen passengers and crew were killed during this final assault, including a second US citizen, fifty-year-old Surendra Patel, the father of three children. Two of Patel's children were seated next to him on the aircraft that day. They watched him die. The remaining eighteen victims came from half a dozen different countries and included children as young as seven.

Scores of other passengers were injured, including seven Americans. These survivor's wounds were grotesque and horrifying: heads opened, faces ripped off, limbs lost. Some surviving passengers and crew, including seventy-six US citizens, escaped through several of the plane's cabin doors, which had been forced open in the melee. They then faced a twenty-foot jump from the wing of the aircraft onto the tarmac. Pakistani security forces had, unaccountably, not been poised to raid the aircraft. One wonders what they were thinking—or doing. In any event, they only entered the plane after it was emptied of passengers.

Safarini's three fellow hijackers attempted to blend in with the fleeing passengers and make their escape across the grounds of the Karachi airport. They didn't make it. Terrified victims identified them to Pakistani authorities, and they were subdued immediately. Safarini, wounded by one of his comrades and found immobile on the plane, was transported to a local hospital for medical treatment. He was carried into the hospital still wearing the Semtex explosive belt. Perplexed hospital staff presented the belt to security officials at the hospital, and Safarini was arrested while still awaiting treatment for his wounds. A week later, Pakistani authorities arrested Wadoud Muhammad Hafiz Al-Turki, the operation's logistical support leader.

At their joint trial in Pakistan, Safarini, his three fellow hi-jackers, and Al-Turki voluntarily submitted a nineteen-page state-ment to the court saying they had traveled to Pakistan to hijack an American airplane, hoping to draw the world's attention to the Palestinian cause. In a prophetic foreshadowing of 9/11, the state-ment noted that the aim of the hijackers was to fly the plane into a "sensitive strategic centre of the Zionist enemy and to blow it up there with us inside"; their goal was to "destroy . . . through an American weapon, i.e., the explosion of American aeroplane." The joint statement expressed regret over not being able to use the aircraft as a bomb. "No doubt, this time, we failed; but one day we will be successful," the statement concluded.

. . .

FLASH FORWARD

Eighteen years after the horrific events in Karachi, in September 2001, nineteen men, driven by an unquenchable hate similar to the hate extolled by the Pan Am 73 hijackers, were successful in using aircrafts as weapons of mass destruction. Their war against America was spawned by rhetoric, as well as by their leader's narrow reading of the Quran and their own ignorance of historic Islam. It was to this new and unpredictable war that the rest of my career, both at the FBI and later at the CIA, would be devoted. A "Global War on Terror," our president and the press called it. But I thought of it, at times, as a personal war: it had come to me in Beirut as early as 1979; but September 11, 2001, was when it came to all of us.

I was ready to do my part. I was ready to bring Safarini and his gang to America to face the scales of American justice.

LATE AL QAEDA NIGHTS 7

My involvement in the USS *Cole* investigation required me to travel to Islamabad to gather intelligence on Al Qaeda's leadership. I left Washington on January 27, 2001, and arrived in Islamabad on January 29 for one of the most important debriefings of my career. Al Qaeda's leadership had roots in both Pakistan and Afghanistan. As a result, it was not uncommon for sources to report information on where they were hiding in South Asia.

The asset was reporting on the senior ranks of the Al Qaeda leadership, and this debrief was done jointly with an elite cadre of counterterrorism officers from the CIA. The information we received from this source was critical to our efforts to track and—we hoped—trap Al Qaeda's leadership. I would later learn that the president of the United States was being briefed on our day-to-day accomplishments.

The day of our meeting with the asset, I was walking around the embassy looking for a copy machine because the machine in the legal attaché's, or Legat's, office was broken. When I finally located one, I heard someone call my name.

"Hello, Nada!"

I turned around and looked up.

"Remember me? From Aden?" Gordon asked.

How could I forget this tall, fair-skinned man with the piercing green eyes?

"It's Gordon, right?"

"Right. I worked with you on the *Cole* investigation three weeks ago."

"And graciously fetched some of the ingredients to help me make my hummus," I added.

I was a bit surprised that Gordon remembered *me* from Aden. We had worked together only briefly but had shared dining facilities for part of my temporary duty assignment (TDY). "Yes, that's me. By the way, your hummus was delicious," he replied.

"Thank you," I said, hoping he did not see the blush I could feel racing to my cheeks.

"Are you having dinner at the Embassy Club tonight?" he asked. "I'm eating with a group of friends, and the special today is quite good. You should join us." It was a tempting invitation.

"I think work is going to keep me from making it tonight," I responded, trying to look as disappointed as I felt. Had he just asked me out? Or was he only being friendly?

"If you finish in time, please feel free to join us."

"I'll try my best, but it doesn't look good," I admitted.

"Well, keep up the good work. Maybe we'll see each other later," he said. But duty called. Informant debriefings, more often than not, are long, tedious processes; given this asset's travel schedule, we met with him on an infrequent basis. We had been fortunate to secure a meeting, and we needed to make the most of it. For security purposes, our meetings were held at night and often went into the wee hours. At this point, Andrew and I had been separated since April 1999, and the idea of getting to know someone new was appealing. I felt that I was ready to date and meet new people, though frequent travel made it difficult.

The debriefing went extremely well. I was proud of the intelligence collected and impressed with my CIA colleagues. At one point the CIA officer on the debriefing team looked at the informant and, using nearly flawless Arabic, said, "With your permission, I will leave the room but will shortly be back." This method of paying respect while maintaining authority and control demonstrated a sophisticated understanding of Arab interpersonal relationships.

Being assigned to the FBI's Extraterritorial Terrorism Squad exposed me early on to CIA operations. I was struck by the CIA's emphasis on teaching its officers foreign languages and immersing them in foreign cultures. In my experience, FBI management did not fully understand the value of these skills, something I believe limited our ability to accomplish our mission.

I returned to my hotel room just before dawn, and by the time I had showered and crawled into bed, my adrenaline had finally stopped pumping. As I drifted to sleep, I thought about Gordon and his colleagues and how important social get-togethers were for government employees serving in foreign locations far from friends and family. I thought about my sisters and told myself that I needed to visit them in Detroit more often. I looked at my watch, and when I saw the date, it hit me. I had missed my birthday! I had been crossing time zones, and January 28 simply got lost in midair—literally. Before falling off to sleep, my thoughts drifted back to my childhood and memories of how my parents had "celebrated" my birthday.

Although my parents celebrated my brother's birthday and made a big deal out of the occasion, they ignored the birthdays of their daughters. Strangely, my parents felt compelled every year to promise us that they would celebrate our birthdays, but inevitably the day would pass with little or no celebration. We girls burned in anticipation of a surprise party that never came. With the innocence of a child, I always believed parental promises to celebrate my birthday the following year, but the next year would come and no celebration would take place. After I left Lebanon and my parents' house, I promised myself that I would always celebrate and make a fuss of my birthday; but somehow, after joining the Bureau, I let go of that promise. Upon reflection, I saw a telling repetition in the fact that the Bureau had replaced my parents as the "agent" that kept me too busy to think about birthdays.

At lunch the next day, I spotted Gordon and his colleagues and decided to join them. They were obviously a close group, and I enjoyed seeing them interact with each other. I sat there wishing my squad's members could be as close. When I traveled with John, for instance, I had the unfortunate opportunity to hear him criticize almost everyone on the squad. He told me that Karen was having an affair with a married member on the squad—Ken—adding that Karen was an alcoholic. He informed me that the squad's relief supervisor, Izzy—who was in great shape, by the way—had been "seriously fat" as a teenager and was "using" exercise to compensate for a painful adolescence. I invariably tuned him out after a few minutes, but I had already made a mental note to never reveal anything about my personal life to John. I would later learn that my efforts to keep my personal life private were futile: after I began seeing Gordon, John started spreading rumors about my having had an affair while I was married, even though Andrew and I had been separated for nearly two years and our divorce was impending. Andrew was aware of my relationship with Gordon and was happy for me. Our divorce would become final a few months later, on June 5, 2001.

That day, January 30, I also briefed the chief of station and his top managers on the FBI's *Cole* investigation to date. I answered their questions and pointed out the areas where their expertise would help. I finished my assigned duties and arranged to return for the next source briefing several months hence.

I flew back to Islamabad in the spring of 2001 and again conducted a successful and productive debriefing. I ran into Gordon in the cafeteria again; we spoke for a bit, and he asked me to dinner that night. It was hard to say no to his big smile and warm green eyes, but, once again, I had to work that night. I had volunteered to use my language and cultural expertise to help the CIA with an operation. In fact, I was working the next two nights with the CIA on other cases, and I turned down Gordon's offer for dinner two more times.

Finally, on Friday night, after finishing my numerous write-ups, I headed to the Embassy Club for dinner. I ran into Gordon, who was having dinner with his colleague Chris. Chris called me over and asked me to join them for dinner. We had a great conversation, and I did not realize how hungry I was until I finished my salad and helped myself to a third serving of the fresh local bread. I was hoping Gordon would ask me whether I had plans for the weekend, but when he didn't, I volunteered the information anyway, telling him that, for a change, I was not working. He immediately caught on and asked me whether I wanted to go hiking in the nearby Margala Hills. I readily accepted. Gordon picked me up from my hotel Saturday morning, and we headed to the Margala Hills. These foothills of the distant Himalayas arc around Islamabad to the north of the city and are known for their dense greenery and rocky outcroppings. We drove to a trailhead, parked, and began a leisurely ascent. It felt strange to be in such an isolated place. I mentioned to Gordon that I was armed with my Glock, and it turned out he was an avid shooter with long experience serving in hostile parts of the world. We talked for an hour about all sorts of weapons and how their presence and use had influenced our work and our lives. We were a couple of gun geeks, and I thought, *What a refreshing discussion for a first date!*

Gordon and I met for dinner several times after that, and the more I got to know him, the more I liked him. On my last night in Islamabad, Gordon took me to a local Afghan restaurant where we enjoyed a delicious meal and talked the night away. I felt genuinely happy. I knew that I was going to miss him when I left Pakistan.

ROCKET AND ROLL OUT

Before I had a chance to leave, I was asked to perform an extraordinary task—an exfiltration related to the November 12, 1999, attack on the US embassy in Islamabad. In a series of coordinated and near-simultaneous attacks on US and other international targets, seven rockets had been fired from homemade launchers that had been crudely welded to the backs of three vehicles positioned around Islamabad. The US embassy, the US cultural center, and the UN offices in Islamabad were the intended targets. The rockets largely missed these targets but managed to seriously wound a guard at the American cultural center. Still, the attack was a brutal shock to American and UN staffers in Islamabad. I heard about it firsthand from Gordon over dinner one night. He explained to me that upon hearing the rocket blasts, he recalled the 1998 US embassy bombings in East Africa, in which smaller detonations set off by attackers were followed by a massive bomb causing catastrophic damage. Gordon had heard cries of "Stay away from the windows!" and "Get on the ground!" echoing in the embassy hallways. He and his colleagues quickly crawled to the locations they judged safest and braced themselves to be entombed by whatever might come next. Gordon described these moments as a lifetime, a wait no one should be subjected to.

But the follow-up explosions never came. The rockets used by the attackers would have caused massive damage if they had directly impacted their targets. Instead, they flew wide of their targets and detonated around the city, causing a good deal of terror but little serious damage.

Given the sharp focus on US targets, the Legat's office made investigating the attacks a priority. Eventually, Mike, the FBI assistant legal attaché in Islamabad, developed an individual source who bragged that he could solve the crime but then refused to cooperate out of fear for his life. With the passage of time, this individual's position in the terrorist group responsible for the attack became untenable. He was a known murderer, a serious criminal moving in a circle of terrorists prepared to kill him as readily as they would kill their enemies. Eventually, when the source's balance of fear tipped in Mike's direction, he demanded, in exchange for information about the attack, that a loved one be moved to a place of safety and that he, the source, be allowed to join the loved one outside Pakistan.

The language and cultural demands necessary for moving the loved one were daunting. First, it required a native Arabic speaker. A woman agent was the preferred choice; consequently, I was asked to undertake a multinational trip. Operating under an improvised cover, I would accompany a known terrorist's loved one to safety. The individual was not able to travel alone: most likely, such travel would have raised red flags, thereby compromising the entire investigation. Later, when I joined the CIA, I was taught that this kind of clandestine movement, called an "exfiltration," is one of the most politically risky and most physically dangerous operations possible. These missions demand meticulous planning and a great deal of luck.

The planning was left to me, and, as it turned out, I was very, very lucky. Generally, the FBI doesn't do exfiltrations overseas; that's left to the CIA. But the FBI moved ahead with this operation to avoid subordinating itself to the CIA. With only a naïve understanding of the potential risks, I accepted a diplomatic passport and enough contact information to get me started. After that point, I was pretty much on my own.

The person I needed to move was young, scared, and uneducated and had no reason to trust me. I was traveling on a diplomatic passport because the FBI lacks a critical capability, which the CIA has, that would have provided me the absolute minimal required level of protection while en route. But, since diplomatic immunity only applies to individuals permanently assigned to a particular country, my travels would leave me dangerously exposed to local security organizations. Furthermore, the diplomatic passport draws undesirable attention—in this case, it would elicit even more attention since I would be accompanied by a nondiplomat of a wildly different social background.

Such subterfuge would be impossible for the "average" FBI agent. For a white male without international experience and zero language capability, a badge and a gun weren't going to open the necessary doors. As soon as I met my strange traveling companion, I started to modify and refine my behavior and my plans. I had the individual discard traditional clothing, and I purchased clothing less likely to highlight our disparity. I then faced the most dangerous point in the trip—initial departure. If we were stopped at this point, the entire plan, including apprehension of the terrorists responsible for the rocket attacks, would fail.

The first things you lose in a sensitive journey like this are your sense of security and your ability to feel clean. My journey started with a terrifying risk and with a stifling heat that bathed me in sweat. Under harsh fluorescent lights, I walked with my charge up to the immigration line at the airport. Lazily spinning fans pushed warm, dusty air and clouds of flies down on the travelers. I could feel my pulse rate climbing, and I struggled to affect an unconcerned appearance. I knew that as soon as I presented our documents, there was no going back. If my ruse failed, questions would be followed by detention, detention by investigation, and investigation by an international incident that would place both my life and my charge's life at risk. In the midst of all this anxiety I kept having the strangest thought: Would I ever see Gordon again?

I refined my plan as I stood in line and closely observed the customs officers: officious, petty, and mean, they used their power over departure stamps to extort subservience and bribes. While it made my skin crawl to consider it, I knew that I would need to "play to type"—to appear weak and unintelligent in order to corroborate the official's cultural perceptions of women. As I feared, the customs official quickly questioned why we were traveling together and looked at my companion with a suspicious eye. I launched into a glib explanation. Using a light, falsetto voice, I spoke of my excitement at being able to go overseas for a shopping spree.

I watched understanding settle over the officer's face. He stamped our passports, and I moved my charge into the business-class lounge, with instructions to speak with nobody and to quickly feign a pre-departure nap. The overcooled air of the lounge turned my sweat cold. I quickly stepped out of the lounge to case the route and situation at our departure gate. I expected additional layers of security. Now that we were trapped inside the airport, I didn't want to be surprised.

The rest of our departure was highly uneventful. There was a cursory document check at the gate before we boarded the plane. The doors were sealed, and we started our taxi out. My fear of flying started to buzz in the back of my head, but the extreme delicacy of the departure and the need for me to be focused on the next step of the journey pushed it away. I knew we had a couple of hours to rest; after that we needed to pass through the next layer of security. At this point, the risk for extended detention had largely passed, but it was still possible for the operation to fail. A problem at immigration could mean deportation of my charge back to the country of origin. That would be a serious setback, one I was determined to avoid.

When we completed the first leg of our journey and arrived at our first stop, a country in Southeast Asia, we moved through immigration quickly and exited customs. I started scanning the crowd for the local FBI Legat and hoped that he would be out in front, supporting us upon our arrival. He would have real diplomatic immunity, local expertise, and could take over until the next leg of the journey—lifting the crushing load of responsibility I was carrying. But nothing about this operation turned out to be simple.

As time passed with no Legat in sight, it became obvious that we were on our own. I grabbed our bags, flagged a taxi, and headed to the preset hotel where I hoped to find I had reservations. At the hotel I spotted the Legat furtively peeking around columns in the lobby in a failed attempt to be discreet. Until I realized it was the Legat, I briefly thought we were certainly under some kind of local surveillance. I was shocked at the Legat's fear of approaching us; I suddenly realized I was being offered as bait to see if there had been a problem with the plan's security measures. Perhaps someone associated with the embassy rocket attack had gotten wind of our deal with the incriminating source and had tipped off one or another government about the exfiltration. In these situations, one has to make quick, strategic decisions. My focus narrowed. I stashed my charge in a room at the hotel and headed to a travel agency to reserve and purchase our tickets for the second leg of the flight. I really was going to have to do this on my own.

Luckily, things went smoothly. I left our Southeast Asian hideaway and traveled with the subject of the exfiltration to our next stop, an island in the Pacific Ocean. The flight was uneventful, and when we landed, I finally felt a sense of personal accomplishment. On one front, I had received sincere appreciation from the subject of the exfiltration. After all, I had reunited my charge with a loved one. But, to my surprise, I received little appreciation from the organization that had assigned me this difficult task, a task that more senior and ostensibly more capable agents had avoided or simply refused to do.

That Pacific island was a popular diving and tourist destination that also boasted a historic World War II site. I took advantage of some free time to tour the island and enjoyed its world-renowned diving spot. Diving was a hobby I enjoyed, but my schedule had always been too hectic to be able to devote enough time to becoming an advanced diver—something I really wanted to follow up on. I knew that Gordon was an accomplished diver, so here was another hobby we had in common. I found myself wishing I could have shared the beauty of the dive with him. My loneliness was catching up to me. All these dangerous missions and beautiful stopovers left me wanting a companion to share things with.

The rare opportunity to dive was a reminder of how my personal interests had been almost totally subsumed by my professional duties. The dizzying pace of the travel and my obsessive need to be on top of every move in every investigation were draining my energies and eliminating any sense I had of myself as a private person. I was also feeling some disappointment because I observed that many of my coworkers didn't share in the intense sense of mission that drove me to seek out challenging assignments. For some agents, it seemed, personal interests came first and work came second or, even worse, work became an opportunity to "work the system" by using government assignments to further personal agendas. Some agents would meet sources in areas chosen ostensibly for security but actually selected for the overseas shopping! It was not uncommon to see an agent place a golf bag in a Bureau car on top of his or her weapon, apparently because it was more important to the agent to get to the golf course ten minutes early than it was to be ready to grab his or her MP5 submachine gun to respond to a bank robbery.

I guess I resented the relaxed lifestyle most agents enjoyed. At the very least, I knew I wouldn't be diving again anytime soon. I believed in the idealized FBI mission, and I was going to sustain my current pace of investigatory work because I thought my personal sacrifices were a necessary part of working for justice. The FBI, for better *and* for worse, was my family.

After conducting a successful exfiltration, I returned to Washington to continue working on the Pan Am 73 investigation. Gordon and I stayed in contact via email, and I enjoyed waking up and going to bed reading emails from him. Getting to know Gordon from what seemed like millions of miles away was easy and comfortable. There was no time pressure, which, given the hours I worked, was perfect. I found myself uncharacteristically attracted to him. The more we talked, the more I was drawn to his life story, especially to the many experiences he shared with me concerning his years of living over-seas. I felt I could trust him.

While working on the exfiltration project, I had learned that in the summer both the Legat and the ALAT were going to be on vacation at the same time. Their office would need a highly capable Bureau agent to manage local law enforcement relationships and to execute the important tasks assigned to it by FBI Headquarters in Washington. The Legat is the senior US law enforcement repre-sentative assigned by the FBI to a US embassy in a foreign country. The primary duty of the seventy-five Legats around the globe is to foster cooperation with the leadership of the host country's law enforcement organizations to further investigations of crimes with ties to the United States. Legats are also responsible for represent-ing the FBI's equities to the various US government agencies that make up an embassy's "Country Team." Legats tend to be very se-nior and experienced agents, since a Legat's missteps or omissions can easily give rise to international incidents. Given my repeated visits to Islamabad and owing to the quality of my work, the Legat was confident that I would be able to properly represent the FBI and encouraged me to apply for the temporary assignment as legal attaché in Islamabad. He had witnessed my work in handling the innumerable leads sent to Pakistan from the dozens of FBI field offices in the United States. In fact, I was by this time accustomed to arriving in Islamabad to find a special file set aside just for me that was filled with tasks sent to the Legat office for completion. These were special tasks, many requiring language capability, or were particularly sensitive assignments requiring my foreign-area knowledge and understanding of our Pakistani hosts. While many agents would object to these extra duties, I did not mind. I wel-comed the challenges, recognized I had special capabilities and skills in running leads to ground, and had little or no personal life that might interfere with my duties.

In June 2001, my supervisor called me to his office with news on the Legat position. I fully expected him to tell me that he had handed the assignment to a more senior agent.

"Nada, congratulations. You've been chosen to travel to Islamabad and be the acting legal attaché for a six-week period," he told me.

I told him I was surprised and honored to be chosen. It was the truth. Among those who applied for this assignment, I had served the shortest Bureau stint. Generally, time-on-board was the standard criterion used to select among competing agents. In fact, seniority determined not only mundane things, like the location of your desk or the quality of your Bureau-provided car, but very important things as well, like future office assignments.

Well, I said to myself, *so much for standard criterion. For God's sake, with less than two years at WFO, I'm still a probationary agent!*

LADY BOSS

I arrived in Islamabad to start my part-time duties in early June 2001. I was as excited to see Gordon as I was to run such an important office. Gordon picked me up at the airport, and my heart skipped a beat when I saw him. He gave me a big hug and handed me a cup of coffee. We drove to the embassy and had breakfast together. I shared the excitement of my new assignment with him and then headed off to the office.

When I got to the office, I examined and prioritized all leads, then hit the ground running. In reviewing the leads, I was disturbed by the apparent lack of understanding of the Legat's role among the various offices in the FBI. As an example, there were several requests from various FBI field offices to locate and interview Pakistani citizens—although under Pakistani law (and the laws of most nations, including the United States) these kinds of interviews were prohibited and illegal unless done in direct partnership with the host nation's accredited law enforcement. Moreover, the Pakistani government (like the governments of most developing nations) did not have a centralized computer system that could easily locate a given individual. Generally, they used word of mouth, especially the familial and tribal contacts of their officers. Needless to say, locating a specific person, not to mention giving the Legat access to interview him, is a process that consumes significant time and resources. To maintain a positive relationship with his or her host country, the Legat must understand and accept the hardships that the host country might face in responding to requests.

Demanding undeliverable results is always counterproductive, and while it was clear to me that Mike had built a solid working environment in Islamabad, it was not clear that Washington understood the facts on the ground. In an attempt to prod its Pakistani law enforcement partners, Washington continually delivered sharp rebukes and made empty threats of sanctions if demands for information were not met faster.

GORDON AND I WERE SEEING EACH OTHER on a regular basis, and I knew, after a few dates, that he was the man for me. We shared similar views on almost every issue, we both spoke Arabic (and English, of course), and both of us were ready to settle down and start a family.

On one of the few nonworking weekends we had together, Gordon and I decided to visit the famous Khyber Pass, the strategic corridor running between Pakistan and Afghanistan. I was not afraid to venture out, especially with Gordon by my side, into the more remote areas of Pakistan; in fact, I believed getting outside the diplomatic compound would have its benefits. First, it would present opportunities to build rapport with Pakistani officials whom I might sooner or later do business with. Second, because these officials were proud of their heritage, they were excellent sources of information about the complex government versus tribal relations in Pakistan. The Khyber Pass would be as good a place as any to start my education.

The pass, a winding, thirty-three-mile passage through the Hindu Kush mountain range, connects the northern frontier of Pakistan with

Afghanistan. On the north side of the pass rise the towering, snow-covered peaks of the Hindu Kush. Alexander the Great descended this pass on his way into India nearly 2,500 years ago. More recently, from the 1980s on, the pass served as a supply line to Islamists fighting the Russians in Afghanistan. Osama bin Laden had traveled these mountain roads many a time as he built up support for the *mujahedeen* fighting the Soviets. At the time, Bin Laden had been a dangerous but effective ally in America's cold war support of the Afghan rebellion against the communists. Now, with the Russians gone, it was anybody's guess as to who would dominate this paradox of a region: a crossroads of world history so out of the way that 90 percent of Americans had no idea it existed.

Today it is America that travels the pass, now from south to north, using the artery to help supply its sometimes nebulous war against the Taliban and other shadowy forces in the heart of Afghanistan.

My first view of the pass that day in June 2001, a mere three months before the day the world changed, gave shape to my imagining of the birthplace and home of Al Qaeda. My thoughts wandered to the dozens of highly classified operations that I knew of that had, at some point, crossed this ground. In the afternoon, we hiked to a mountain top where we were fed a traditional Pashtun meal of grilled meats and fluffy seasoned rice while watching a folklore dance group. The dancing went on for hours, and Gordon and I talked away the time, enjoying the vitality and beauty of the dancers. For a long time, perhaps for all my life, I had carried with me a sense of need for a safe nest away from the terrors of war and family strife. Basking in the pleasure of the moment, I realized suddenly that it was with this new friend and colleague that I felt at home. I knew right then that there was no one else in the world I wanted to share my life with but Gordon. I think, as we drove back to Islamabad that day, we both realized that in the crazy wide world we each had come to inhabit in so singular a fashion, we had finally found a bond we could nurture and build our lives, both personal and professional, around.

To parallel my growing relationship with Gordon, I had growing work responsibilities as I settled into my role as acting Legat. I made an appointment to meet with the director of the Pakistani national police. The national police were, in part, the Pakistani Federal Investigation Agency (FIA). I had reviewed, prior to this appointment, a lengthy list of "demands" from FBI Headquarters and numerous field offices. I was determined to build on Mike's positive approach with the Pakistani agencies, so as I drove to FIA headquarters, I contemplated how to recast the Bureau's PowerPointed demands in a softer, more respectful light.

After a long introductory discussion ranging from the director's family to Pakistani history to my travel to the Khyber Pass, I politely asked the director for his help in furthering American interests in serving justice and in providing both his country and mine with useful information. When I assured him that the FBI appreciated all his efforts, he quickly assured me that *he* appreciated my easygoing manner and professional courtesies. To further build on my rapport with the director, we agreed to meet at his firearm's range for some recreational shooting.

During my time as the acting Legat, I naturally worked on many highly classified terrorism cases; after all, it was the summer of 2001, relatively close to what would later turn out to be the Al Qaeda camp where the 9/11 plot reached its final stages. Though the intelligence on that attack was, tragically, always a step behind the perpetrators, plenty of intelligence concerning Al Qaeda was filtering into our offices.

As my assignment in Islamabad drew to a close, Gordon too was preparing to change assignments. Because he and I would be returning to the Washington area around the same time, late July 2001, we decided to travel back together. We had grown a great deal closer during our time in Pakistan. This return trip felt so different from any other. I felt as if I were arriving in a familiar place for the first time in that I would now be making a home with Gordon right here in Washington. I would never again dispassionately return after a mission to an apartment where I lived temporarily. On the first weekend back, after dinner at a local restaurant, Gordon got on his knee and took my hand in his. I remember his words perfectly.

"Nada," he began, "the first time I laid eyes on you, you had dark circles under your eyes, you wore soot-stained dirty pants from being on the *Cole*, and you had an odor of diesel about you, from the ship's engines. When we spoke, your genuine and caring personality shone through that rough facade. You always had a kind word, a bright smile, and a positive attitude. Thirty-five hundred feet up in that beautiful air of the Khyber Pass, I knew I'd found the woman for me. I am a better man because of you. Your passion for justice and your love of our country inspires me. There is no one else for me. I want to spend the rest of my life with you."

Tears of happiness rolled down my cheeks as I accepted Gordon's proposal. I was very happy and wanted to share my news with my family, but I waited to do so in person. I knew my parents would not approve of a non-Druze, let alone an American, as their son-in-law. But I was finally beyond their barbs. I was a woman who had it all: a perfect companion, a challenging job, and the energy to embrace my future, whatever it might bring.

Wanting to put down deeper roots, I decided to purchase a modest townhouse in Northern Virginia. I did not travel during August and was lucky to spend my free time with Gordon. We were getting to know each other in the context of a daily life that moved happily forward. Our work worlds meshed seamlessly. I was scheduled to close on my house in mid-September and move shortly thereafter. And I would be building a future with a true soul mate.

SEPTEMBER 11, 2001 8

I was sitting in Joe's office, speechless and suddenly afraid of everything around me, as we watched the South Tower of the World Trade Center collapse in a rush of smoke and cinder. Both the North and South Towers had been hit by this time, and news reports were filtering in of additional planes having been hijacked. A single, clear thought pierced my fear and disbelief: this was the work of Al Qaeda. Osama bin Laden's audacious plan to attack us in a place symbolic of our power and reach had come to pass. Within thirty minutes of the attack on the World Trade Center, a third plane slammed into the west side of the Pentagon, less than five miles from the Washington field office where Joe and I were sitting. We stared at each other in shocked silence. *Are we the next target?* I thought to myself.

A number of employees had already fled their offices in panic. Many of them later confessed that they too thought Capitol Hill would be targeted. I immediately called Gordon and checked on him; he also was in a federal building that was a potential target. But he was staying put, he said, and he told me to do the same. We made tentative plans to check in with each other as the day wore on. When I got off the phone with Gordon, I went back to watching coverage of the growing disaster with Joe. After a fourth and then a fifth hijacked plane, I wondered where it would all end. Not until the fourth plane crashed in a field in Pennsylvania and a report came through that all planes were accounted for did I start to feel some of my fear dissipate. A feeling of numbness replaced the fear.

When Joe and I got our voices back, I remarked to him that the sites chosen by Al Qaeda made sense to me, but I wondered about the terrorists' choices of both the date and the airlines. Could United Airlines and American Airlines have been chosen because their very names represented our nation? *United . . . American?* Having worked on several investigations relating to Palestinian terrorist groups, I recalled an offshoot group of the Fatah organization named "Black September." The group had derived its name from the timing of a conflict between the king of Jordan and the Palestinians who had tried, unsuccessfully, to overthrow the Jordanian state in a coup d'état in the early 1970s. Could Bin Laden be using the date of the attack to build a strong symbolic bridge of support throughout the Middle East? It was too early to tell, Joe remarked. He offered a more practical observation: everyone was back at school, and these flights had probably been half full, which would make taking over the planes easier. (It turns out that Joe had a point. Three of the four planes had very limited passenger lists.) In any event, speculation would be the order of the day for some time. A massive new case was about to overwhelm every branch of the government.

The Pentagon attack site was now a crime scene that needed to be protected as soon as the search and rescue efforts were completed. A senior squad mate and I immediately headed to the Pentagon and were among the first FBI personnel to arrive there. As I stood looking at the destruction, I felt my rage rising. How dare these terrorists come to our country, take advantage of our freedoms, and use them to attack us? I found myself hoping the president would order immediate military action against all areas where we suspected the presence of OBL and Al Qaeda. The circumstances were extraordinary, I told myself. Even innocent civilians there would probably have to die. It was what it was. The attacks had pushed the uneasy truce between East and West out the window.

Of course, a part of me wondered if revenge at any cost was what I really wanted. In truth, I didn't know at that moment. I could only feel that my colleagues and I should have gone after Bin Laden when we had an opening after the attack on the USS *Cole*. I was also angry with and ashamed of Arab media for displaying disturbing footage of the so-called man-in-the-street celebrations in the West Bank and other locales. How dare these journalists show no respect for the families of the victims? And I was furious with extremist Palestinians, who applauded their "hero" Bin Laden.

As I helped to cordon off the area around the Pentagon and prepare the site for an investigation, I realized I was angry with God, too. Our God, their God . . . it didn't matter. Life was sacred, and these acts had unfolded with no sign from any protecting agent on high. *We are all on our own now,* I thought. I did what I could at the Pentagon before heading home to share my grief with Gordon.

I did not know how to deal with my anger, and so for the next few weeks, I buried myself in work. Because of my language skills, I was asked to examine official documents, analyze intelligence, and interview witnesses.

One morning, I got a call from my real estate agent telling me that everyone was waiting for me to sign the contract on my new home. In all the work and confusion, I had nearly missed my house closing. I rushed to the meeting, signed the paperwork, got my key, and went right back to the office. When I got there, the ASAC— assistant special agent in charge—walked over to my desk and told me I had an immediate assignment.

"Pack your bags, Nada," he barked, "you are going back to Islamabad. They asked for you by name. They need you!"

And that was it. Back to the front lines. My gut told me Bin Laden was hiding out somewhere in Pakistan or Afghanistan.

I called Gordon and told him about the house and my upcoming travel. I was anxious about moving; now, it would have to wait. Gordon told me not to worry, assuring me he would take care of everything while I was gone. Having an understanding and unconditionally supportive partner made life easier. I was not ready to discuss my unresolved anger with Gordon or anyone else, so in a way, flying to Pakistan actually seemed like a good idea. I would be far from my new home, but closer to OBL. I would work on my anger there on that frontier where the glorious and the vanquished had lined up throughout history, and I knew perfectly well into which camp Bin Laden would eventually fall.

I was in Islamabad for six weeks. As I suspected, the pace of work helped me deal with my roiling feelings. I buried myself in the details. I did not mind the endless hours; in fact, I sought them out. But what I really wanted to do was pick up a weapon and head to Afghanistan. The thought occurred to me a number of times. I wanted to defend my country by attacking and eliminating as many AQ members as possible. Although I knew that the paperwork I was doing also had an impact on the fight, I was still profoundly enraged. As an Arab American, I believed that anything short of firing a live weapon in the direction of an AQ fighter seemed like sitting on the sidelines.

After six weeks in Islamabad, I returned to the States. The matter of the Safarini case was coming to a head. Perhaps a victory of some sort could be won in that battle. I was ready to celebrate something, for sure.

TOURISTS

Safarini was scheduled to be released by Pakistani authorities on September 25, 2001, just two weeks after 9/11. He would be traveling to Amman, Jordan, via Bangkok; in order to apprehend him in Bangkok, our team left Washington on September 23, arriving in Thailand the next day. The team consisted of me, John, two hostage rescue team (HRT) agents, a senior Washington field office agent (Paul), and a physician. (The physician was responsible for attending to Safarini's medical needs: our team had to determine whether he was psychologically fit to be interviewed following his capture.) Upon our arrival in Thailand, we moved to finalize the details of the rendition plan in a meeting with officials from the US embassy and representatives of the Thai government. Paul, although only vaguely familiar with the case, was to interface with both the US embassy and the Thai officials. I was very protective of the case and naturally worried that with Paul in charge I didn't have total control. The slightest mistake or misrepresentation, especially by some team member who was not up to snuff on the case, could prevent a successful rendition.

After freshening up at our hotel, we traveled to the embassy, where we learned that Safarini's release had been delayed a day. That made me even more anxious: I'd be worrying over every essential detail for an extra twenty-four hours. On the other hand, the delay would give me some time to finalize my strategies for a potential in-flight interview with Safarini aboard the FBI aircraft we were taking back to the States. The next day was a bit of a circus. We were all still a bit jet-lagged, but more importantly, not everyone on the team shared my concern and focus. Paul, a robust man with an apparently insatiable appetite for all things Thai, was adamant about eating, shopping, and touring Bangkok during our suddenly "free" day. I burned with embarrassment at one of our initial meetings when Paul, instead of refining the details of our planning with our Thai hosts, questioned senior US embassy officials about good restaurants and stores. When he managed to arrange for transportation to a local shopping destination and insisted we tag along, I decided I did not want to make waves. I followed orders.

I am sure he noticed my air of quiet exasperation as we spent hours in the bazaar, followed by a lengthy meal at a local restaurant. I ate enough Thai food at home not to feel impelled to search it out in Bangkok. And shopping for a housewarming gift for my new home—the house I had not officially spent a night in—was the furthest thing from my mind. I cared only about the man of the hour—Safarini himself.

"I KNEW YOU WILL BE WAITING FOR ME"

On September 28, 2001, I was in hiding at the Bangkok International Airport. I was in the back of a van, parked inconspicuously on the tarmac, clutching the partially open door and peeking out furtively in an attempt to identify Safarini as he exited his flight from Islamabad. A Thai intelligence officer sitting in the driver's seat was communicating via a handheld radio with a number of other Thai police officers stationed at various locations on the tarmac and around the plane. I waited as the passengers deplaned, but Safarini was not among them. I was worried. I could hear my heart beating, and my mind was racing in a million different directions. Where was Safarini? Had there been a problem on the plane? Did he know we were stalking him? Given all we had invested in this operation, I was not going to allow Safarini to slip through our hands.

Suddenly, without warning, the Thai officer slammed down the accelerator, and the van hurtled toward the front exit stairs of the plane. The van door swung open, exposing me. I quickly slammed it shut, pinching a finger in the process, but so much adrenalin was rushing through my body that I didn't feel any pain at the time. I looked at the blackening nail as I pulled my hand from the door and knew I was in for a world of hurt later.

The van lurched to a stop at the front exit stairs, and I leapt out of the door and greeted Safarini. He recognized me immediately.

"Ok, ok, you got me," he quickly said in English. "I knew you will be waiting for me."

Two agents from the FBI's hostage rescue team gathered around Safarini. After quick visual, document, and fingerprint identification—as required by DOJ regulations—Safarini was officially arrested and transported across the tarmac to a US government plane prepared for immediate takeoff. We had to move quickly. If Safarini collected his wits and asked for asylum in Thailand, we would be required by international law to hand him over to the Thai authorities. Packing Safarini onto the waiting plane, we began the first leg of a long journey that would end with this notorious felon facing the full weight of the American justice system. Soon after the plane gained cruising altitude, I began my rapprochement with our captive.

PIG AND PORK

"Thanks, Miss Nada, for the sandwich; does it have any pork in it?" Safarini asked me, in Arabic.

Clean-shaven, with clothing laundered, Safarini looked and smelled quite different from the last time I had seen him at Adiala Jail. He now resembled the pictures we had in his file, which for some reason helped me focus on the interview.

"No, it is pork-free," I told him. "I don't eat pork either, Zayed, and so I made sure there would be pork-free food on the plane." He was appreciative and, surprisingly, visibly relaxed.

I had built good rapport with Safarini during our previous interview at Adiala Jail, and I hoped that, building on our previous foundation, the interview to follow would be productive and successful—and it was.

After I served Safarini his food, I realized that one lunch package was missing. I was famished and exhausted. As I looked for the missing food package, I realized that Paul had taken two lunches and was feasting on both as he reclined in a luxurious aircraft seat. At that point, I was fuming. I had had enough of him. This rendition was apparently nothing but a "box-checking" exercise for him, a stepping stone to his next assignment at Bureau headquarters. To me, it was about achieving justice and giving closure to the many victims of Flight 73. I was honored to be part of this case; I knew I was making history. I found Paul's behavior insulting and his casual attitude disrespectful of the work the other agents and I had put into the case.

Putting these thoughts behind me for the moment, I calmed myself and channeled my energy toward preparing for the upcoming arraignment hearing in front of a federal judge in Anchorage, Alaska—our first stop in the United States. We arrived in Anchorage on Saturday, September 29. We were greeted by the FBI Alaska Division special agent in charge (SAC), a professional, no-nonsense, warm man. In preparing for the Safarini rendition I had had the opportunity to work with numerous law enforcement agencies, and I could tell that the Anchorage SAC ran a tight ship. *What a relief,* I thought to myself. I felt proud to work alongside this agent—even for the short time we were in Anchorage. His help was instrumental in getting Safarini transported by Bureau of Prisons officers to a local holding facility where he awaited his arraignment.

That night, we all met at a local steakhouse that Paul had extensively researched and selected as a proper venue for celebrating our successful rendition. Paul surprised us all by announcing that he would be returning to Washington the next day. He would miss the arraignment.

I was a bit taken aback. Why wouldn't he wait until Monday? Why the rush? Why spend additional funds for a commercial ticket when a US government plane was returning to Washington the following day? It seemed to me that Paul simply wanted to spend the remaining part of the weekend with his family and sleep in his own bed. I had been baffled by his disinterest in the Safarini case, but now I felt he just didn't care. I was offended that American taxpayers would be footing the bill for what I considered a personal trip, but I kept quiet and reminded myself that one does not criticize "family."

On Monday, October 1, 2001, Safarini was arraigned before a federal judge. He was ordered to be held without bond and transported immediately to the District of Columbia to face the charges pending against him. We flew Safarini to Washington, where, on October 2, he appeared before a second federal judge and entered a "not guilty" plea. He was remanded to a federal holding facility, and there he would await his trial.

JUSTICE AT LAST

On May 12, 2004, more than three years after we had arrested him on the tarmac in Thailand, Safarini was sentenced to three consecutive life terms plus twenty-five years—a sentence totaling 160 years. Back in December 2003, Safarini had changed his "not guilty" plea and entered a "guilty" plea to all ninety-five counts against him in the superseding indictment. The change in plea spared him the death penalty. Additionally, he agreed to cooperate with the US authorities "whenever, and in whatever form, the United States shall reasonably request," including testifying against his co-defendants, if and when any of them came into US custody.

The federal judge presiding over the sentencing proceedings agreed to let about twenty passengers testify in a session that would eventually run over two days. Perhaps the most moving testimony for me was that of flight attendant Sunshine Vesuwala.

I first met Sunshine in August 2001 when I interviewed her in Canada, thanks to the diligence of the Royal Canadian Mounted Police. She was a charming Asian woman who had saved a number of American lives on Pan Am 73 by hiding the individuals' passports. Her memory of the incident was incredible, and her eagerness to help was touching. The interview must have been very hard for her, as she had to relive the terrible details of the incident. Listening to her was like watching a movie. It was all there: the sound, the colors, and the terrible action. And she spoke so knowingly. Honest and straightforward testimony, I thought. After the interview—the information from which would be used to begin building a case against Safarini— I reflected on the vividness of such memories. Sunshine's cool recollection of the events on that plane struck a chord in me. I, too, had been a witness to murder. Despicable deeds seen more than once had left deep memories. Pictures of rocket attacks and street gun battles ran together with Sunshine's depictions of the hell inside that plane. Somehow, I had filed these pictures in the back of my mind, as if they were a lesson of some sort. Sunshine's testimony reminded me that certain memories never pass.

On the stand in court during the sentencing hearing, Sunshine eloquently narrated the psychological and physical effects of the Flight 73 ordeal on herself and on her family. Toward the end of her statement, she turned toward Safarini.

"It may seem a long time ago to most people, but it's like yesterday to me," said Sunshine. She pointed at Safarini and told a packed courtroom that he had shot Rajesh Kumar in the head, at point blank range, after asking the terrified Kumar, "Are you a man?"

Sunshine, pointing toward Safarini with a steady hand and speaking in a voice rising to a near shout, demanded answers from Safarini.

"What makes a man?" she asked him, directly. "A weapon?" And then she turned back to the packed courtroom and uttered her verdict: "He's no man. He hid behind flight attendants when the plane door was open." Without his guns and grenades, Safarini was helpless in front of Sunshine. He simply watched in dejected silence as she stepped down from the stand in triumph. Sunshine's story of overcoming adversity and resettling in the West evoked memories for me of my uneasy personal journey in overcoming the ordeals of the Lebanese civil war and in resolving the sometimes bitter memories of my Lebanese upbringing. The words of Sunshine and the others made me feel like the events of the rendition had come full circle: the long hours, the stress, and the anxiety investigating the case had all been worth it. I had helped Sunshine and others bring closure to this chapter of their lives.

GREEN WITH ENVY

My ties to the Safarini case will never leave me. As I write this, I still am proud of what we did. But at the time, after we had brought Safarini back to the States, I was ready to be done with the whole matter. The story of why I didn't drop the case at that point has to do with the way I value the emotional aspects of a case. But there was a time, shortly after returning to Washington with Safarini in tow in October 2001, when I very nearly ended my association with the case.

"I am officially asking to be removed from the Safarini case," I told Bob in October. Bob was the relatively new supervisor who had replaced Joe as my immediate squad supervisor. "I already put the request in writing. The EC is on your desk waiting for your approval."

I had been thinking about my decision for months, and finally, shortly after I had arrested Safarini and brought him to Washington to stand trial, I took action. In my mind, I had fulfilled my commitment to the victims. I stood in Bob's office until he located the electronic communication and signed it.

"Before you leave, Nada," I heard Bob say, "I want to assign you to another case."

As Bob spoke, my thoughts raced back to my contributions on the Safarini case. I wondered where the investigation would go after my departure. I felt good walking away from the case. Certainly, the rendition operation had been successful. Safarini was awaiting trial, the evidence against him was overwhelming, and a conviction was a certainty. At the time I put in the request, I didn't know that justice would take three years to be final. It would take that long, but it would come. Looking back now, I saw that I had done all I could on the case.

But I was not entirely happy. Yes, I had done my job. But I had also stood up for myself and my beliefs, and this had created waves. After putting up with a potpourri of degrading incidents throughout the rendition process, I had come to believe that the so-called partnership between John and me was hurting the case instead of helping it. I thought the time was right for me to direct my efforts and skills toward something more productive. I did not reach this decision overnight; in fact, on a number of occasions, when I was close to marching into the supervisor's office and demanding reassignment, I reversed my thinking and gave myself more time to analyze the situation. I felt I could only move on after my emotional obligations to the victims of this terrorist attack had been tended to, and I wasn't sure whether John—or anyone else for that matter—was thinking of the victims. Sure, the case was airtight, but who would keep up with those who had survived? Who would speak for them?

But I had serious reasons for wanting to move on. Our investigative approaches were different, and I worried about some of John's judgment calls. As an example, one of the main witnesses we interviewed, a foreign Pan Am employee, requested our assistance in "fixing" his US immigration status. He explained to us that he had been a resident alien for years, but he had not been able to obtain his US citizenship because he had actually been living in Pakistan. The law required him to reside in the United States, so his foreign residency disqualified him from becoming a US citizen; he was looking for our help in getting around the law. The witness explained that he had tried to use a P.O. Box as an address on the immigration application in an attempt to falsely show his "residence," but that P.O. Box addresses were not recognized as proof of residency. I was about to tell the witness that he would have to find another way, a legal way, to reside in the United States to meet the residency requirement, when John quickly agreed to the witness's deal: "Don't worry," said John, "we'll take care of it."

Upon our return from Pakistan, John approached the Immigration and Naturalization Service (INS) officer assigned to the Joint Terrorism Task Force at WFO to discuss the situation. I later learned that John and the INS agent found a "creative solution" for an address to be used by the witness on his immigration application that would fly under the INS's radar and get the witness his citizenship without his having to fulfill the residency requirement. This maneuver was a serious problem in my view and could spell trouble for our case if it came to light—especially if a defense attorney extracted it from the witness during his testimony. Even if Safarini were to reach a deal that spared his life in exchange for a life sentence—even if the case did not go to trial—I felt that John's actions were witness-tampering violations. I found his behavior totally unacceptable.

Although I did not realize it at the time, John was hung up on competing with me. It became clear when I later reflected on an incident that had occurred on one of my TDYs to Pakistan in May 2001. I had been in Islamabad working on the USS *Cole* investigation when the Legat informed me that the Pakistani government had given us unanticipated access to a number of Pakistani law enforcement officials who were involved in the Pan Am 73 case. The Legat immediately tasked me to travel to Karachi and conduct the interviews.

I was ecstatic when I heard the news. Securing interview access to foreign officials is a complicated and unpredictable process that requires rapid exploitation to avoid losing critical information. As such, the Legat appropriately determined that we needed to proceed with the present interviews without delay. I frantically made travel arrangements to Karachi and started to work on preparations for the interviews. I could not wait to call Washington and tell Joe and John the good news. Given our time difference, it was too early to call; however, I could not contain myself, so I dashed off an email instead. I then headed back to my hotel and packed some clothes for the two-day trip before returning to the embassy to tie up any loose ends prior to my departure.

When I walked into the Legat's office, the administrative assistant met me with a sigh.

"You got a response to your email from John."

"Great! I've been waiting for it." My excitement must have been quite evident.

"I hate to break it to you," she continued, "but it's not one to look forward to."

John's email, sent to me but copied to both the Legat and to Joe, was a thinly veiled ruse designed to get me into trouble with the senior agents. In the email, John complained about my acting without consulting him and charged that I was intent on "taking over the case." I was shocked. The Pakistani interview offer was not about John or about me; it was about a rare chance to help bring justice into the hijacking victims' lives. I was angry and disappointed. The Legat saw my reaction and tried to make me feel better by joking about Joe allowing "childish behavior on his [Joe's] squad." The Legat then turned serious. He told me he wanted to respond to John's message and tell John that I was simply following the Legat's order to conduct the interviews. I thanked the Legat for his offer of support, but I told him I wanted to respond to the email myself, adding that because I was tired of John's juvenile bickering, I realized I must face John or things would continue to get worse. The Legat saw my point and left the matter of a reply to me.

Fortunately, John's plan to undermine our investigation had backfired. Here was another brick in the wall of his obvious non-empathy with the suffering victims of the Pan Am attack. As I sat at a computer terminal ready to compose my salvo to John, I really, really, really wanted to send him an email telling him I was done with the Pan Am case and with his bullying. I wanted to challenge his mock seriousness: if you want to travel to Pakistan and be ready to conduct the interviews within the next few hours, then you are more than welcome to do so, I would write. But I didn't write that. Instead,

I simply explained in my response that we had been granted access, the situation was fluid given the political environment in Pakistan, and it was my assessment that the interviews had to be conducted immediately. That was my way of standing my ground.

Meanwhile, the real ground I stood on was anything but still. I ran to the embassy gymnasium for a quick workout. On my eighth mile on the treadmill, I calmed down and focused on the upcoming interviews. I went back to the office to find additional immature—and aggressive—emails. After several not-so-polite email exchanges with John, I left for Karachi. The interviews with the officials came off as planned.

When I had time later to reflect on John's hostility toward me, I recalled that a squad mate of mine had once confided to me that both the Legat and the ALAT had routinely called my supervisor after each of my trips to Pakistan to compliment my work. John, who accompanied me on these trips and eventually learned of the phone calls, was never mentioned in the conversations. I could imagine how glowing compliments about my work must have made John irate and green with envy. I could hear him saying to himself, "How dare a junior agent, let alone a *woman,* show me up?" But what had really showed him up, I came to believe, was his attitude, an attitude that was on high-def display for all to see in the dustup over the police-official interviews. I would eventually link this incident to other incidents that I felt revealed John's serious lack of concern for the victims of terror. I hadn't backed down and kept quiet about his behavior. If he refused to show any concern for the human side of our professional duties, I told myself, he had better get used to my critical attitude. I was through with keeping my feelings under wraps. If we succeeded in delivering Safarini to the American court system, I was ready to end my association with John.

ACCESS GRANTED

While I was in Karachi working on these unanticipated interviews, I met the police official who had made them possible to thank him for his cooperation. We met over a luncheon at his residence. The official told me that he was surprised that an American representative would actually feel comfortable outside the security of the consulate, let alone at an official's modest home.

"You ate our food and entertained my daughter's million questions about the FBI. I consider you family now," he said.

It was a pleasant compliment, and I took note of it. Using the customary Pakistani forms of address for family members, I asked that "my brother" locate the remaining witnesses I needed to interview for "his sister."

"Consider it done," he assured me. After saying goodbye to his wife and daughter, I went back to my hotel, packed, and walked to the consulate to wait for my ride to the airport.

On the way to Karachi International Airport in the consulate's bulletproof SUV, I thought about the email exchange with John. What impact might that exchange have, I wondered, on my continued involvement in the case? I was lucky, I mused, to have discovered early on in my career that working overseas in a cross-cultural environment was where I was able to contribute the most. It was also my good fortune that I loved the immense level of detail surrounding the work. I appreciated the sometimes elusive nature of evidence and enjoyed gathering clues and facts despite the long, tedious hours in some very dangerous environments. As I stared out at the labyrinthine streets of Karachi flashing by me through the SUV's tinted windows, I concluded that I really liked starting at the beginning. I loved wondering where the threads of evidence would all lead. Maybe it was this love of beginning a quest that caused me to feel less attached to the Pan Am case as it wound down. Well, that and John's apparent disenchantment with the case.

As it turned out, our squad had a number of cold cases. Taking on a new challenge became a very appealing alternative to continuing my Pan Am 73 investigation. I told myself that when I arrived in Islamabad, I was going to ask Joe to remove me from my Pan Am 73 assignment. Given the success I had enjoyed in Yemen, perhaps I might land on the Cole investigation on a full-time basis. That would be the ticket, I thought to myself.

My flight from Karachi to Islamabad was delayed, and as we sat parked on the tarmac, it suddenly hit me. From my seat, I could see the gate where the Pan Am 73 incident had unfolded. I was within fifty feet of where the hijacking took place. When I closed my eyes, I could hear the screams and the explosions and visualize the chaos. I was replaying the hijacking incident again in my head, just as I had in my dreams for months. My heart skipped a beat. *Nada, you waited so long,* it said. *Be patient,* it cautioned. *Wait till you have Safarini in custody,* it advised. *Now is not the right time to leave.* My heart had made its point.

After I landed in Islamabad, I did not call Joe; I did not, later, ask him to remove me from the case. And when I returned to Washington, John remained petulant over the Karachi interviews. In the end, I stayed on the case.

Even after Safarini's arrest, it was still not easy to let go. I felt as if I was neglecting my obligation to the victims of Pan Am 73. Having said that, I also knew that after the subject of a case is in custody, FBI agents play—more or less—an administrative role. Agents help locate and transport the families of victims to the trial. Agents also assist prosecutors in mundane legal tasks. Additionally, federal agents may be called on to testify on each other's behalf. For example, an agent who obtains a confession or an agent who conducts an interview need not be present to testify to the content of the confession or interview. The transcripts of those encounters stand on their own, and another agent may, in fact, describe the evidence to the court. For the most part, prosecutors prefer to limit the testimony of case agents because case agents know too much and are subject to the scrutiny of defense attorneys.

The confession I had obtained from Safarini could be introduced into evidence by any agent; what concerned me was the rendition of the three remaining terrorists from the Pan Am 73 hijacking. They were not in our custody, but I rationalized that their confessions, unlike the Safarini confession I had secured, would not be critical to making the case against them. Prosecutors could simply use Safarini's confession to implicate the others. In the post-September 11 environment, and given the involvement of Gwen, the DOJ attorney, I was certain that Safarini, to avoid the death sentence, would take a plea deal requiring him to testify against his accomplices. When it came to rendering Safarini's accomplices to the United States, I thought that I had already paved the way with the first successful rendition; rendering the other three members of the hijack team should be an easy task.

As it turned out, I was wrong.

BACK TO THEIR OLD TRICKS

"Nada, come to my office. Now, please!" said Bob, sounding flustered.

I saw my squad mates rushing around the office and knew something was wrong. My head was buried in a pile of notes. I was responding to a tasking related to a suspected Hizballah cell in the Northern Virginia area, which had possible ties to a cell in Michigan.

"I'll be right there," I answered. I wondered what had Bob so agitated.

"We are going to get the remaining hijackers of Pan Am 73," he said.

"Excellent. What great news!" I had been waiting to hear of this development for a while; I was happy that the year 2002 would get off to a good start for my squad.

Deep down, I was worried that he was going to ask me to accompany the team on the trip—I had made the mental break from the Pan Am 73 case after Safarini's capture and wasn't eager to be drawn back into the case. I was relieved when I heard my new assignment.

"I need you to run the squad when I am gone, Nada," Bob said.

Thank goodness. Bob seemed bewildered by the number of tasks necessary to pull off a successful rendition, so I told him that he need not worry about anything at home. Focus on the mission at hand, I said. He instructed me about his daily meeting schedule, handed me his office keys, and noted other management-related duties. He also showed me where he kept folders carrying the Top Secret/Sensitive

Compartmented Information (TS/SCI) associated with the cases on the squad.

Bob avoided my gaze during this conversation. He had recently replaced Joe as the supervisor of our squad, and he had already suffered an embarrassing incident in which he had exposed classified material. Bob lacked experience investigating terrorism—he had only worked criminal cases—but that did not prevent him from becoming the supervisor of the FBI's elite Extraterritorial Terrorism Squad. (The Bureau did not differentiate between the two fields, and assignments were made based on seniority, not on expertise in the subject matter.) Soon after his arrival on the squad, Bob, unfamiliar with the proper security procedures, had left TS/SCI material on agents' desks for review, sometimes overnight. Anyone—including the office cleaning crew—could have picked it up. When a fellow agent realized what was happening, he cautioned Bob, who then started keeping the material in his office.

No one reported this incident to the Security Division for review of possible compromise. The lack of reporting itself represented an additional security violation. Unfortunately, serious security violations were common on the squad. It was my understanding that taking classified information out of the Washington field office by members of other squads also was not unusual, and the fact that no one I knew to have taken such information had been punished further solidified my understanding. As revealed in an Inspector General Report dated August 2003, the FBI did not place importance on following security procedures or enforcing them because security was viewed as an "impediment" to investigations. In fact, many agents on my squad took classified information home with them and routinely discussed classified information in prohibited environments, such as restaurants and coffee shops.

So I'm sure Bob was happy to put some space between himself and the office. I eagerly awaited his and the team's return. But after a week of waiting in a Middle Eastern country, spending millions of dollars to rent a dedicated airliner, and wasting hundreds of hours, the dozen or so members of the rendition team came back to Washington empty-handed. Although, as I've made clear, I did not care for John, who had served on the team, the enormity of this debacle made me feel sorry for him. Apparently, John had misunderstood a message sent from the Legat in Pakistan and had launched the rendition mission without confirmation that the Pakistanis planned to release the remaining three terrorists. This was a serious miscalculation. I naïvely thought someone's career would end over this disastrous outcome. I thought accountability for this mistake was the least we owed our real bosses—the taxpayers. Imagine my surprise when the resilient WFO bureaucracy simply swept this mess under the rug.

While the failed rendition was a crushing blow to the morale of the squad, it didn't prepare us for what happened next. We thought that we would have another shot at bringing our quarry to justice, but we were proved wrong when Pakistani authorities freed Safarini's accomplices based on a March 18, 2002, decree from the Lahore High Court. The Rawalpindi bench had ordered the release of the remaining Palestinians—who had completed their sentences at this point—and directed the federal government to make arrangements for their deportation. The men were escorted to their homeland by Pakistani military personnel to ensure their arrival at their planned destination. The judge's actions came in response to an Amnesty International report that had questioned the legality of the transfer, by Pakistani authorities, of a number of Arabs to the United States. The Amnesty report prompted another judge of the Lahore High Court in Rawalpindi to call on the government of Pakistan to explain the circumstances under which Safarini had left Islamabad and landed in the United States. While the Safarini rendition was a done deal, the actions of the Lahore court meant the remaining hijackers encountered no resistance to their deportation.

Safarini's three accomplices were freed, and, according to Arab news media, they received a hero's welcome in their homeland. I knew when I heard this that, absent other legal options or rehabilitation programs, these men would again engage in terrorist acts against Americans.

My worst fears were realized when I heard that one of Safarini's accomplices, Jamal, was reported to have been killed in a suspected US drone attack on January 9, 2010, in North Waziristan, the lawless tribal region of Pakistan that serves as Al Qaeda's safe haven. Jamal's presence at the drone strike was a strong indication that he had not only returned to terrorism but also was living among the most dangerous and hunted terrorists, probably providing leadership and inspiration to Al Qaeda's murderous cadres in the tribal regions of Pakistan with his firsthand accounts of killing Americans. I couldn't help but feel that the FBI's mismanagement in the failed rendition of Safarini's accomplices had costs far beyond the financial and personnel resources that were squandered. Jamal had returned to his mission, and we had missed the chance to stop him. A few days after these depressing results, I was called into Bob's office to receive my new assignment. I quickly read the case title of the thin file Bob handed me.

"It's a kidnapping case, and the suspects live in, uh, a jungle," Bob reported. "I only expect you to update the file when the biannual file review is due."

"Thank you, Bob. I'll take a look at it. It may turn out to be interesting—you never know."

As I walked out of Bob's office, I said to myself, "Updating the file? Yeah, right. How about catching the suspects?" With a twinkle in my eye and a smirk on my face, I went to my desk and started to read the case file. A trip to the jungle sounded pretty interesting, I concluded.

And, so, Africa came calling.

VANISHING ACT 9

. . .

I did not understand all the details, but I knew someone "bad" had taken my cousin Sami against his will. No one would admit to knowing anything about the kidnapping or about Sami's whereabouts. Speculation in the village centered on the Syrian military forces occupying the area. Syria had, for many years, illegally occupied parts of Lebanon. Damascus was a hotbed of terrorists and plotters behind much of the terror of the 1980s. The masterminding of the destruction of Pan Am Flight 103, which exploded over Lockerbie, Scotland, in 1983, killing all 274 passengers on board, took place in a quiet Damascus neighborhood. Most signs pointed to Damascus as the origin of the attacks on the Marine barracks and the killing of French paratroopers in Beirut in 1983.

Sami had openly criticized the Syrians for their brutality against innocent Lebanese citizens. He was not shy about criticizing political figures and the violent factions active in the Lebanese civil war. So these figures did what they do best: they used kidnapping to silence the truth.

What I understood best was the kidnapping's impact on Sami's family: it ruined them. They were quite modern by village standards. His mother always dressed fashionably. She wore beautiful makeup, her hair always looked professionally done, and her nails were always painted with vibrant colors to match her outfits. She and her husband were happy people, boisterous and proud. They loved to entertain, were very generous, and played music and danced. I knew there was no crime in that, but until you live in a war zone—especially a civil war zone—well, you don't know just how precious that vivaciousness can be. The war had tainted everything. Sami's family had put their best face forward at all times, but Sami's disappearance put an end to their joys.

Sami's home was near our home, so we drove by it often. I loved seeing the family's beautiful garden. It was filled with exotic flowers, and I always rolled down my window to breathe in the scent of the many varied blossoms. The parking lot in front of their home was always full of cars, and, nearly as often, their balconies were filled with people listening to music, drinking, and laughing. With a child's wonder, I swept Sami's life into my family's not-so-happy orbit. I imagined things could be different. My family seemed so much the opposite of my cousin's. For me there was little gaiety. My family seemed to suffer through dooms of foreboding. It was this uneasiness that would eventually be ratcheted up to the point where I had to leave my family behind—for my own sanity. Like Sami, I too was to become a victim of war but I was also another sort of victim: I would need to run away from a family that devalued women's freedom.

After my cousin's disappearance, I would see cars parked at the house, and I would know these were the cars of elderly people in the village who had stopped to offer their support and wisdom. Eventually, I did not see any cars there. I would hear at the fruit market that people were afraid to offer help because they feared that whoever took Sami would hurt them or their families. I could not understand how people could turn their backs on Sami's family. They were such a giving family; most of the folks in the village had been guests at their lavish gatherings or had benefited from their generosity in some way. How could they ignore the family in its time of need?

The atmosphere of fear created by the kidnapping had sent an effective message to the villagers. I felt disappointed in the villagers and thought they were selfish. Above all, I wanted Sami to come back home—I wanted things to return to normal.

As weeks passed into months, the beautiful garden suffered neglect. Few flowers survived the kidnapping. Dull shrubs choked the life out of the neglected flowers. The shutters of the house were permanently closed, and the balconies accumulated dirt, leaves, and dust. Sami's home began to resemble a dark, dreary, unkempt ghost. I remembered seeing Sami's mother moving awkwardly about on one of the balconies, often standing frozen beside the choked and silenced flowers.

Sami's mother vowed to wear black until her son's return. Her fashionable clothes were given away to villagers who clandestinely received these gifts, fearing the kidnappers could link their new clothes to Sami's family. My aunt's hair was now pulled back in a stiff, tight bun; she wore no makeup, and her nails were cut short and remained unpainted. Years and years passed, but Sami never came home. Seeing Sami's mother pacing back and forth or waiting by the window was heartbreaking. The woman aged decades in front of my eyes. Her hair became disheveled, and she developed a hump that made it hard for her to walk. When she moved away, the house was locked and abandoned. My eagerness to peek at their home and wonder at their marvelous lives disappeared.

As Sami's mother descended into her own private waking nightmare, I grew more fearful. I had many terrible dreams. I would dream about faceless people in dark clothing taking my sisters away from me. I could not stop these dreams. They recurred with terrible regularity. I could not tell my parents about the dreams because my parents would only mock me and call me paranoid. I did not want to tell my sisters about the dreams because I did not want to scare them. I resorted to a strange tactic to ward off dreaming—not sleeping! If I could keep myself awake at night I would not have to face the horrible dream people. This strategy failed me initially—I would tire and fall asleep. I was resourceful, however, and I devised a master plan to deal with the problem. I convinced my two sisters to share a bed; then, I decided to tie myself to them. I reasoned that if anyone took them, I would most certainly feel the tug of the rope. I would wake up and fight the kidnappers off. I was ready for battle.

I eventually overcame those fears when I had to face more challenging ones. As the war became even more a part of our day-to-day reality, I gradually let go of my nightmares. Or, I should say, I began living them in the waking world. There seemed to be no difference between the visitations of horrible dreams and the visitations of horrible events surrounding us. Lebanon, and Beirut in particular, had descended even deeper into chaos and brutality. Sami's disappearance and his mother's descent into depression were the war's initial experiences for me. I wanted to help my relatives; I wanted the fun-loving Sami back. But I was surrounded by violent men with violent agendas and violent philosophies. I hated it all so much, and I vowed to someday make the world safe for the likes of my cousin's family—and for myself, I suppose.

My family, meanwhile, was not acknowledging the war at all. Some say that war brings out the community, heightens the socially driven behavior of humans, and that is true, I suppose, but our family remained isolated, and I saw more clearly how dysfunctional we were as a family. My father was preparing to marry me to a much older businessman. My mother ignored my feelings, refusing to acknowledge her own anxiety. My brother tormented me, no doubt playing the role of the awful Syrians or the PLO or the Hizballah guerrillas. No, he was not consciously identifying with these intruders. He was simply exercising his dominance over me and my sisters, perhaps displacing his fear and anger onto us, acting in a way that he thought saved him from the neurosis of living with war. For me, these fractured relations were yet another sign that one day I would have to escape not just Beirut and Lebanon, but my family as well. If the terror of war had not brought us together, supporting each other, then I supposed nothing ever would. I would go somewhere safe and free. The frustration of not being able to help Sami or my aunt weighed heavily on me. I wanted so much to be a child, but children were not allowed to be children in Lebanon in the war years. We were prisoners. And I was a prisoner on still another level—I battled my father and my brother for my own right to be recognized for the feelings I did have. The tyranny of fractious battle descended on

my family as well, and I could do nothing to turn that around. My
nightmares returned, and I was unable to sleep.

. . .

RETHINKING THE MISSION

The Africa case Bob handed me related to the October 1992 kidnapping of Brent Swan, a US citizen working as an aircraft mechanic in the Cabinda enclave of Angola for PHI Petroleum (a subsidiary of US Chevron Corporation). In a matter of months, I was able to locate the subjects, designate the case as Major Case, and render one of the subjects, Arthur Tchibassa, to face trial in the United States.

Weeks after the Tchibassa rendition, Gordon could tell that I was distracted—more so than usual. He didn't like it when I brought work issues home, and lately it seemed like I was doing that every night. But I couldn't help it—he was my sounding board and an excellent objective advisor. I came to him to discuss strategies for investigations, and I always valued his advice. He always had good ideas, and he directed me to the right people when he didn't know the answer. I was hoping he could help with my biggest dilemma.

I was busying myself with dinner preparations and trying to avoid talking about what was on my mind. But Gordon knew something was eating at me.

"You need a break from work, Nada. Twelve hours a day is enough. You will not be able to sustain this schedule over the long run."

"Spoken like a twenty-year veteran of the wars," I observed.

"It's true."

"I know it is, and you're right," I agreed.

Lately, I had been consumed with so much work that I had a hard time winding down at home. An occupational hazard, I had been telling myself. Burnout, maybe. But it wasn't the work environment or cases or time I wanted to think about.

"I'm not thinking about my cases," I replied after a brief silence. "I've been thinking about my future with the FBI. I'm questioning whether my skills are best used on the squad that I am assigned to now. I think I can contribute better to the mission elsewhere."

Gordon was now my confessor.

"The mission? What exactly do you think the mission is?"

"Well, cases, mostly. Bringing criminals to trial, you know. Policing the world. I don't know. Maybe that's the problem. I am not sure the mission is clear anymore—or if I am on the right mission at all."

"Investigating crimes overseas is very challenging," Gordon said. "I know you enjoy the long hours and don't mind working across two and sometimes three different time zones."

"Gordon, I've been thinking about the future for some time." I looked him straight in the eye. "I want to make a difference."

"You made a difference for Brent Swan."

"Sure, I did. But that was after the fact. Swan had already suffered. I didn't make a difference in his suffering."

"You're splitting hairs now, Nada," Gordon argued.

"Look, my dear, my interpersonal skills along with my language abilities and cultural understanding are my strengths. I know this. Using these capabilities to represent the FBI overseas has served the FBI's mission. Gaining access to crime scenes more rapidly, interviewing witnesses on an immediate basis, and interrogating suspects directly after the commission of a crime in an overseas location are all critical elements in achieving successful investigations and prosecutions. That is my mission. More importantly, building solid relationships with our partners overseas based on mutual respect and understanding is a strategy that would most certainly be beneficial for the FBI in the long run. I want to continue doing that—but I want to do it on the ground."

Gordon had heard me complain for months about a lack of cultural understanding and the language barrier during FBI investigations, so he quickly agreed.

"I can work overseas if I join the FBI legal attaché program," I told him.

"Well, that should not be hard. All the Legats you have worked with have written glowing letters of recommendation for you. You would be a welcome addition to the Legat program. Is that what you want? To join the Legat camp?"

"It's what I've been thinking lately. But . . ."

Gordon had always been supportive and went out of his way to accommodate my crushing work and travel schedule, which was quite generous considering we were newlyweds.

"But joining the Legat program would probably mean we would have to spend even more time apart? Is that what's eating at you?" He cut to the point.

"Yes, yes, that worries me. You've already made sacrifices this past year. Maintaining our relationship hasn't been easy on either of us. I don't know what to do."

We had married months after the September 2001 attack, and over the past year and a half we had barely seen each other. Our work and travel schedules were downright crazy. The only thing that made it bearable was that each of us understood our responsibilities and accepted them happily.

As if reading my mind, Gordon told me, "I understand your passion for justice, I know how much love you have for our country, and we will work this out."

"You think we can?"

"I think we most certainly can. I will look for another overseas post. Perhaps we can serve together . . . or at least on the same continent," Gordon laughed.

"The dream team," I said. "You make things easy, my love." I kissed him softly on the cheek.

"Well, easier maybe. So, you have your new mission. Explore that assignment with the FBI Legat program."

And I kissed him again.

STALKING

I watched him for a long time. I knew his every move. I knew what time he woke up, what time he ate breakfast, what time he left for work, what route he took to work. I waited and waited some more so

I would know what time he left work, what route he took home, and what time he got home. I learned all his habits, and I came to recognize his friends. I discovered what he liked to do, where he liked to shop, and what he liked to eat. I knew everything about him. I could predict his daily schedule to the minute.

He, on the other hand, knew nothing about me. He had seen me a number of times; I had caught his eye in a crowd once, but the next time we shared a glance, he treated me as a stranger, as if he had never laid eyes on me. This is what I wanted. He did not know me, did not know what I was doing or why I was surveilling him. My cover gave me power. It gave me confidence for what I had been planning all along. Although we came from different cultures, he was not different from me. He was a human being who lived a normal life; he could be my friend, my neighbor, or even a colleague, but I could not think that way. I did not want to develop any feelings for him. I did not want to compare his likes and dislikes to mine. Any emotional bond could distract me from my mission.

I had worked on this mission for a long time, and nothing was going to derail me. I had received extensive training and had traveled across the borders of Jordan, Syria, and Iraq successfully without bringing any suspicion on myself. On one of these border crossings, I had successfully snuck the weapon I needed to complete my task into Jordan. Everything was on schedule. I had staked out the location and practiced several dry runs of my task. I say task, but in reality, I had come to feel this task was bestowed on me as a duty, an honorable duty. I was chosen among many, and I was special. My dedication, my commitment, and my loyalty were all factors in the decision to pick me. I believed in my duty and was devoted to it without hesitation or doubt. When I had my final meeting with my boss, he knew by the look in my eyes that I was ready, and he dispatched me to fulfill my calling. I had been praying throughout my training; I put my fate in God's hands and deployed to complete my undertaking.

On October 28, 2002, I was up very early. "Today is the day," I said to myself after I finished my prayers. I left my house and was dropped off at the location I had become very familiar with over the last few months. I was ready. I jumped the closed metal gate and hid, crouching, behind the rear passenger wheel of the mid-1990s burgundy Mercedes. I would not be seen by anyone approaching the car from the residence, and I was invisible to anyone passing by on the street. I was where I was meant to be. I waited. I stared at the diplomatic license plate; the number 109 was displayed in Arabic and English. "I am very familiar with this number," I told myself. He had parked the vehicle the night before in the usual spot, the courtyard of his home with the engine facing forward. I looked at my watch; it was a little after seven in the morning. The waiting time was about fifteen minutes, but it felt like an eternity. I heard the front door of his house open, and my heart started to race. My heartbeats seemed loud and distracting, and I was afraid he might hear my tension. But nothing was going to stand in my way now. When I heard him saying a farewell greeting to his wife, I drew the gun from my loose-fitting jacket, thinking how short a window I had to do this thing and do it right. I quickly played out, in my mind, my daring escape. I had to get out fast if I wanted no witnesses to my actions. The construction workers across the street hadn't arrived yet, but I knew they would be there any minute, and I sure did not want them to see me. When he opened the driver's door, I jumped out from behind him and opened fire. I wanted to make sure that I killed him, so I shot him once, twice, three times, and then I stopped counting. He fell to the ground, and I looked at him closely. He was dead. I was satisfied, so I quickly jumped the gate and ran down the empty street. No one had seen me, I hoped.

Later that evening I finally regained my normal breathing. I did not want to think about him; I knew that I had done the right thing, and I convinced myself that my act was politically justified. I did not want to think about the impact my enemy's death had on his wife, his children, his family, his friends, or anyone he knew. I needed to focus on the good that would come out of my actions. I was making a difference in the world, and I knew my colleagues, especially my boss, would all be proud of me. My boss told me he would have done this act himself, but because of his high profile, he couldn't risk carrying out the attack. I believed him. Why should he lie to me, one of his chosen ones? My boss had plans, big ideas, great dreams for what he called "the big picture" or the "cause," and I wanted him to dedicate his time and efforts to that cause. I admired him and I idolized him, especially when he lectured us on our duties and responsibilities to our homeland.

THE TONE OF HIS CONFESSION was both morose and matter-of-fact, the hypnotic delivery chilling me to the bone. But it also angered me. I wanted the man behind the lone assassin brought to justice. Yasir Fathi Ibrahim's murder of Laurence Foley, a US diplomat working for US Agency for International Development (USAID) in Amman, Jordan, was ultimately the work of his boss, Fadil Al-Khalayleh, aka Abu Musab Al-Zarqawi, the future leader of Al Qaeda in Iraq. In hearing Ibrahim's confession in the winter of 2002, I heard a foreboding example of the fanaticism and violence Al-Zarqawi had in store for the United States.

YOU, ME, AND ZARQAWI

The day of Foley's assassination, Bob had called me to his office and told me that he was assigning me the case.

"We have some idea of who killed Foley," Bob said. "The Amman Legat, Wayne Zaideman, is working on the case but needs help. I need you to depart for Amman on the next available flight. Will is going to act as your co-case agent; he is new to the squad, so you have to work closely with him."

I went back to my desk and called Gordon immediately.

"I am off to Amman as soon as I can reserve a flight," I blurted.

"Will you be back in time for our anniversary?" he asked.

I was touched by his eagerness to celebrate our first wedding anniversary. I had been working so hard lately that I had completely forgotten about it.

"I don't know, honey. I will certainly try."

I hung up the phone and walked to Will's desk. Will had zero experience with overseas investigations, so I asked him to shadow me for the next few hours as we got ready to deploy. I made a list of items often needed to process evidence outside the United States, items that are not typically in the evidence response kit. I had Will gather these and get them ready for overseas transport. I prayed that the Jordanian authorities would process the crime scene as close to US standards as possible. Having worked with them on the Tchibassa case, my impression was that they were a professional, competent, and capable service. I was hoping they wouldn't disappoint me.

I called a colleague at the FBI laboratory and explained my assignment. He made a list of the relevant departments within the lab, such as DNA, fiber, fingerprint, and fragment analysis, that I might need. I reached out to each department and secured a point of contact and telephone number. Having an actual person to call can make an investigation much easier—especially when an agent is on a different continent and in a different time zone. In order to ensure that I had access to every possible resource on the ground in Amman, I also called my State Department and CIA colleagues, who connected me to trusted colleagues at the US embassy in Jordan.

Finally, I contacted Zaideman in Amman and spoke with him about any updates in the case. At the end of our conversation, he made one thing clear.

"We need you on the ground as soon as you can be here," he reminded me.

"My next call is the travel office; we'll be there as soon as we can get a flight," I promised him.

I booked a flight arriving on October 31, 2002—just three days after Foley's murder. After completing preparations for the deployment and walking Will through all the steps, I was ready to start reading the intelligence reports on the murder and writing up our investigative plan. I asked the squad's intelligence analyst, a very bright and energetic guy, to pull all the intelligence reported thus far. The case was a headline story on every media network. Foley, reports said, had been killed by gunshots from a 9mm silenced handgun outside his Amman home. Over the next few hours, I was able to piece together a rough trajectory of the murder.

By the time I finished writing requests and communicating with key FBI management personnel, it was evening. I had called Gordon earlier to compare schedules; neither of us was going to get home until well after 7:00 P.M. I considered staying at the office for an additional hour or two, but I decided against it. I was already feeling guilty about the prospect of missing our first wedding anniversary because of the investigation. So, I stayed a bit longer and then left and picked up some food from our favorite Thai restaurant to surprise Gordon. Despite my best intentions, I got home a little before eight o'clock. Gordon was rummaging through the refrigerator looking for dinner ideas.

"We need to go to the grocery store," he declared.

"We are pretty much out of anything that resembles real food," I confessed, "so I got some Thai." Gordon closed the fridge, looking pleased. I had not been to the grocery store in weeks, and clutter was slowly accumulating throughout the house. I felt bad about neglecting my home, but I wanted to spend my free time, little as it was, with Gordon, not cleaning. We sat down and quietly started to eat our dinner. Both of us were physically and mentally exhausted. Gordon broke a growing silence.

"I know you have to leave again, leave right away, and I want you to know that there is no better reason for you to leave—to leave me here for a while—if you can bring some justice to the family of Laurence Foley while you are out there turning up the heat on you know who."

Gordon's voice sounded a little shaky, and I wasn't sure if it was just fatigue or if Foley's murder had impacted him more than I had originally thought.

"Are you excited to be working against Al Qaeda again?" Gordon asked me. "Media reports are saying that Al Qaeda is claiming responsibility for the attack."

I smiled at his insight.

"Yes, my dear, I am very happy to finally be back in the game fighting Al Qaeda."

I pushed the uneaten hot peppers around on my plate, and Gordon sat back and smiled. He liked it when I got my game on. Our brief conversation and the good curry had brought both of us out of the fog a bit.

"Do you remember," I asked Gordon, "how disappointed I was when Joe instructed me to disassociate myself from the *Cole* case? It was the first thing he said to me, and I didn't care for it. Remember his excuse, that the New York FBI leader who supervised the *Cole* case, John O'Neill, would use my work in Yemen to justify a request for my transfer to the New York field office? 'O'Neill has the juice to pull you to New York in a heartbeat,' he told me." The Washington and New York field offices were fierce rivals, and when FBI Headquarters assigned the OBL case to the New York office, the rivalry reached new heights.

"It all goes back to Al Qaeda, my dear. I wonder what would have happened if O'Neill had got hold of you," Gordon said, somewhat absently.

We looked at each other, eyes growing wider by the second.

"Right," I finally said. "I might have been in that tower with O'Neill on 9/11. I might not be having this conversation with you right now." For a second we both had the same thought—O'Neill had died that day, at work in his World Trade Center office.

"But you are here, for a few hours more. Then it is back on the same trail O'Neill was forging."

"Right," I said.

As Gordon got up and began to clear the table of our plates and take-out containers, I continued, thinking out loud, "O'Neill was one of the few FBI managers who understood the threat of Al Qaeda and was willing to fight the bureaucratic battles necessary to devote resources to it. But I was new at the time, so I just deferred to Joe. Well, in any case, I am glad to be back on the scent of these killers."

Gordon, having cleaned up, returned to the table with two glasses of wine, handed one to me, and proposed a toast.

"I know you are happy to be back on an AQ case. You missed an opportunity coming off the *Cole* case, but here is to a successful run in Amman. There is no use getting upset about the post-*Cole* dustup. I know that whatever assignment you work on, you will give it your all. That is what matters."

I needed that toast. Gordon could read me like a book.

ONE GOAL, TWO TEAMS

I was up bright and early and was able to get my run in before stopping at my desk to read the overnight updates on the case. On the bureaucratic side, all my travel and investigative requests had been granted "officially," and I was ready for the trip. I drove my Bureau car to Washington Dulles International Airport and arrived early in order to check in all the equipment we were carrying. I was checked in when I spotted Will. He appeared nervous, so we sat and talked for a while before our flight was called for boarding.

We arrived in Amman in the early morning and were met by the Legat and an embassy expediter. We waited for our luggage to be processed, and when it was cleared by customs, we loaded up a massive SUV and headed to the Legat's embassy office. Buildings in Amman are constructed from cream-colored limestone, and in the reflected morning light, the city had a strikingly beautiful glow. As we approached the city from the airport, I was struck by the disparity between the beauty of the awakening city and the ugly reasons for my trip to Amman. Will and I dropped the work-related luggage at the embassy and headed to our hotel. I took a quick shower and had breakfast before Will and I returned to the embassy.

The first thing I wanted to do was to get a briefing on all investigative efforts and intelligence gathered to date from embassy officials. I met with State Department officials, visited the embassy's Regional Security Office, and talked with CIA officers. I documented these updates in writing and sent a written report to FBI Headquarters and the Washington field office. I knew I needed to feed the bureaucratic machine early and often; if I didn't, demands for updates would be on Washington's schedule—late in our day or, worse, at a time when typing up reports could interfere with the investigation. Using the time difference between Jordan and Washington to my advantage, I was determined to send daily reports prior to their opening of business. Having a full investigative report waiting on the desks of the key managers in D.C. kept the beast happy and kept me focused on the investigation.

Later that morning, meeting with the Jordanian investigators brought me much comfort. The crime scene had been processed to the high standards I had hoped I would find. The FBI Academy and my field experience had taught me how important it is to process a crime scene accurately and how crucial it can be to collect evidence meticulously if you wanted to successfully apprehend and prosecute a criminal. Contrary to the glitzy Hollywood version portrayed on television crime shows, crime scene investigations are often complex, dirty, and tedious. In my discussions with the Jordanian investigators, I found that their methods mirrored the training I had received from the FBI in almost every way.

The first step in processing a crime scene is to secure the scene. Once secured, an initial walk-through will determine whether the scene had been disturbed and, if so, who and what caused the disturbance. I learned from my Jordanian colleagues that immediately after her husband's murder, Mrs. Foley had contacted an embassy colleague, who came to see her. Other embassy personnel had also stopped by to check on Mrs. Foley when they heard the tragic news. I needed to interview each person who had potentially disturbed the crime scene, and I noted that on my "to do at the embassy" list. After the walk-through, the investigators thoroughly recorded the crime scene via photos, sketches, and videotaping. After the recording was completed, the local police collected all potential evidence, tagged it, bagged it, and transported it to their crime lab where it would be analyzed. This entire process, conducted by the Jordanian officials, was completed with exceptional professionalism and competence.

The high standards of the Jordanian services stood in contrast to the low opinion held of them by a majority of FBI managers and fellow agents. Non-Western security services were largely viewed stateside as incompetent and corrupt, a generalization I feel is based on little more than racism. I had experienced nothing but positive relations working with foreign services in the Safarini and Tchibassa cases. My genuine love for the Bureau and its mission made it very difficult for me to reconcile this patronizing attitude with the work I knew the FBI needed to be doing overseas. In an age of international crime and global terrorism, the FBI leadership clearly saw the need for positive engagement with overseas partners, but they had failed to instill the changes in FBI culture needed to achieve the necessary level of emotional intelligence. At the same time that I was finally coming to grips with my own destructive upbringing, I was starting to see the challenges I faced in carrying out the FBI's mission overseas. Initially, I did not want to face the faults of my FBI family any more than I had wanted, earlier in my life, to acknowledge the dysfunctional nature of my real family, but they were getting hard to ignore. My capabilities as an investigator were blossoming, and my role as a spouse was maturing. I felt like it was time to examine where I stood in relation to the most important aspects of my life.

Our investigation gradually revealed more and more about the perpetrator and about the mastermind behind Foley's murder. In my examination of the crime scene, I took a walk around the property and found some undisturbed cigarette butts and soda bottles close to the carport area of Foley's house, a possible location for someone to hide while stalking him. With my evidence-gathering gloves on, I collected these items, sketched their location in comparison to the crime scene, and bagged, tagged, and packaged them in a diplomatic pouch for transport to the FBI laboratory for processing. I needed DNA, fiber, and fingerprint analysis on these items to determine if they were relevant to my investigation.

In the aftermath of the rush of activity that follows a homicide, the investigation reached an expected lull. I took advantage of this downtime and hand-carried evidence collected in the investigation back to Washington. I was waiting for the results of the autopsy and for the accompanying analyses conducted in Washington. All the information had to be viewed together. Together with the evidence collected in Amman, the Bureau's processing of complete forensic evidence would help to develop the most comprehensive understanding of the murder possible.

LEGAL DELIBERATIONS AND DEBILITATIONS

When I arrived in D.C., I drove directly to the FBI lab at the headquarters building. After entering the evidence into the case log at the lab, I stopped at WFO to find most of the squad gone for the day. I returned some items from the evidence collection kit and headed home.

The flight back home had been exhausting, but jet lag kept me from sleeping. I sat at my kitchen table and ran through the case in my head again and again. I was anxious to see Gordon, and when I thought of him, I smiled. I was going to be home for our anniversary. I wanted comfort and hugs, but mostly I wanted to fall asleep in his arms.

During the Amman investigation, staying busy helped me focus on the investigation and helped me deflect my emotions. Foley was loved by his family, and friends described him as having a heart of gold. To have him taken away from his loved ones so unexpectedly, and in the most cowardly way possible, was abhorrent. Watching Foley's colleagues grieve was not an easy task, and it evoked memories of the lives I had seen lost when I lived through war in Lebanon. I wanted to help them, to hold their hands, to talk to them at length about grief; but I also knew that becoming too emotionally attached could cloud my judgment and jeopardize the investigation. So I grieved for Foley my own way. I cried, I welcomed my anger, and I thought of revenge. I questioned God's way, and I imagined justice for the killers. But these solitary emotions belonged in another place. They belonged with Gordon and me talking and reflecting. The emotion of dealing with murder is a different kind of emotion. You share it in a different way, if you share it at all.

Waiting for Gordon to get home, I finally found the energy to unpack, shower, and start dinner. I lit several candles and opened a bottle of wine. When Gordon arrived, I jumped up and greeted him, feeling like it had been a year since we had seen each other. As we ate our anniversary dinner, Gordon listened to me talk about my work, my travel, and the investigation. I went to bed that night feeling relaxed and relieved of all the stress and emotion that I had bottled up inside, and I slept well, for a good eight hours. I had forgotten to set the alarm, and Gordon did not wake me when he left for work in the morning. I woke up energized, downed my breakfast fast, and headed to the office.

I had so many things to do and did not know where to start. My indecision was quickly resolved by a summons from WFO management requesting briefings on the Foley case. After finishing the briefings, I went to my desk and checked on the status of my other cases and the leads assigned to me while I was away. I proceeded to work on my to-do list for the Foley case, setting up appointments and identifying time-sensitive matters I had to address before I could shift my attention from Foley to my other cases. I scheduled a meeting with the AUSA assigned to the case and reviewed the results of the interview with Foley's wife that had been conducted by two colleagues on the squad. I had to determine whether I needed to conduct a follow-up interview while her memory of the tragic event was still fresh. I also contacted the Legat in Amman for any updates on the case, and we discussed developments in the investigation in general.

It took me a week to cover leads on other cases assigned to me and bring all of these files up to date. After completing these tasks, I was back working on the Foley case full time. I learned that the Jordanians were on the trail of the assassin, a Libyan citizen, and his accomplices, two Jordanian citizens. I was not surprised at the investigators' swift pursuit of justice. Lawrence Foley had been a guest in Jordan, and the Jordanian officials were treating his murder as a personal affront to the honor of their nation.

My next step was meeting with the AUSA assigned to the case to discuss the possibilities of securing an indictment of the individuals responsible for the murder. When I met with the AUSA, Mickey Sang, and discussed the progress of the case thus far, she told me that Gwen Cohn was the DOJ attorney assigned to the case, which made me very happy. I told Mickey that we owed it to Foley's family to indict the subjects, adding that I was willing to work around the clock to get the AUSA's office the evidence it needed to pursue a successful prosecution.

I asked Mickey to let me know, very specifically, what her office needed, given the unusual circumstances and conditions of overseas investigations, to secure a grand jury indictment.

"I am not sure," I told Mickey, "whether I will have direct access to interview the assailant or his accomplices. If not, I may secure indirect access or even transcripts of the Jordanian investigation to date. I need to know, from you, what is needed to obtain the indictment."

Mickey pulled out a law book and looked up the elements of the crime under "Murder—Title 18, Section 1111: Intent, act, and causation." We discussed each element and examined the procedure for establishing the presence of each element during a potential interview or confession.

"I may not be able to ask the questions directly, but I can certainly have the questions asked on my behalf. In my presence, I mean. Is that satisfactory?" I asked Mickey.

"As long as you are able to testify that you heard the subject or subjects confess, I am fine with that," Mickey said.

"What about the conditions in which the interview takes place?" I asked.

"Again, if you can testify that the assailant was not under duress or coercion and that he was interviewed under reasonable conditions, then we are good," Mickey declared.

Mickey's broad generalizations gave me pause. I knew from my successful overseas cases that a great deal of planning and meticulous execution of a suspect's interview were the only ways to ensure that a prosecutor could tell a cohesive and complete story to a jury. The location of the interview, the people present at the interview, and the physical state of the subject are factors that must be taken into consideration. The case agents and the AUSA must focus on any element of an investigation that might allow a defense attorney to persuade a judge to throw out a confession. I took notes from my meeting with Mickey and fretted over whether I would get a chance to directly interview Foley's accused killer. I felt certain I could obtain a confession, and I knew that my hearing the suspect's words would help make a better case for admitting it at trial.

Although the United States did not have an extradition treaty with the Kingdom of Jordan, I still wanted to pursue an indictment. I knew there was a chance the US government might be able to convince the Jordanians to hand over the assailant, especially if he was not a Jordanian citizen. Historically speaking, the Jordanian government has not extradited its citizens to any country. But if indicted in a US court, Foley's shooter, a Libyan citizen, could very possibly be handed over to us based on an Interpol arrest warrant—commonly known as a "Red Notice." Although I worried about Mickey's limited experience with this type of prosecution, I followed her instructions precisely. I assumed she had confirmed them up her management chain given the very real challenges we were facing in trying to secure the indictment.

PRIDE AND PREJUDICE

In early December 2002, I was on a plane to Amman to continue the investigation and share the results of our evidence analysis and testing with our Jordanian colleagues. At a meeting with the director of the Jordanian General Intelligence Directorate (GID), I shared reports relating to bullet trajectory analysis. After hours of discussion and multiple cups of Arabic coffee, I secured the director's commitment for an interview of the assailant, Ibrahim. This effort was exhausting. The director was determined to protect the integrity of the Jordanian investigation, and I used every bit of experience and cultural understanding I had to convince him to trust me and make me a partner in the interview process. My native Arabic opened the door to understanding his concerns, but I found myself scrambling for the vocabulary and nuance, in Arabic, needed to express complex ideas about the US legal system and the intricate requirements of FBI investigations. I was sure, as the meeting closed, that I had made the best case possible, and I made a note to be prepared the next time I needed to make this kind of request to a senior Arab official.

My efforts paid off. The director granted me indirect access to and, most importantly, control of Ibrahim's interview. He told me that I could not directly interview Ibrahim, as he did not want to jeopardize the legal case they were building against him locally. Because Ibrahim had committed a crime on Jordanian soil, he would be tried in a Jordanian court. I respected the director's concerns and coordinated with him my meeting with the working-level investigators prior to the interview. I felt a rush of relief that the case was still moving forward.

I met with the investigators that same day and went over questions I needed answered in order to satisfy Mickey's requirements. I gave them a quick tutorial on FBI legal requirements, and they immediately understood. Ibrahim, it turned out, was eager to discuss his deed, and I was pretty good at reeling in a talkative suspect.

We set up the interview room and an adjacent room, where I would witness and hear the interview via a closed-circuit television (CCTV) camera. Water was provided for Ibrahim, and the table in the room was set up so I could view him and the investigators at the same time—I didn't want a defense attorney claiming that Ibrahim could have been "convinced" to confess. The investigators were accurate in their assessment of Ibrahim's willingness to cooperate; he took pride in his act. After a few simple questions I had provided to the investigators, he confessed his role in its entirety and in great detail. I was elated.

I left GID headquarters with my notes and replayed the interview in my head on the way back to the embassy. It all seemed just right. I sent a message to Washington, outlining the result of the interview, and knew that I had done my part. I now looked for DOJ and all its might to pick up the case from this point. I prepared myself to be available for testimony or follow-up investigations when needed, but expected the case to move forward smoothly.

A CIA officer in Amman had played a key role in introducing me to the GID director, a meeting that was directly responsible for my ability to secure Ibrahim's confession. The CIA officer, who I will call "Sam," was particularly helpful and was a close contact of one of my friends in D.C. In celebration, I decided to invite him to dinner and thank him for all his support. We met at The Terrace, a restaurant located in the Hyatt Hotel where I was staying. We ordered the vegetarian mazza plate and enjoyed a selection of hummus, baba ganoog, grape leaves, falafel, and fool mudamas. I ordered fresh juice to go with the mazza and relaxed in my lounge chair, drinking in the cool breeze. I wanted to bask in the feeling of a mission accomplished for a while.

I thanked Sam profusely for his assistance on the Foley case. It was refreshing to see someone set aside the politics, ego, and turf issues that far too often poisoned FBI/CIA relationships and focus on doing the right thing. Sam was not obligated to help me or the Bureau; in fact, he could have suffered some consequences for it, given the rivalry between the two agencies, but he had jumped in to help at every opportunity. We discussed the investigation, and I explained the legal requirements for indicting the subjects in this case. I told him how impressed I was with the Jordanian authorities, and he agreed that some folks in Washington did not give the Jordanians enough credit as equal partners with common interests. Sam asked me about the type of investigations I worked on, and I told him that I worked on an elite squad investigating crimes against US citizens and interests overseas.

"You show up after the fact," he said.

"I guess I do," I replied.

"Given your skills, you should think about working for the CIA," he offered. "By collecting good intelligence you might prevent these kinds of attacks."

"I have been thinking about joining the Legat program. I could work overseas and use my language skills," I informed him.

"To do what?" he asked. "To catch the bad guys *after* they commit a terrorist attack?"

I didn't know how to answer his question. Until that moment, the goal of catching the bad guys had seemed sufficient. Sam's challenge to me—that I might contribute to preventing attacks instead—stuck with me. For the remainder of the evening, I was distracted by the thought that I could better serve my country playing on his team.

After dinner I retired to my room. I could not fall asleep right away, even though I was pleasantly full and rather tired. Would I be of greater service to my country if I worked on a prevention team? Was I really happy working on the reaction team? I knew that focusing my efforts on preventing attacks would be more challenging, which appealed to me. I already knew I could use my language and cultural skills to effect a more comprehensive degree of security for my country.

Emotionally, however, I could not see myself leaving my FBI family. The Bureau had taken me in and provided me with the means for achieving justice for terror victims and their families. At a time in my life when I had been struggling to find purpose and harmony, they had given me stability and pride. I believed (and I still do believe) in the core values of the FBI motto: "Fidelity, Bravery, and Integrity." Like many families, the Bureau got the occasional bad apple; in general, however, agents had good intentions. Unfortunately, the Bureau's male-dominated bureaucracy meant good intentions too often remained just that.

I was at a crossroads. I wanted to call Gordon to share my good news—and ask him what he thought—but given the time difference, I'd have to wait. Since I couldn't sleep, I decided to go to the gym. My treadmill session helped calm me, but I kept revisiting the conversation with Sam.

Although I had worked closely at times with CIA operatives, I did not know a lot about the CIA's physical and mental requirements, training, or team operation. I wondered how it felt to be a spy. Would I simply be a ghostlike presence shadowing through a world of other ghostlike presences? Since Agency people work overseas, alone and undercover, are they in constant danger? Who rescues an operative when he—or she—lands a mission that goes sour?

The treadmill slowed to a stop. I was surprised to see I had completed a ten-mile run; the time had flown by while I imagined life in the CIA.

Back in my room, I listened briefly to Jordanian news coverage of the Foley case. That brought me back to reality. The capture of Ibrahim had ignited a new wave of media. I called Gordon.

"Hello, sweetie," Gordon said.

"How did you know it was me?" I asked.

"Oh, is this my gorgeous, globe-trotting wife? I thought you were someone else," he joked.

"It *is* someone else, someone who has something she didn't have a few hours ago," I teased. I could not discuss all the details of the investigation, but I wanted to let Gordon know that I was bringing a confession back home with me.

"I got what I needed for the AUSA."

"I knew you would," Gordon said confidently.

"I am so happy and can't wait to get back to D.C. and discuss this with my legal partner," I confessed.

"Which legal partner would that be?" Gordon's tone was disappointed. "Are you putting work ahead of me, again?" he grumbled.

"No, no, sweetie, I'm not! You know you are my one and only legal partner. I am just so excited for the Foleys. I think I have a good chance of putting this guy behind bars where he belongs." Although I had not meant to, I knew that my focus on the case and my elation at my success had hurt Gordon's feelings. I was disappointed with myself even as I celebrated the confession. Sometimes, I felt like my work was all I could think of and all I could do; it was my number-one priority. My successes were arming me with a new identity. I was a better, stronger, and more determined agent. The feeling of satisfaction I derived from justice being served was a powerful tonic for me. Every time I was able to do right by someone, I felt as though I shed a little more of the wrongs done to me. I was repairing the damage, bit by bit, but I knew I had to be careful. I needed to share with

Gordon the things in our relationship that existed outside of work. I needed to show him that he, too, was a big part of the repair I was undergoing.

"I love you, Gordon, and I need your support. I don't mean to put us on the outside of all this work."

"Well, OK," he said. "That sounds better. I sure do miss you."

"I'll be home soon. Keep those home fires burning—I am going to need some good time with my man."

We ended the call on an up note, but it had reminded me how fragile relationships can be. I knew I was going to be very busy with the Foley case upon my return; I would need to make it up to Gordon by planning a trip for the two of us somewhere far from the pressures of D.C.

DROPPING THE BALL

"We cannot use the confession to indict." Mickey spoke in a low voice, almost inaudible. I looked around the room at her boss, Norman Spear, and the DOJ attorney, Gwen. I was completely bewildered.

"Why is that? Why can't we use it?"

My voice sounded polite, but in my head I was screaming the question. The media attention this case was getting was hot. I wanted to capitalize on that attention, get the indictment, and move the case to the rendition phase. What I understood from Gwen was that Mickey had failed to sufficiently coordinate with either Gwen or Norman the requirements needed to indict and subsequently render the subjects that she had spelled out to me. I felt like I'd been kicked in the gut. My cooperation and partnership with the Jordanian investigators, my endless hours of work, the confession—all of it had come to nothing.

Normally, when I hear disappointing news, I try and salvage the best outcome from the situation, however furious I am. In this case, however, I said nothing. I simply sat there as Mickey explained why the confession would not be enough to move forward on an indictment. In that moment, something became clear. At the CIA, I could work on preventing attacks like the Foley murder. Yes, I felt attached to my cases and I wanted to see them through, but I felt like the hoops I had to jump through to reach a successful prosecution were getting smaller and smaller. Mickey's news was the last straw. My current work did not align with my feelings about where I could most contribute to the mission. When the meeting ended, I said nothing to anyone about my state of mind. There was only one person I could work this out with. I left work early and headed home. It was strange to be home so early, but it felt good to sit on the couch and think. I knew what I had to do, but I wanted to talk things over with Gordon first. It was Friday, and I had planned a weekend trip to the Poconos. I thought perhaps we could talk about it on the drive. It helped that I found our drives relaxing. Sitting alongside Gordon with the landscape flashing by loosened my tongue. I could say things at such times without too much self-editorializing. I packed a small bag for our trip and made dinner before Gordon got home. We had a quiet night, watched some television, and went to bed early.

The next morning, we grabbed a couple of coffees and were on the road early. I liked the constant gliding motion of leaving the city by car, of getting outside the Beltway by some means other than an international flight. I liked looking at the myriad of roads and businesses, the tree lines and open fields, the people going about their Saturday morning routines. We were headed to wooded peace in the Poconos. I sat back and enjoyed the ride, getting ready to pop the question. Then Gordon surprised me with a question of his own.

"Are you ready to start our family?"

My mind immediately raced back to one of the darkest moments of our lives.

I was in Rwanda the day I learned that I was pregnant for the first time in my life. I had missed my period, so I walked to the pharmacy next to the Hotel Rwanda for a pregnancy test kit. It was positive. I immediately wanted to share the news with Gordon, but, given the time difference, I decided it would be best to call later. Thoughts of balancing my work and travel schedule surfaced; however, what worried me most was whether I would be a good mother. I was certain Gordon would make a wonderful father, and that reassured me.

I eventually decided to put off telling him until I returned to the States. I had to shift mental gears and focus on getting confessions from suspected murderers. I placed the pregnancy test in an evidence bag and closed it with evidence tape. I decided to surprise Gordon by handing him the evidence bag rather than telling him the news on the phone.

After returning from Rwanda, I handed Gordon the bag. He was elated. For the next few weeks, we endlessly discussed the baby and how she or he was going to change our lives forever.

Then one day, all our excitement and anticipation changed 180 degrees. I discovered that I was bleeding and called my doctor. I pushed down my fear and worked to stay calm. She asked me to come see her immediately, and I called Gordon and told him to meet me at the doctor's office. There, our worst fears were realized: the doctor was unable to hear the baby's heartbeat and made an appointment for an ultrasound. That night, the bleeding got so much worse that we decided to go to the emergency room. We registered with the front desk and sat in the waiting room to be called. Emergency rooms on weekend nights are horrible places. The waiting went on and on. In the end, unable to secure any help from the hospital staff and suffering from waves of intense cramps, I was forced to retreat to the public bathroom, where I passed the fetal tissue.

We were devastated. I had lost my baby at a very early stage, with all the promise of what could have been. It was a harrowing experience. We had been so ready for a child, in every sense. Even though I had never seen its face, I had grown to love this child. Gordon and I grieved together. We went through shock then anger before coming to terms with God's will and plan for us. I immersed myself in my work and did not take any time to myself; this was my way of dealing with tragedy. Gordon did the same.

We hadn't talked about trying again for a good while.

"It's been a year and I don't want your fear to make the decision for us," Gordon ventured.

"Fear will not make the decision. You and I will," I replied.

"Well, that's OK by me."

"I feel like we both dealt with it as best we could, and I'm ready to move on. That way we can make a good decision," I continued.

"So, we will talk about this?" Gordon asked.

"Yes, my dear, we will talk about it. I think your idea is a wonderful one."

We stopped for lunch and enjoyed the scenic views from our restaurant and got back on the road. I felt at ease mentioning my plans of changing careers from the FBI to the CIA. As expected, Gordon supported my move and jokingly started calling me Janet Bond. Our Pocono weekend was just what we needed: calm, relaxing, and cheerful. We drove back to D.C., talking about our future family together and where we might retire surrounded by our grandchildren.

OVER TO THE DARK SIDE 10

On May 15, 2003, I was on a charter jet along with a number of other FBI special agents heading to Riyadh, Saudi Arabia, to investigate attacks on the US compound in Riyadh days earlier. Although I was prepared for and quite familiar with the intense work schedule ahead of me, I could not help but question how this work could be the most effective way to deter terrorism. My understanding of the purpose of this specific FBI mission did not help to ease my concerns. My FBI team was directed to assist the Saudis in conducting their investigation. The US and Saudi governments had reached an agreement that, despite the number of Americans killed, no individuals found guilty of participation in this attack would be extradited from Saudi Arabia to face trial in the United States; moreover, any evidence collected during the investigation would not be provided to the FBI's evidence response team to process. Instead, we would simply assist our Saudi counterparts in their investigative efforts. None of the information gathered by our team was to be used in a US court.

During our several-week stay, we were housed at the Guest Palace in Riyadh. We were broken into teams of three, and each team was responsible for investigating one of the three locations that had been attacked: the Dorrat Al-Jadawel (a compound owned by the London-based MBI International), the Hamra Oasis Village, and the Vinnell Corporation compound. The Vinnell Corporation compound was also known as the "SANG compound" because it was used by a Virginia-based defense contractor as a training site for the Saudi Arabian National Guard (SANG).

I was assigned to the SANG compound team and traveled daily in a caravan of SUVs accompanied by two jeeps filled with armed Saudi security personnel. At the site, our Saudi partners would make witnesses available for us to interview. A team of evidence response agents was also present at the SANG site, and they processed the crime scene. I worked with this team at times, mostly while my team was waiting for someone on the Saudi side to find witnesses to interview.

During one of our drives from the Palace to the SANG site, I noticed a vehicle driving close to our caravan. I kept an eye on the driver and its occupants. Subconsciously, I noted the model, color, and any other distinguishing characteristics and started repeating the license tag to myself. When they drove very close to our SUV, I looked the driver, and then the front-seat passenger, in the face. I realized that they were trying to tell me something. The passenger rolled down his window and made an explosive gesture with his hands. I read his lips and understood quite well the familiar rhetoric: "Death to America." I immediately alerted our driver, who radioed the chase vehicles and informed them of the incident.

Moments later, the suspicious vehicle was stopped, and I saw the occupants step out of the vehicle with their arms up. Where these guys trying to tell me that another explosion was going to take place? Were we being targeted? Or were these guys punks playing games? *Time may tell,* I told myself, *but I won't be there for it.*

After a long day of interviews at the SANG site, we would head back to the Palace and write down the results of these interviews. Because of my language capabilities, I had a considerably larger number of interviews to document. I was also often required to translate for FBI management when they held multi-hour meetings with senior Saudi investigators. In the typical FBI fashion, it was left to me, despite my workload, to document these meetings in English for the record and then transcribe the notes into official reports.

Owing to the large number of terrorist attacks against US citizens and interests overseas, FBI HQ management came up with what

I felt was a very shortsighted strategy to deal with the constant demand on its staff. They formed a "travel squad" whose duties were to immediately respond to the site of an attack, conduct initial investigative steps, and then turn the investigation over to agents from the FBI field office that would be assigned the investigation. The travel squad would consist of agents with language capabilities and travel experience. As a result, we had several agents among us from the newly formed travel squad, and one of these agents (who was introduced to me as an Arabic speaker) was assigned to work the SANG location with me.

When we were given access to the main witness at the SANG site, I wanted to ensure that the interview was conducted by two Arabic-speaking agents in order to have the most unassailable legal case possible. A petite Saudi male, with a long beard and dressed in the traditional garb, walked to the interview room and sat across from us. I took the lead in the interview while my partner looked at me in bewilderment. I was not sure how this witness would initially react to a woman interrogator, but I spent some time assessing his demeanor and body language and felt confident that the witness was comfortable with me asking him all kinds of challenging questions. Over the years, I have often been asked whether my gender affected my ability to work interrogations. I reply that in my experience I had found my gender to be an effective tool for conducting successful investigations. For instance, playing to the culture, I knew that Arab males generally did not want to disappoint someone playing the cultural role of a "sister." So, I often played that role and got what I asked for when other interrogators had been refused.

During the four-hour interview, I frequently looked at my partner for follow-up questions, additional explanations, or advice on anything I might have missed. To my surprise, throughout the interview, he looked back at me with confusion. I did not address my concern during the interview and continued on with my questioning. Owing to the level of detail provided in the interrogation, I asked the witness to walk me through what he had witnessed at the scene. At the conclusion of our long walk-through in the brutal desert sun, I was happy to confirm that what the witness had told me in the interview room matched what I was seeing on the ground; most importantly, I confirmed his ability to see the perpetrators from where he had hidden at the crime scene. Upon completion of this essential interview, I thanked the witness and walked with him to where he was scheduled to be picked up. This gesture showed my appreciation and respect for our witness. I did not think that sitting in a room and having the witnesses come, be interviewed, and walk out on their own was appropriate. Certainly, such dismissive behavior lacked cultural sensitivity.

When I finally questioned my partner about his lack of involvement in the interview, he confessed to me that he did not understand the "Saudi dialect." I explained to him that the witness had spoken in Fusha (the Modern Standard Arabic, which is in wide use in the world) and not in Amiyya (colloquial Arabic, which is uncommonly used in Saudi Arabia). After some digging, I learned that my partner had taken no more than a few basic Arabic classes. Basically, he could say hello and order at a restaurant. This was inexcusable on several fronts. First, I was disappointed with FBI management for falsely representing the skills of the newly formed travel squad; and second, I was ticked, maybe even more so, with my novice speaker of an agent who went along with the charade. A defense attorney with even moderate skills would destroy the credibility of this "Arabic-speaking" agent. The failure to have top-notch agents on the job could potentially imperil the entire multi-million dollar investigation.

After more than two weeks of assisting the Saudi government and getting precious little for our sweat and hard work, we all departed for Washington on a chartered FBI jet. On the flight back, I had a lot of time to reflect on what had taken place on the ground. I found myself becoming more worried than usual about America's battle with terror and our citizens' safety. Terrorist violence was escalating as major attacks now came with depressing regularity. As I gazed out of the jet's tiny window into an endlessly clear blue sky, I began to have disturbing visions of a series of laudable FBI convictions that did nothing to put a serious dent in terrorist activity. I was now sure that my skills would be better used contributing to the prevention of terror via the gathering of intelligence, as opposed to being used in investigating attacks that had already taken place. I now felt that after-the-fact investigations, especially those without critical intelligence sharing, were doomed to solve only a small part of the problem. I was certainly determined, perhaps unrealistically so at the time, to solve all of the problems. Unrealistic or not, my thinking led me to see the Saudi investigation as my last FBI round-up.

My thoughts were spinning in all directions. We were at war, our enemy was sophisticated, and time was of the essence. We needed an effective plan to eliminate this evil. The battle was unconventional (in great part because our enemy was so unconventional), and we needed to understand that centuries-old rules of war had been radically altered. We required an imaginative network of creative and forceful means to be successful. We could no longer go home at the end of the day, speak of how we had put a counterfeiter or a crime boss in prison, and pat ourselves on the back. Most importantly, I was coming to believe that we needed to engage the enemy in his backyard in ways that were legal, effective, and creative.

I finally fell asleep and had a vivid dream about another attack involving a US embassy overseas where both adults and children were killed. I woke up covered in sweat and hoped that no one on the plane, especially the agents sitting close to me, had noticed my agitated state.

I was looking forward to being home with Gordon and called him immediately after I arrived. I stopped and picked up some takeout before I made it home. Given my travel schedule, home seemed, at first, to be yet another hotel room. I unpacked, tidied up the place a bit, and started to feel at home. I was happy to see Gordon, and after we sat down at the dinner table, I talked about the Saudi Arabian heat and played absentmindedly with my food. Gordon sensed that something was wrong. I was always excited to tell Gordon how justice had been served by my work and how perpetrators would be suffering the consequences of their crimes, but this time I barely mentioned the SANG case.

"You don't seem enthusiastic about this case," Gordon observed.

"This case is a mess."

"Aren't you happy about building a case against these terrorists and extraditing them or, even more exciting, rendering them to face our legal system?" he asked.

"Unfortunately, that is not going to happen with this so-called investigation," I replied.

"I don't understand, Nada."

"I don't understand it either; I don't know why we traveled to Saudi Arabia and spent millions of dollars when we were so obviously not going to be allowed to do our job." I was getting upset and struggling to make my point. Gordon started to say something, but I interrupted him.

"We will not be indicting, rendering, or extraditing anyone," I fumed.

"Then why did you all go there?" he inquired.

"Good question. The only thing that I can think of is the role of politics. When my office investigated the 1996 Khobar Towers bombing, there was a lot of speculation about whether the Saudi government had tried to steer that investigation away from OBL—to allegedly protect him—and toward a dissident Shi'a group that was opposed to the Saudi monarchy," I started to explain.

I could see concern on Gordon's face, and I continued explaining my theory.

"Bin Laden has always claimed responsibility for the acts that he has committed, and he claimed responsibility for the Khobar Towers bombing. It made sense to have the FBI's OBL experts, the New York field office, look at that possibility, but the Washington office blocked New York out of the Khobar Towers investigation. So, the rivalry between the two offices grew even sharper. It was a turf war, plain and simple. I can see how, in the present case, the Washington office, wanting to prove something to NYFO, dispatched all of us—to a pretty dangerous spot I might add—to make the point that we were looking at things firsthand and not simply relying on the information received from the Saudi government." I threw my hands into the air. "It's just a game of one-upmanship, Gordon."

"I don't know what to say," Gordon mumbled.

"There are better ways for our government to check whether the information we are receiving from the Saudis is truthful; it is called intelligence." Despite my efforts to make our first dinner together in weeks a pleasant one, I could hear myself lecturing.

"On the subject of intelligence, good news that you heard back from the CIA," Gordon offered. I had opened a letter from the CIA when I got home. I was glad he was changing the subject. I was getting more and more upset talking about my trip.

"They did offer me conditional employment," I said, a little more upbeat now. "All that's left for me to do is to pass the last portion of the background investigation." I even managed a slight smile delivering this bit of news.

"Look, Nada, that's great. Things change and you know they need to change. I know you can really make a difference," he said firmly.

We spent the rest of the night talking about everything but work.

I successfully completed my CIA polygraph exam on June 6, 2003. Unlike the test that I had taken four years before with the FBI, this exam concentrated on questions about classified information. I was now someone in the know. The CIA exam wanted to assure all concerned that I knew how cautious to be in protecting and handling classified material. I passed.

Gordon had fully supported my transfer to the CIA, and the Saudi trip had reinforced my feeling that I was making the right decision. I regretfully left behind the cases I was attached to, but I viewed my transfer as moving deeper into the frontline battle. In June 2003, having completed all the necessary paperwork, I joined up. The Bureau communicated to the CIA that they had "lost" my personnel file but confirmed that I had a valid security clearance. As such, no mention of my first marriage followed me from the Bureau to the Agency. I was now a CIA operative.

RUNNING AND GUNNING

In the calmest voice I had ever heard, Dave called over the radio for "react" forces. He then switched off the lights of the SUV, put on his night vision goggles (NVGs), and hit the gas. Once we reached the dead end, he informed our rescue team of our rally and rescue location. At that point, he turned and looked at me.

"Don't worry; they have to get through me before they get close to you."

"OK, Dave," I heard myself saying. I pulled my Colt Commando machine gun closer to my body, checked the Glock on my waist, and started pulling additional magazines for both the Glock and the Commando out of my backpack for easy access. I had been in Iraq only a matter of weeks, but I knew how to be armed and dangerous. Dave looked at my arsenal approvingly.

"I will fend them off, but if I am down . . ."

"Let me come out and help, Dave, please!" I interrupted.

"You stay in the armor. The react forces are on their way, and there is no need to expose more of us to danger," he said firmly.

"Do not let them take you hostage," he added. "Fight till the end."

I immediately thought of William Buckley and how he had been tortured. And I thought of my cousin Sami.

"You will never see the orange jumpsuit on me," I assured Dave.

I will ignore Dave's instruction, I told myself once he vacated the safety of the vehicle, *and I will get out of here to help if he takes fire and is injured.* I would not be able to live with myself if Dave bled to death in front of my eyes. I imagined myself telling Dave's children that their dad died protecting me while I sat like a lump in the relative safety of my heavily armored SUV. It wasn't a picture I wanted to be in.

Dave got out of the darkened vehicle and, laden with his "battle-rattle" equipment, assumed a tactical position. While it might take some time for help to arrive, I knew I was in good hands: after all,

I was working with one of the most decorated Navy SEALs in the service.

The encounter that presently beset us had started close to midnight. We had just dropped off an asset after a very long debriefing, and both of us were beyond exhausted. The intelligence gathered was of utmost importance, definitely worth our time and trouble. Being able to gather information about the intentions and abilities of various groups that were forming in Iraq after Baghdad fell was vital to both policymakers and troops on the ground.

Unfortunately, our drop-off site that night was in one of the most hostile locations in Baghdad, a location relatively safe for the asset but quite dangerous for us. Suddenly, after our asset had disappeared into the smoky Baghdad night, we started taking fire. Almost immediately, it seemed, I was looking right at the men firing on us. The whole attack seemed to unfold in slow motion.

Two Iraqis had spotted our vehicle from a distance of about 200 meters, picked up their belt-fed machine guns, and sprayed fire in our direction. We decided to get off the "X" immediately but our choices were limited. Backing up would get us closer to the assailants but nearer to a familiar route to safety. Going forward would get us away from the shooters but leave us in parts unknown. Dave had decided to go forward, and we rapidly ran into a dead end, where Dave took over. Now he was outside, ready to exchange fire.

The assailants, surprised by our maneuver, did not want to take a chance and get close in on our location. They were looking for victims, and we weren't acting like victims. In fact, they were so confused that after surging toward us from the area where they had initially launched the attack, they melted away into the alleys of their neighborhood. This allowed me a moment to exhale, but I knew they could return at any moment. If they returned, it would be with more friends and more firepower.

Our react forces finally made it to our location. Dave had given them coordinates, and they found us with little difficulty. We were escorted back to the relative safety of Baghdad International Airport, where I wrote up the intelligence collected from our asset after the adrenaline passed. Having lived in war-torn Lebanon for almost twenty years, I was oddly comfortable with the daily possibility of violence and danger. I had not realized how accustomed I was to it until I saw the impact that constant violence had on other CIA officers. Some had a hard time adjusting to the stress. The war severely disrupted their eating and sleeping habits.

But for me, living with the potential for danger isn't the same thing as actually being attacked. The brazen shooting made me unspeakably angry. And, because I liked Dave's cool manner and selfless courage, I wanted to take on any shooter who would send a volley of fire Dave's way. I hadn't fired any of my weapons, but I was ready and prepared if need be. I ran over the event in my head a few times before hitting the stuffy track that ringed the airport tarmac. Running helped cool my temper even as the temps on the track reached well over 100 degrees. As I ran myself to exhaustion—assuring me of at least a few hours of blessed sleep in this stultifying desert—I thought of Dave's children. I hoped they were proud of their old man.

The conditions on the ground that July were austere, befitting a startup war zone CIA station. We worked in a blast-resistant, generator-powered pod shaped like a shipping container. The pod was equipped with narrow racks of computers and chairs for the officers' use that made the already tiny work space even more confining.

The kitchen, a defunct cooking/catering area within the airport terminal, was briefly staffed by one cook who departed at the end of his TDY and left us without any help. To say that sanitary conditions in the kitchen were primitive after the cook departed would be generous. I quickly acquainted myself with the Meals, Ready to Eat (MREs) and found them to be surprisingly tasty. I also ate tons of peanut butter and jelly sandwiches for breakfast, lunch, and dinner. I did not want to complain about our food situation. In general, I do not like to complain about issues unless I have a solution to the problem at hand. In this case, I knew that CIA management was doing everything in its power to rectify the situation, and I viewed complaining as distracting to the mission. More importantly, I thought of our military personnel who ate nothing but MREs because they did not have a choice in the matter; I believed that complaining was flat out disrespectful to our soldiers.

Our sleeping quarters were converted shipping containers that contained a single cot and an area that resembled a shower stall. To cool these containers as they baked daily in the hot desert sun, a hole was roughly made in the wall and an air-conditioning unit was installed. In my container, the hole was a bit bigger than the AC unit, and I often came home to my pod to find various insects—such as beetles, mantis, and hornets—exploring my bed or making nests in other areas of my little home. I made several unsuccessful, albeit feeble, attempts to plug the gaps around the AC, but not until the day when I woke up with a camel spider on my chest did I find the motivation needed to get my pod sealed up.

Initially, we did not have running water for showers, so we all took what we dubbed "baby-wipe" baths or "pit showers." Actually, wiping your body down with baby wipes left you surprisingly clean and refreshed. It was also amusing to have enormous, heavily armed gunmen walking around smelling like a fresh diaper. Conversely, the outdoor portable toilets that cooked in the hot desert sun were vile, even from several yards away. When I used them, I held my breath as long as I could. I limited my visits accordingly.

After some adjustment, I fell into the routine of a seven-day work week with multiple asset meetings per day. My adventure with Dave took place shortly after my first month in Iraq.

SIX MONTHS EARLIER, I HAD BEEN sitting on the couch at home with Gordon and watching on TV then-secretary of state Colin Powell's speech and slideshow at a packed meeting of the United Nations Security Council. Powell's February 5, 2003, presentation inspired both of us. It inspired a lot of folks. We were ready to join in the fight against Al Qaeda in the upcoming mission to liberate Iraq from its sadistic dictator, Saddam Hussein. (As recent reports confirm, however, Powell's all-important presentation in the run-up to invasion was riddled with misinformation. Lies told to American intelligence by an informant nicknamed "Curveball" were put forth as truths in Powell's briefing to the Security Council—and to the nation. Curveball, a disgruntled Iraqi businessman, had invented the weapons-of-mass-destruction (WMD) story in the hopes of getting America to invade.)

Secretary Powell's speech linking the WMD charge with an Al Qaeda connection to the Iraqi regime had framed Saddam Hussein as a viable threat to the US homeland. At the time, I agreed with Mr. Powell's assessment that WMD and AQ were not a good mix. Both Gordon and I wanted to make America safer for everyone and especially for the family we were starting together.

We stepped forward to meet the challenge.

On Friday, June 27, 2003, I handed my gun and my FBI badge to an office administrator and walked out of the Washington field office. I still loved the FBI and what its ideals stood for. The good men and women of the FBI work hard to provide justice for citizens and the families of those who have been victimized. I was proud to have been a special agent for the FBI and was also proud of all my accomplishments. I was now embarking on a new mission. On Monday, June 30, 2003, I reported to a CIA facility where I was briefed and processed.

Prior to my departure for Iraq, I had confided in my sister Lola, and in my mother, that I had transferred to the CIA. I had designated Lola as my secondary beneficiary (for insurance purposes), and I wanted her to know who to contact should anything happen to me or to Gordon. Gordon, who was extremely sensitive about my security, was not fond of the idea of my confiding my work-related life to my family. He knew that my mother would most likely tell my father and, similarly, that Lola would tell her husband, Talal Chahine. Gordon understood enough about Arab culture to realize that the relationship between a husband and wife meant full disclosure by the unequal female partner. I understood his concern about security, but I did not think I had a choice.

"Be realistic. You know the level of violence in Iraq," I told Gordon. "We started our relationship back in Yemen, working on a mass casualty attack. What if you and I were both to die?" I asked him. "Lola would not know what to do."

Gordon shrugged his shoulders and accepted my decision. I asked Mother and Lola to not discuss my employment with anyone, but I too knew that in the end they would likely confide in their spouses. I knew that keeping such a secret, especially in the culture of Arab marriage, was an almost impossible task, so I did worry about it. In fact, I was reassured when I discussed with other CIA officers the issue of breaking cover with family members. They noted that there is always a chance that someone will discuss your true employment. And the reasons people blab are both good and bad. I heard stories of proud fathers bragging at family gatherings about their child's employment, and I heard stories of siblings who had had too much to drink announcing their brother's CIA affiliation to a crowded bar.

Culturally, I would not expect my parents to brag about my CIA employment; the fact was, they had never been proud of me. On the other hand, I was a little concerned that they might try to use my CIA employment as a tool to frighten others in the Arab community they wished to manipulate. My mother had once called my desk when I was with the FBI and asked me to call and scare a relative she had gotten into a fight with. Similarly, I could expect Talal, should he learn of my employment, to potentially brag to his buddies that he "knew" someone in the CIA in order to create the false impression that he had connections, or *wasta,* in the government. But my options were as limited as the trust I put in my family to remain quiet. I needed to prepare them rapidly for my impending deployment, and I had to make sure they knew how to handle my affairs if Gordon and I returned from Iraq in caskets.

So, in the wake of the American-British invasion, and more or less immediately upon my transfer to the CIA, I volunteered to serve in Iraq. After successfully completing additional firearms training, I arrived in Baghdad within weeks of my first day at the CIA. Gordon had departed to serve with his team in Baghdad ahead of me, and I was happy to see him when I got there. We were lucky to be able to work in the same location and, more importantly, on issues that we both believed in strongly. It was going to be an interesting ride.

ABORT MISSION—WINTER 2003

The caller's words were indecipherable. An agitated voice crackled over the encrypted hand-held radio of the security officer driving our vehicle, who quietly relayed the message to his partner in the front seat. Seconds later, the black bulletproof Mercedes G–500 was speeding so fast over Baghdad's pockmarked roads that pothole recoil was launching the heavy vehicle high into the air. The crash landings repeatedly jolted me and my asset in our backseat cocoon.

I put my hand underneath my armored body vest and felt my heavy belly. The repeated bouncing was causing my baby to kick me repeatedly; it was as if she understood what was going on and was complaining about the bumpy ride. I had felt nauseated before I got into the Mercedes, and the wild ride—along with the stench from the open sewage and the mountains of garbage—made my nausea unbearable. I threw up in my plastic bag and put the first bag in another bag before setting it under my seat. By this time, everyone was familiar with my vomiting spells. In fact, colleagues often brought me extra bags, just in case.

Gordon had been worried about my pregnancy and my work schedule. I had lost fifteen pounds by the time I was six months pregnant. At 5' 8" and 105 pounds, I looked emaciated. Gordon asked me to speak to a physician about my weight and insisted he be with me when I went. It was not my weight that alarmed the doctor—anti-nausea pills would allow me to keep food down. He was more concerned about the effects of possible trauma. The doctor bluntly told me that if I were seriously injured, the trauma doctors would do everything possible to help save my life, but the limitations of combat medicine meant the same could not be said about saving the life of our baby. The doctor's words made a difficult decision even harder. Gordon had expressed his concerns multiple times and assured me that my assessment—that I would be "abandoning" the mission if I placed our future child's safety above my duties—was not accurate. But having worked with Navy SEALS, Army Special Forces, and the Marines that stood guard near our station, it was inconceivable to me, knowing how important my contributions were, to desert the mission. This disagreement was a sensitive topic for us. In the end, Gordon, although he did not approve of my decision, supported my stay in Baghdad. His support allowed me to remain in Iraq despite increasing risks to my pregnancy.

I leaned forward into the front seat and asked the driver to explain what he had heard over the radio. He responded by telling me to keep an eye on the asset seated next to me, to keep my hand on my weapon, and to not ask any more questions. This response did nothing to ease my concerns. I was told only that we were heading for the nearest "safesite." Although moving at ballistic speeds, I was able to check my map: it appeared that Baghdad International Airport was our likely destination.

I had just completed the latest in a series of several meetings with the asset seated next to me. He had always provided actionable intelligence relating to planned attacks on US military sites and personnel; in fact, it is safe to say that the intelligence he provided had saved the lives of some of our military men. For that reason, I always looked forward to our meetings. He was very organized, and he provided great detail. He brought out my business side. Working with multiple assets in a war zone, I had contact with diverse personalities, requiring a lot of skill and patience to deal with differences in background, motivation, and expectations. I often felt like a roving psychiatrist, picking up patients along with intelligence. I heard of wives who did not give the asset enough attention and of mistresses who were cheating on the cheating asset; I knew of contacts taking on a second or third wife; I was regaled with stories of problematic children and rebellious teenagers. The ability to listen deeply is an essential tool for CIA case officers. Knowing your asset's family circumstances and understanding his or her needs is key to recognizing the motivation behind their cooperation and understanding how best to gain useful information from them. Showing interest in them moderates their behavior and creates trust. As exhausted as I often was, I wished I could simply meet the asset, gather the information, and be finished. But, from both an investigative and a human perspective, I knew that I had to reestablish rapport every time we met.

In the backseat of the speeding Mercedes, I reflected on how my morning had started—with a bout of sickness and a review of my next contact meeting. "Moe" was on time, and we picked him up at an agreed-upon location. I greeted him, and he jumped into the backseat with me. In typical fashion, he quickly had his notebook out and was thumbing through page after page of his cryptic notes. He had beautiful handwriting, and he always color-coded his various tasking points. I told him I wished that all my agents were as organized as he. Moe liked to have long political debates and discussions—my least favorite kind of conversation in a war zone. Sometimes it felt like he wanted to test me on what I knew of Iraq's political history; other times, I felt like he wanted to show off his knowledge of emerging political figures. On this particular day, I listened a lot and engaged him here and there with simple questions. I could tell he had been thinking hard about his ideas and had to get them off his chest before we dove into the real purpose of our meeting.

After asking him several security-related questions to ensure he had arrived at the meeting site without any problems, I returned to the information I had previously tasked him with. He opened his notebook, and we went down the tasking list and discussed each topic at great length. Of course I wanted the information, but I was also interested in how he collected it. I wanted to know more about *his* sources. As I did not want him to confuse his personal assessment of a topic with the facts, I ever so gently asked him the how, where, and when of his gathered information, allowing him time after each answer to editorialize about the source's reliability or his own take on the value of the information. I engaged him thus in order to make sure *I* could differentiate between actionable intelligence and friendly observations. It was necessary to do this sort of double-entry note-taking for a cultural reason (I wanted to show him I respected his networking acumen) and for a security reason (I wanted to ensure that

I was properly vetting his reporting). It took me about two hours to gather, clarify, and document his information. Once that was done, I issued him new tasking, reminding him that if he received any information regarding imminent attacks on the military or any US person or establishment, he needed to contact me immediately.

I began to relax as our meeting drew to a close. I was happy with the information gathered and knew that I had a long night ahead of me documenting all the raw intelligence. I asked Moe to repeat his tasking to make sure he understood exactly what I was looking for. I found that this precaution generally prevented any disconnect between the asset's hearing one thing and thinking something else. Moe repeated the assignment, and I tweaked a couple of the requests. Once satisfied, we headed to the drop-off site. We were almost there when the emergency abort call came in.

When we reached the entrance to the airport, we enjoyed the safety of the 20mm cannon overwatch and the active Coalition military forces located there. Only when we arrived inside the airport's relative security did the security contract officer explain that we had been "set up." Had we remained on our planned route to the drop-off site, we were told, our vehicle would have become the target of a RPG–7 rocket-propelled grenade attack. I asked the officer for more information, and he replied that he did not know who had compromised the mission, adding that all efforts were being made to find the source of the leak.

For a brief moment, I seriously questioned whether I had made the right decision to place my child so much in harm's way. But I quickly pushed these thoughts aside. I had to focus now on my efforts to uncover by whom or what, when, why, and how my mission had been compromised.

Initial evidence indicated that Moe had been involved in the planned attack. I had doubts about that theory, but I knew I had to think objectively. Moe was placed in a room under armed watch while a polygraph expert was dispatched to our location. At one point, I was sitting with him in the old dusty room used as storage for extra cots and other furniture when he looked me in the eye and asked me what was going on. I told him that I did not know enough of the details to say. I didn't want to believe I had misjudged this man, and as I looked at him, I thought that he certainly did not act like someone who had been involved in a plot to kill me. He looked genuinely confused, even ashamed. He just stared at the floor, not moving. I left the room long enough to make some calls, hoping to determine how we had heard of the planned attack. I learned that another CIA officer had been contacted by one of his assets. The asset had informed the officer that "some men" were setting up to ambush a black Mercedes SUV. The aim of the ambush, the asset had reported, was to kill the female Arab "traitor" helping the US government.

Hearing these words made me feel numb. I was in shock. I had been in life-threatening situations before, but I had never felt so personally targeted. I could feel the numbness spreading as I hung up the phone.

The situation was surreal. I couldn't feel a thing. The odd thought occurred to me that I must not value my life very much to be reacting in so muted a manner. Maybe, I thought, my longstanding battle with low self-worth was manifesting at last. I could still hear my father wishing failure on me as I left for America. Was this investigation telling me I had lost control in some way? My instinct that Moe was on the level, my desire to bury a cold-blooded sniper, my sense of being so right about my decision to stay in a war zone while pregnant—were these less signs of courage and determination than signs that I had misjudged and overstepped? If the planned attack had come off, I thought, I would be dead. So would Moe and the two officers driving the vehicle.

A sick feeling started to creep into my numbness. Our deaths would have confirmed my father's judgment that I was ultimately too weak or too headstrong for success—my father would have it both ways, no doubt. I chewed on that thought as I sat at my borrowed desk and awaited the arrival of the polygraph examiner.

Gradually, I began to see the bright side of disastrous fate avoided. I was not dead. Moe would be exonerated—or not. I had survived quite a bit of horror already, and I would see my way through the current confusion. I would work with my team to get to the bottom of how the mission had so very nearly gone so terribly wrong.

I set aside for the moment my self-analysis and returned to Moe's room with a bottle of water. I wanted, for my own reasons, to look him in the eye again and know whether I would be able to see for myself if he had betrayed me. Moe thanked me for the water and asked me again whether I had learned anything new. His questioning eyes seemed to say he was sorry for any trouble he might be causing. I thought I caught in his tone of voice an honest appeal. *He is innocent,* I thought, but all I said was that they were still looking into the matter. The polygraph expert finally showed up, and I briefed him on what we knew so far. I gave him Moe's biographical information, which he needed as part of his testing.

After an intense debriefing session with Moe that lasted for the next four hours and included a polygraph examination, we determined that Moe was not "bad." He had not passed any information to our enemies. I was more than a little relieved. However, our finding was of only temporary comfort. I would later learn that Moe's associate, who had sold him out, was the cause of the compromised mission.

Dangerous men all over the country knew things about all of us that made our every move outside the Green Zone potentially our last. That was the way it was that summer of 2003. The war, which was to last another eight years, was just gearing up. For many of the men and women I came to feel close to, the war would never be over. An insurgency, which few had foreseen, was looming. Prison fiascos would tarnish the nation's image. Roadside bombings, mass firefights, and sectarian violence amounting to a civil war would claim the lives of thousands and send many more thousands home to a frightful reckoning. My CIA experiences in Baghdad demonstrated that dangerous missions and risk-taking were necessary to gather real-time intelligence. The skill I had developed through good, honest police work was the touchstone I kept close to my breast. I had to trust others, to whatever degree I was capable, to help prevent attacks against our troops. Given what I saw on the ground as the positive results of our focused missions, I was prepared and willing to take the associated risks. It was the least the Agency could do to help our military men and women who were taking even greater risks daily.

WEAPONS OF MASS DECEPTION

"I am a bit disturbed about the increasing violence I am seeing on the street," I confessed to Gordon. "I know mission priorities can change, and I am happy to adapt to these changes, but it seems to me like the entire mission has changed."

I tried to explain my lingering doubts over Operation Iraqi Freedom—Secretary of Defense Donald Rumsfeld had given the operation this tagline—during one of the few times in early 2004 when Gordon and I were lucky enough to have dinner together.

"I came here to flush out the relationship between AQ and the Iraqi regime. I came here to gather intelligence on Iraq's WMD program. And I came here to make America safe for everyone, including the baby."

I patted my growing belly as I made this last observation. "I don't think Iraq has any WMDs. And I have not uncovered any convincing evidence of a direct relationship between the Iraqi regime and AQ. I am not the only one now in that camp," I sighed. "In fact, I think we may have created a breeding ground here for AQ. If that is the case, then part of this mission has almost certainly failed."

"I'm seeing the same problems," Gordon agreed. "I cannot tell you how many 'yellow cake' scams are out there, and I'm afraid that one of these scams could be a lure designed to capture or kill CIA officers who respond to these calls."

I took a deep breath and confirmed Gordon's take on the matter.

"Right. We have dug site after site," I continued, "where alleged WMDs supposedly existed and have found nothing. You know, we are sitting ducks for snipers and terrorists when we go and spend long hours at these sites. I just don't understand it!"

Gordon was silent. I knew he was thinking as much at that moment about our baby as he was thinking about WMDs.

"The main mission," I concluded, "is to gather intelligence about planned attacks against our troops. Don't get me wrong, I feel honored to be part of this mission, but, at the same time, I feel a bit deceived."

Gordon put his hand under the table and on my belly and asked me if the baby had been doing her typical aerobic exercise movements that day.

"Of course," I replied. "Do you expect anything different from our offspring?"

Gordon helped me shift my focus to our domestic priorities—our careers and our baby to be. I slowly began to unwind. Later, I was happy to nestle in Gordon's arms. As I drifted off to sleep, I recalled one of the more harrowing missions of my FBI career, a mission that had resulted in similar gnawing feelings of being deceived about what was right and what was wrong when it came to the subject of a different unconventional weapon with a potential for mass destruction.

. . .

The task was not complicated, but it had a potential for being fatal. As a diplomatic courier, I was to transport the white powder on a commercial airline flight from Pakistan to the United States, with a plane change in Europe. The powder, I was told, might be anthrax. It would be "secured" inside a medical box placed in a bright-orange diplomatic pouch. In the post-September 11 environment, where all packages were searched, the diplomatic pouch would provide high assurance that its contents would not be disturbed. I was advised that diplomatic pouches "are immune from searches and seizures," as I also would be. I was told that such pouches are not "x-rayed, searched, or scrutinized in any way, shape or form."

When I said I hoped the rules on pouches were still being honored, I was assured that I would encounter no obstacles. I reminded *my mission supervisor that it took only one uninformed clerk to open the package and expose travelers at the airport to the powder. They, in turn, could expose others, who in turn would expose individuals traveling to dozens of countries scattered around the world. I was told no such thing would happen as long as I was cool, kept my head, and professionally showed my IDs and authorization letters. I knew that people had already died in the States, and I was afraid something, any-thing, might go wrong. I was worried that I would be traveling aboard a commercial jet, with families and students and elderly folks going to visit their overseas relatives. I was again assured I would handle the task just fine. "We trust you," they had said.*

Departing Pakistan was easy; after all, I told myself, I was leaving the country, and any concern regarding the pouch would be the arriving country's problem. The Pakistani government was sen-sitive and eager to help the American government in the war on ter-rorism. An official FBI courier with an official pouch would be fine. Still, in the waiting room, I held the pouch close: I was willing to physically defend any attempts to tamper with the bag. The depar-ture went smoothly, and I sat in my window seat gazing out at the warren of Islamabad's ancient suburbs slowly being obscured by clouds. All I could think about was the closed air of the cabin, the possibility that some jolt of turbulence would contaminate these innocent passengers. I settled in for a grueling flight.

I kept the pouch in sight and held it close to my person. I refused the flight attendant's polite offer to stow the pouch in the luggage compartment and requested cup after cup of coffee. The inevitable bathroom visit drew stares from passengers. I felt awk-ward walking down the plane's narrow aisle, clutching the bright orange bag and wrestling it into the bathroom. I sat there, in that tiny cubicle, and for a moment I prayed hard that nothing would go wrong. I drew more stares as I returned to my seat. I wanted no more of those stares, so I would have to make the rest of the trip without the benefit of caffeine. Every remaining minute of the flight was a struggle. Finally, the plane landed. I was halfway home.

I anxiously deplaned, grateful for the opportunity to walk. Walking would help anyone stay up, I thought. It was adrenalin, though, that kept me up and, more importantly, sharp and ready to face any hiccups in the mission. There would soon be customs agents and, possibly, government officials to address. Airport patrons eyed the bulky orange pouch with curiosity and distrust. Walking from the arrival gate to the departure terminal, I encountered a long line of passengers waiting to be screened and patted down. Mounds of luggage were being tossed on conveyor belts and were moving slowly through x-ray machines.

I could not miss the armed police officers who were walking around at the airport visually examining passengers and looking for any signs of nervousness or apprehension. An airport employee, eager with his search wand, was one cause of the long line of waiting passengers. I was becoming uneasy, envisioning potential problems ahead. When I reached the checkpoint, the young airport employee insisted the pouch be put through the x-ray machine. Immediately, in a business-like manner, I handed the employee letters clearly stating that the pouch was not to be searched in any way, shape, or form. When the documents were just as immediately questioned, I braced myself for a confrontation. The wand-toting employee called in two armed police officers for support. With my heart racing, I could feel sweat coming warm to my hands, and I hoped and prayed, silently, that my discomfort was not visible to others who would no doubt interpret sweat as hard proof that I must be hiding something. It wasn't until one of the senior officers took the time to read the documents that I was allowed to pass through the checkpoint without a search of the pouch. Breath came a bit easier then. I thanked the officials for their cooperation and then found a bathroom, followed by another cup of coffee, before retiring to the lounge to await my flight to America. One more step, I told myself, just one more step and it will be done. You are nearly home. You've done well. And the adrenalin was still there, stronger than ever, the rush from the checkpoint encounter flowing through my body. I looked at the coffee in my hand and gave a sharp laugh before tossing it away in a nearby trash receptacle. I would fly home on my emotion now. One more step, I said again. You will be home before you know it.

When my flight was called, I waited a few minutes before heading to the gate. Getting there early would invite onlookers and being last to board would also raise eyebrows. Arriving in just the right time window, I boarded the United States–bound flight without any problems. The flight was uneventful, but I remained anxious, the package still held close to me. Processing through immigration in the United States went smoothly. It wasn't until all the bars had been crossed and I handed the pouch to another courier that I felt a final sense of accomplishment. It was now up to the big boys to deal with the package and its contents.

The new courier seemed hesitant and appeared anxious to transport the package to its next location, a relatively short distance compared to its journey from Pakistan. Perhaps agitated by the contents of the package and in a rush to deliver the pouch to the next team, the receiving courier got into a spectacular accident and flipped his car. He was unconscious when the police arrived on the scene, and officers very nearly opened the pouch before realizing they were in possession of something they had to be cautious with. They called in the FBI, and the unconscious courier was transported to a local hospital. The pouch then disappeared into the maze of evidence and international accusations swirling about everywhere in those weeks immediately after the AQ attack on our homeland.

. . .

WHEN I CONSIDER THIS MISSION NOW, I understand things about it that I couldn't understand when it was unfolding. I see the whole event as a confounding blend of organizational achievement and personal exploitation. Things have come to light, as they often do. And I am a different person these days.

The powder in the pouch, touted to me as "suspected anthrax," had first been discovered in a letter addressed to the US embassy in

Islamabad. The letter had been opened by a secretary, and a white powder had fallen on her hands and on her desk. She was immediately sent to a local hospital for treatment. (Early and continuous antibiotic treatment is generally antidotal to anthrax poisoning.) I had been following Bureau orders when I acted as the pouch's courier.

Although I had not agreed wholeheartedly with a decision that could conceivably result in exposing innocent airline passengers—not to mention myself—to potential danger, I followed orders. America was less than two months removed from the devastating attacks by AQ, and I was nothing if not an FBI foot soldier. People had already sickened and died in America from anthrax-laced mail sent to newspapers and to Capitol Hill offices. I did not question the necessity for quick action, but transport on a commercial airliner seemed strange to me.

At the time, doubting my superiors' judgment meant not being faithful to the FBI mission. The approval to transfer such a potentially dangerous substance on a commercial airline came from FBI Headquarters, and I could not help but think of the role of politics in such an irresponsible, haphazard decision.

Soon after the first anthrax attacks in the United States, in October 2001, the Bush administration started pumping the media full of suggestions that Saddam Hussein was behind both the domestic and international anthrax attacks. In retrospect, I can see that the administration was making these highly public charges with little or no evidence concerning who was really behind the anthrax campaign. In October 2001, suggestions that Iraq was engaging in bio-terror would convince a large part of the American public that Saddam would eventually have to be dealt with. This sort of trial-by-headline strategy, in which Saddam was guilty not only of poisoning American citizens with anthrax but also with having mailed anthrax-laced letters all over the world, was the kind of public calling out that would lend the administration's broader war on terror a decided credibility. Even the British, in early November, were expressing alarm at how single-minded Bush and his advisers were being in tarring the Iraqi dictator with responsibility for the anthrax attacks. The looming war against the Taliban in Afghanistan was practically a given at the time. Payback was popular—extraordinarily popular. But a campaign against Saddam would be a much harder war to sell. The president was, I came to believe, quite aware that anything he could do or say to cast suspicion on Saddam was smart policy.

Just as I felt deceived in Baghdad, when I looked back at my participation in the suspected anthrax transport, I believe that I had unwittingly played a role in the campaign that convinced the American public of the legitimacy of Operation Iraqi Freedom.

After seeing what I did of the "WMD Mission" in Iraq, I knew that I should have followed my instincts back in 2001 and asked more questions when I was selected as a courier. And I came to believe, while rummaging around Iraq, pregnant and putting my life on the line and not finding any signs of WMD, that politics and some politicians did not hesitate to endanger both civilians and government employees to further their causes. Between the anthrax incident in Islamabad in later October 2001 and the WMD searches in Baghdad, I came to my own conclusions. And these conclusions disturbed me.

In June 2004, Gordon and I departed from the Middle East and headed to Michigan to deliver our first child. Our townhome in Northern Virginia was rented, and we were waiting for the lease to expire so we could move back in. Also, I wanted to be close to my sisters in Michigan during this special time of my life. Leaving Baghdad was difficult, but there came a point when my pregnancy had the potential to jeopardize missions, and I was not going to take risks that endangered my colleagues. The oversize bulletproof vest I was using was dubbed the "pregnancy vest" and, because it wasn't really designed to fit a pregnant woman, it wasn't providing even marginally adequate protection to me or the baby. If I caught even a small piece of fragmentation, I would be forcing everyone to deal with an emergency that a normal officer would easily avoid with proper protective equipment.

I sometimes thought about how women "nest" and prepare for the arrival of their children. I was in my last trimester of pregnancy and had not bought a single item for the baby. Shopping was not something many of us did in Baghdad. I felt guilty and was anxious to begin getting ready for our new arrival. Gordon knew how I felt and continually assured me that everything would be all right. Finally, I was able to let go of my Iraq mission—I was given a leave long enough to deliver and spend a month with my newborn. As our plane landed in the United States, Gordon and I felt the stresses of Iraq momentarily melt into the background. I would be able to enjoy the peace I fought for, and so missed, when I was serving my country on the front lines.

Or so I thought.

FAMILY AFFAIRS 11

After their arrival in Detroit in 1992, my parents declared that they wanted to remain in the United States. They found that as dual citizens, they could enjoy free first-class medical care (Medicare) while easily traveling to and from Lebanon. In the meantime, Father happily paid Fadi's expensive tuition at a local college and reasoned that Fadi also needed to become a US citizen, since he faced a dim future in Lebanon given his academic performance. Father consulted an immigration attorney and learned that, based upon my US citizenship, both Mother and he could apply.

However, Fadi, a sibling over the age of eighteen, could not. Instead, the attorney suggested that Fadi apply for political asylum by pleading the history of the conflict in Lebanon. The asylum process required a one-year waiting period before one could travel outside of the United States. Unwilling to restrict his travel back to Lebanon to see his friends, Fadi disregarded the attorney's advice. Father, ever loyal to his only son, completed Fadi's asylum paperwork and, in an attempt to bolster Fadi's asylum claim, fabricated a story about Fadi's having been kidnapped and tortured by Syrian forces occupying Lebanon. Upon his return from vacationing in Lebanon, Fadi's status was questioned by immigration officials. Despite spending tens of thousands of dollars in attorneys' fees and his genuine marriage to a US citizen named Mary, Father could not prevent Fadi (who had had numerous run-ins with local law enforcement) from being processed for deportation.

Somehow, during this legal imbroglio, Fadi managed to graduate from college and was working as an executive for Talal at Talal's successful La Shish chain of restaurants. Fadi had stars in his eyes: he wanted to become a franchisee of the La Shish restaurant chain, but, given his immigration problems, among other issues, he could not.

Rula started working immediately upon her arrival in the United States in order to contribute her share of the rent and pay the bulk of her college tuition. She had difficulty making ends meet, and Father grudgingly helped her, but he made it clear that his assistance was temporary. Rula also faced pressure from Fadi. My brother believed that Father's money belonged to him, given his role as Father's heir. Consequently, he hatched a plan to palm Rula off on someone, whereby the union would reduce the expenses that Father was paying. Fadi introduced Rula to a friend and pushed hard for her to engage in a sham marriage. Rula did as she was told, but when she learned she was entitled to apply for political asylum, she annulled her marriage, applied for asylum, and lawfully obtained her US citizenship. Rula had always dreamed of becoming a physician, and when my father refused to help with her tuition, she took out a maze of loans to finally achieve her dream.

In contrast, Lola was making some pretty bad decisions with fateful consequences. When Lola called me in 1999 to let me know that she and Talal were married, I wanted to be happy for her, but I knew deep down that she would ultimately face the same heartbreak she had suffered during the ten years they had been dating. Talal had repeatedly cheated on her during their prolonged engagement (some of these episodes even produced children), and I believed that it was only a matter of time until he reverted to his old ways. Why would he change? Why would you be any different from all the other women he dated and cheated on? Why would your children's fate be any different from the fate of the multiple children he had fathered and emotionally abandoned in the past? I would have liked to ask Lola these questions, but I knew that all she wanted to hear was my congratulations and my wishes for her happiness. I heartily congratulated her and silently hoped for the best.

I am, contrary to what you might think, the silent type, at least when it comes to my family. Sure, I was a bit of a prankster around my father when we lived in Lebanon. But really, those were angry pranks. I wanted attention and I liked showing him up. I disliked almost everything about my father, but he was my father. Lola's situation was more difficult. Talal wasn't blood family, so there was no reason to give him the benefit of the doubt, to idealize him, or to make excuses for him. He was trashy, I'd always thought. He still is. But I kept silent, hoping against hope that Lola's marriage might bring her some measure of happiness.

I prayed that Talal would show his true colors before they had children. But soon enough, in late 2001, Lola had her first daughter, and I knew then that she was committed to the relationship forever.

Despite my desire to share in Lola's happiness, her call relaying the news of her marriage upset me for weeks, and I discussed the situation with a trusted FBI colleague at work. My colleague reassured me that things could well turn out differently than I feared. This colleague also reminded me that I was required to update my security file by "tracing" (doing a name search) any new family member—Talal, my relatively new brother-in-law—and to report any derogatory information to the security office. When I did the trace, I did not find any negative information, and as such did not report anything; however, I did see Talal's name documented as part of my pre-employment background investigation.

EYE OF THE STORM

On June 24, 2004, after returning from the Middle East, I gave birth to a healthy, beautiful baby girl, Evangelina (Eva). We stayed at a home, owned by Lola, where my parents lived when they were in the United States. Lola paid the mortgage and the bills associated with the house because, as Father put it, "that was a daughter's obligation to her parents." Lola, like me and like Rula, was always looking for acceptance and love from my parents. She was, perhaps, the most gullible and easily manipulated of my parents' three daughters. But when Father suggested that it was Lola's obligation to share her salary with Fadi, she finally stood up for herself and demurred.

With my new priority, I discovered rather quickly that I was deeply conflicted about my future. I loved my daughter and was thrilled to be a mother, but having grown up in an abusive family meant I had to face the challenge of overcoming my upbringing and ensure that I would never follow in my parents' footsteps. Because of the absence of a loving mother in my life, I questioned my basic nurturing abilities and felt heavily the stresses of motherhood. It was easy for my imagination to run wild. I wished for a sign that would confirm I was cut out for the job, but none came. Instead, I searched my past for any clues that would point to my capabilities for successful mothering.

For me, motherhood was transformative *and* abstract. My previous knowledge of mothering had come from what I saw on television, where mothers are portrayed as ecstatically happy creatures nursing well-behaved babies in gilded rocking chairs. You don't hear about the sleepless nights, the lactation problems, the mountains of diapers, or the colic. So when I entered this new stage of my life and discovered that my daughter cried and had a hard time nursing, I thought I was failing miserably and that my developing maternal instincts must be to blame. But with my sisters by my side encouraging me, helping me, and listening to my concerns, I started to gain confidence and realized that time and experience would give me the skills I needed to be a good mother. Under the best circumstances, the person who plays the biggest role in defining a woman's quality as a mother is her own mother. But I knew I could not be like my mother, who had been, in my long memory, abusive, distant, critical, and withholding. I wanted to be different. I wanted to instill values in my child that I had not been exposed to in my childhood. I didn't want to compromise Eva's future by falling into the role my mother had played with me.

So I read books. I read and read and read. And though I could not follow my mother's example, I did enjoy the support of my grandmother. Teta Nabiha, as I called her, lived about five minutes away from Lola, so in those months after Eva's birth, she often visited and checked up on me. Teta had moved to the States in the mid-1980s to be with her son, Uncle Ned, after her husband died. On one of Teta Nabiha's and Uncle Ned's visits, I was surprised to hear my uncle raise a sensitive subject with Father. Uncle Ned, who had been a witness over the years to the unfair treatment my sisters and I endured from my parents, remarked to my father how ironic it was that his daughters, whom Father had neglected, had all "made something" out of their lives. He pointed out that Rula was to be a doctor, that I was forever secure as a government employee, and that Lola was married to a successful businessman. I was shocked at Uncle Ned's audacity in confronting Father. When Teta Nabiha and Uncle Ned left that day, Teta said to me, "God has a way of balancing life; you will achieve fairness in the end." That felt good—I remember hoping that she would be proved correct.

Father, shocked by Uncle Ned's frank words, let Ned know he did not like to be challenged, especially when the subject matter was his heir. I remember Father becoming quite angry after my grandmother and my uncle left. His son could do no wrong, he told us, and no one was to ever highlight any negatives about his "successor." Uncle Ned's observation was, I am sure, made with the best intentions. Perhaps he thought that, away from the stresses of war and with his daughters' financial independence assured, Father would change his ways and treat his children with equal respect. But nothing could have been further from the truth. Uncle's well-intentioned defense of his nieces would turn out to be a pivotal event in the destruction of my career. I would later learn from Lola that when Father shared my uncle's frank words with his heir, Fadi vowed to "destroy" the very successes my uncle mentioned.

Fadi had compromised his immigration position by running afoul of local law enforcement on an illegal firearms transaction charge. Unwilling to return to Lebanon but now unable to pursue citizenship through the asylum process, Fadi went looking for allies other than Father and found them in Justice Department prosecutors in Detroit. Fadi had always wanted everything handed to him; he was a lazy boy-man who believed he deserved more than the rest of us. Federal prosecutors in Detroit, it turned out, were happy to use him for their ends, ends that meshed with his desires to be granted the benefits of citizenship and to take a share of Talal's lucrative restaurant business.

Talal had been careless with the piles of cash he was raking in, and federal agents wanted to link that money to a tax evasion charge . . . and more. The "more," as it turned out, was Hizballah. It seemed to me that it didn't matter whether it was true; the mere suggestion of a link would be enough to give the prosecutors a headline case and a giant boost to their careers. So, they thought, who better than Fadi, Talal's now-compromised business manager, to advance their case. They pressured him and he caved. Fadi now saw how he might benefit from Talal's downfall—and if that meant dragging me into this mess of a prosecution, even better.

By playing criminal informant for Detroit-based elements of the FBI and the US Attorney's office, Fadi was able to get close to fulfilling his promise to ruin his sisters. It was my brother's good fortune to find a prosecutor who appeared to share much of his jaded and self-aggrandizing view of the world. I believe that the prosecutors and the investigators were obsessed with terrorism conviction statistics and the awards and promotions that such convictions would bring with them. My brother likely saw a chance for a substantial financial reward that might break his cycle of dependency on my parents. Prosecutors told him that he would be eligible for whistleblower reward money related to the tax case. And he no doubt had his sights set on taking over Talal's cash cow—the chain of successful restaurants whose steady cash flow had started this whole affair. My brother convinced himself that allying with the government against Talal would, as my mother relayed to me, be "beneficial to all." His plan, he must have thought, would be simple to carry out in a post-9/11 environment.

With no regard to either the joys or the stresses of my new family situation, Mother, in the midst of all this, announced to me that Lola and Talal were having marital problems. Her concern, in my estimation, was the impact of their problems on Fadi. Knowing that Talal represented little more than dollar signs to Fadi, Mother expressed to me that she wanted Lola to put up with Talal's "mistakes"—that is, his infidelities. Mother knew full well that in addition to cheating, Talal consistently abused my sister emotionally. He was simply a bully when it came to women. He always had been. Lola had suffered through over a decade of dating and breaking up, and I believed that she, like many abuse victims, felt so conflicted in her relations with Talal that she continually gave in to her abuser. Her lack of self-worth, her insecurity, and her fear of men (given our upbringing) made her a perfectly pliable accomplice to Talal's schemes. He took advantage of her and sought to control her thoughts, actions, and every other aspect of her life. But Mother seemed unconcerned about what was best for Lola. As a successful businessman, Talal had connections in the community and had promised to help Fadi with his immigration problem. So, in my opinion, Mother was looking for Lola to put up with Talal's behavior no matter what.

Mother had revealed to me Fadi's plans to "take over" Talal's business. Fadi had implied to her that he had the backing of "powerful" people. Fadi had first sought a part of Talal's business empire through gaining franchise rights. But given his immigration problems and Talal's uncertainty about franchising, Fadi was left out in the cold. Mother told me that some unspecified "luck" had provided Fadi with new and improved plans. When I asked Mother what she meant by Fadi's new plan and by powerful people, she said that she had already said too much. "Fadi will tell you himself," she said. I felt a bit lost at the time, tired from another sleepless night and not wanting to get into it any deeper. I just nodded and said nothing, but the message was clear: the war between Talal and Fadi was heating up.

Lola, who was intensely focused on supporting me and reassuring me that I would make a wonderful mom, would not discuss her marital problems or Talal's business with me at this juncture. I tried on several occasions to bring it up, but she was not receptive. I had not been shocked by Talal's adulterous behavior after the birth of their child; I was, of course, dismayed that Lola refused to confront his infidelities, but I understood something about the way women silence themselves. Her refusals to acknowledge facts or have strong feelings about Talal's behavior were her survival mechanisms. So, although I found it increasingly difficult to hide my fears for her, I recognized that my relationship with Lola had to focus on our children. The subject of the men in the family was taboo.

So it happened that unwillingly, as a new mother, I found myself embroiled in our family soap opera once again. I could never have dreamed that all this drama would lead to my indictment on federal felony charges and to public screeds that I was a Hizballah mole. It was really a family affair. Fadi owed his livelihood to Talal's generosity, but they had some major disagreements. Fadi was jealous of Talal's business success and remained deeply distrustful of Muslims. Like Father, Fadi viewed Muslims as enemies of the Druze. I believed that a nasty business struggle, with Lola in the middle, was brewing. It could get really ugly really quickly. Fadi despised working for a Muslim, and he openly complained about the innocuous actions of his fellow employees who were Muslim. But it never occurred to me that their war would spill over onto me.

COMPROMISED

As if the stresses of motherhood and Lola's marital issues were not enough, weeks after Eva's birth on June 19, 2004, Fadi finally confided to me that, after his illegal weapon possession arrest (he said the crime carried mandatory penalties of deportation and permanent exclusion from the United States), he had been coerced into becoming a criminal informant working for the FBI.

Fadi explained to me that the FBI had specifically tasked him to report on Talal and that he had been doing so since 2002. According to Fadi, Talal was underreporting the income from his restaurant to avoid paying taxes. I would later learn that Talal, who wanted to grow his successful restaurant into a chain, had devised an illegal scheme—in which Fadi played a critical role—to achieve his goal. The monies

Talal did not report in the United States were sent to Lebanon, where they were deposited and then transferred back to the United States, giving it the appearance of income from a legitimate overseas source. These tainted funds would be used to open new restaurants. As Fadi described it to me, he was the electronic brain behind the operation; he had designed a complex computer program that converted the restaurants' earnings into false numbers to be reported to the government. Lola was aware of the scheme, but she mainly carried on the day-to-day part of operating the business. My brother had rarely displayed integrity or honesty in his dealings with me or anyone else, so I was not sure what to believe of his story at the time. Nonetheless, I decided it was time to put on my investigator hat. I questioned him about who else he had revealed his informant status to, pressing until he finally admitted that in addition to my parents, he had also told his wife. Given the ease of his admission, I had a feeling that he had disclosed this relationship to a number of other people, but I figured the FBI agents now handling him would surely learn of these possible compromises as they tested his "validity" as an informant.

I could see the emotional weight of Fadi's baggage. He was my brother, after all, and I well knew the warped sense of loyalty and trust he had inherited from our parents. I also knew, of course, that most informants come with baggage, but US government investigators are required to test informants to prevent innocent people from getting harassed and even convicted. But in this case, my brother was fortunate to be Lebanese. Because the FBI had so many problems handling informants with ties to foreign cultures, the agents basically dropped the ball on verifying Fadi's information. And the case agents appeared woefully lax in their efforts to comprehend what was going on between Fadi and Talal. To protect the status of any possible ongoing investigation, I cautioned Fadi to refrain from revealing to others what he had told me. The authorities, I reasoned, were aware (or would soon become aware) of any legal problems should Talal's "income issues," as Fadi had described them to me, turn out to be true.

Fadi added that his cooperation with the government had benefits beyond his being able to stay in the United States. His criminal record would be wiped clean, and he stood to gain a large sum of money as a "whistleblower" on the evaded taxes, despite the fact that he was a central participant in the tax crimes and had benefited alongside Talal as the business grew.

Later I learned from Lola that in 2003 Talal had received an offer from someone interested in purchasing his restaurant chain and that, in the process of negotiating an appropriate price, Talal had decided to "go clean" on his tax payments. If he reported his true earnings, he would get a much better price for his business. But Lola confided to me that when Fadi learned of Talal's directions to institute proper and accurate tax reporting, he told Talal he was making a mistake and insisted that they continue to underreport their income for at least another year. Talal agreed to postpone his plans to come clean, and my brother had cleared yet another hurdle in his plan to see Talal indicted and himself in the clear. I did not know at this time whether Fadi was told to insist on maintaining the status quo by his FBI handlers or whether he simply saw his whistleblower monies disappearing right before his eyes and was operating without their cognizance.

A lot was unclear to me about how the FBI was handling the investigation. To this day, I suspect that Fadi and his FBI handlers conspired to bring down Talal. A failure at just about everything he had ever tried, I believe Fadi turned out to be remarkably successful at hiding large portions of Talal's income. My guess is that he lobbied the FBI to ignore Talal's "go clean" plan, but I never really did find this out. Perhaps—and I don't like thinking this at all—he told the FBI to hold off because, who knew, there might be even bigger fish to fry by the time the investigation had ended.

Mother, never one to keep a secret and tired of playing second fiddle to Father's alpha personality, would later make Fadi's plan known to nearly everyone in our family. Talk about a warped sense of reality! She bragged that Fadi had hit the jackpot; our entire family would get rich as a result of Fadi's genius "plan." In addition to the whistleblower money, Mother believed Fadi would take over a successful business after putting her troublesome Muslim son-in-law behind bars.

And when the FBI got its conviction, Fadi's immigration problem would go away. He stood to gain a large sum of money, but he wanted more. With Talal behind bars for tax evasion, Fadi, the good Druze son, would purchase the now-immolated La Shish for pennies on the dollar. Fadi needed Lola to achieve this part of his plan. Attempting to capitalize on Lola's marital problems, Fadi had repeatedly prodded Lola to seek a divorce attorney and to begin proceedings against Talal. Fadi's plan was incredibly self-serving: Lola would win a lion's share of the business as part of a divorce settlement, and Fadi would then leverage control of the business from his sister.

Standing with Fadi in Lola's garage after he told me he had become a snitch and asked me to help influence Lola in accordance with his plan, I told him flat out that I didn't want to be involved. I thought to myself that I was an undercover CIA operations officer and did not want a messy family legal fight affecting my career. For a moment, I put myself in the shoes of Fadi's FBI handlers. The last thing they needed was more people aware of Fadi's status as a criminal informant, people who could tip off Talal to the investigation. I didn't like Talal, but I had no knowledge of any illegal activity on his part aside from my brother's admittedly self-motivated allegations. I was in Detroit as a visitor, a visitor who had just given birth to her first child at that, and I was loath to play any game that might jeopardize either my career or my child's future. If Fadi was telling the truth, the proper authorities were already aware of any wrongdoing, and the sooner I distanced myself from this mess, the better. I was dying to discuss this development with Gordon, but he was so focused on being a new father that I didn't have the heart to re-inflict my long-running family crisis on him. I also knew it would be wrong of me to identify a criminal informant (assuming Fadi actually was working in this role), so keeping Gordon out of this situation was the best thing I could do for both of us.

I would not hear from Fadi on this issue again until nine months later, in April 2005, when he called me to feign shock that federal agents had raided Talal's businesses and homes. I instantly saw the call for what it was: Fadi hadn't informed his FBI handlers that he had revealed his role to me, and he was trying not to get caught in his web of lies. I told him that the information he had provided to the FBI had led to the raid and that he should not be surprised. Then he started to tell me things that didn't make sense. At the moment, I attributed his bizarre questions to the stress of the game he was playing with the FBI. I would later learn that the call was being monitored and that Fadi was trying to validate fabricated stories he had been feeding his handlers.

I tried contacting my sister for weeks after the raid, but she would not take my calls. When she finally called me back, she told me what I believe her attorney had coached her to say—that she and Talal were trying to clear some irregularities in their income reporting. I understood and respected her privacy. I later learned that Fadi had told her I was involved in reporting to the FBI on Talal and that I had prior knowledge of the raid.

Lola eventually learned that Fadi was the one responsible for the raid. She had assumed something was up, but she wasn't sure exactly what. During the raid on the restaurant's headquarters, the lead IRS investigator's cell phone had rung and was answered by an IRS colleague in the room at the time. The colleague announced loudly, in front of scores of employees, that someone named Fadi urgently needed to talk to the lead IRS investigator. The dozens of witnesses to this exchange instantly began buzzing, and soon everyone learned of Fadi's role. Indeed, secrets are hard to keep.

Lola and Fadi's problems, on top of the negative environment created by my parents, turned what should have been a joyous and special time—welcoming my daughter into the world—into a complex skein of backbiting and recrimination. Gordon had remained on the sidelines throughout, and I was completely overwhelmed by all the problems in Detroit. I wanted more than anything to simply enjoy our baby daughter.

BACK TO WORK

In early July 2004, Gordon and I returned to Northern Virginia and to work. I was ready to start a new chapter in our lives and try to stay clear of the family meltdown.

I was assigned a desk job at CIA Headquarters and knew immediately that I wanted to get back to the field, although I had doubts about family life in such environments. In talking to other officers at the CIA, I learned that being a mother did not foreclose a successful career as a covert operations officer overseas. I reviewed the available assignments and discussed them with Gordon. When we found a location in which we could both serve simultaneously, I applied and was accepted for a future posting in a country in the Arab-dominated Persian Gulf region. This country had a large Iranian expatriate population and an extremely tense relationship with Iran. I volunteered to study Farsi on a part-time basis, recognizing fluency in that language as a key to collecting the most important intelligence possible, especially as US relations with Iran continued their downward slide, primarily over nuclear issues and Iranian activities in Iraq. A long-range planner by nature, I started the packing process, made the necessary hotel reservations, secured airline tickets, and readied myself for departure. The summer of 2006, when Gordon and I would begin our respective assignments, was still many months away, but I was already excited about the prospects of me, Gordon, and Eva living overseas.

One of my duties while working at CIA Headquarters included handling a US-based agent who regularly deployed overseas. The intelligence I gained from this agent turned out to be of the utmost importance, and I was receiving feedback on my intelligence gathering directly from the White House. I scheduled a meeting with this very productive asset and booked reservations on a train heading to a northeastern US city to meet him. Having met the contact and gathered my information, I took the train back to Washington.

To pass the time on the train ride home, I reflected on how CIA informant–based meetings compared with my meetings with informants when I was with the FBI. While I can't reveal all the differences in detail, it is safe to say that the FBI practice of calling on a government phone and driving a government-issued car to a public place selected for the FBI special agent's convenience would not pass muster by CIA standards. The FBI simply does not place the same degree of importance on clandestine communications as does the CIA. I realized I had grown to respect the Agency's level of care in handling intelligence.

In addition to taking pride in knowing that I was running secure and productive cases—cases, like this one, which enhanced national security interests—I had also finally found an acceptable balance between my responsibilities as a mother and my role as a government employee. The more I pushed the frontiers of what my job could produce in terms of satisfaction and intellectual challenges, the more energized I became about the future of my life with my family. A strange but wonderful symbiosis had set in, blending dutiful work and familial love in perfect proportions, and I foresaw a future of lessening threat from violence and rising faith in humanity.

By the time the train pulled into Union Station, I also had mulled over the Detroit investigation a few times. All I could fathom was that the Bureau's work was indeed shoddy and far too public. Was there something I was missing? The Bureau has its faults, I thought, but all things considered, Detroit was a simple tax case. How messed up could that get? In the weeks and months ahead, the answer would prove to be anything but straightforward.

BULLIES RETURN

In September 2005, I got a call at my desk at Langley from FBI agents who said they wanted to talk about Talal's business. I arranged to meet with them and hung up the phone feeling troubled. The first thing I remembered was a phone call I had received from FBI Headquarters months earlier, in which they told me that during the discovery phase of an investigation into the would-be twentieth hijacker of the September 11, 2001, attacks, agents had uncovered information that suggested my identity had been compromised to Al Qaeda. That had kept me up many nights, worrying what Al Qaeda might now know of my identity and my efforts to uncover the workings of their network. Surprisingly, after that, I was never informed of how the compromise had come about, nor was I briefed on what specific impact being compromised might have on me. No one filled me in on what steps the Bureau was taking to ensure my safety. Instead, I was repeatedly dispatched to trouble spots around the globe to work on Al Qaeda-related matters. Having since learned more about the dangers associated with an identity compromise, I was hesitant, for personal security reasons, to talk to the agents about Talal. I also recalled Fadi's penchant for lying. What, I wondered, had he told the agents to cause them to seek out someone who their investigation must have demonstrated had no knowledge of or association with Talal's business activities? After several more minutes of anxious thinking, I headed down to the main cafeteria to meet the Detroit-based agents.

In the cafeteria, I introduced myself to the two agents seated at the table in front of me. I sat down and quickly realized when I made a joke to break the ice that the two agents looked tense, like they had a definite agenda.

I immediately asked them how they knew that I worked for the CIA. I wanted to make it clear that I was undercover and was concerned with how they planned to document the interview. If the tax-evasion case in Detroit went to trial, I did not want a defense attorney making public my job with the CIA. (Government prosecutors are obligated, in the discovery phase of the trial, to hand over to defense lawyers all information relating to a case.) The agents declined to clarify either their method or the classification level ("Secret," "Top Secret," "Confidential," etc.) at which they would be documenting the interview, so I had to craft my answers at an appropriate level of sensitivity—that is, general and at the unclassified level.

The questioning agent started off the interview by telling me that Talal, Lola, and Fadi were each going to jail for a very long time, and that what I said to him in the interview would determine the length of their jail sentences. I knew right away that his statements were inaccurate, misleading, and deceitful. As a former law-enforcement officer, I was struck by his lack of professionalism. It was obvious that he had no appreciation for the seriousness of a federal investigation. I decided to put my cards on the table.

Both agents appeared shocked when I asked why their informant would be going to jail. They refused to address my question. Apparently, I thought, their informant-handling skills were as poor as their interviewing skills. When informants are not controlled properly, investigations are compromised. Again I wondered whether they had validated the truthfulness of their informant's information. Were they aware of their informant's real motivations? (I later learned that this lead agent had less than two years' experience in the Bureau.)

Given my immediate concerns about the documentation of the interview—as it directly related to my security—and about the agent's misleading and aggressive statements, I immediately requested that a CIA Office of General Council (OGC) attorney join us to clarify these issues. The agents waved off this request and moved on to a new line of questions. They were treating me like the enemy, for sure. Given the sensitive nature of the relationship between the FBI and the CIA, FBI agents were feeling extremely thin-skinned about their investigatory skills. The Bureau did not want anyone—especially the CIA—checking their homework, and I was most definitely checking their homework.

After their initial strategy of bullying got them nowhere, the agents' next line of questioning demonstrated that they had no understanding of or familiarity with my current duties at the CIA or with my former duties at the FBI. Notably, they grossly mischaracterized my work at the FBI as Syrian-focused. When they asked me questions about my CIA work, which is classified, I told them I would not disclose information about my work without prior approval from my supervisors, and I reminded them, for the second time, that they needed to choose a setting appropriate for a classified discussion. The details of my work duties, I added, were available to them from my employer. When I asked if they had approached my supervisor, they ignored the question.

The interview then became disjointed and unfocused. Owing to assumptions the agents had made about my knowledge of the issues in the Middle East specific to their investigation, they followed with a series of questions I told them I was unable to help them with.

Then things got weird. They pulled out several photos of an elderly man with a long beard dressed in Arab garb. *No, it's not Osama,* I thought, *but what the hell are they doing?* When I told them I didn't recognize the man in the photos, they informed me that the picture was of a religious figure with Hizballah ties. They were surprised that I didn't recognize him and suggested that, since I worked for the CIA's Near East Division, I should have.

At this moment I began to understand what was going on—and it was nothing short of the beginnings of a vile smear against me. More than a year earlier, when my brother had confided to me his role as a snitch, I had been surprised to hear that the FBI was investigating a tax-evasion matter; but I had reasoned then, should the tax evasion accusations have foundation, that they were just aiding IRS agents since the suspect in the case had overseas connections. Now, the agents showed me another photo, this one of the elderly Hizballah religious leader in the presence of Talal. I realized they were clearly insinuating that Talal was involved in terrorism.

As a former FBI special agent with a record of successful terrorism prosecutions, I can tell you that if terrorism financing is occurring, and if you have a source inside the organization you are investigating (e.g., my brother), and if the movement of large sums of monies through banks and business institutions over a period of time has been monitored and verified, you will have more than enough evidence for a terrorism financing prosecution. And as an intelligence officer raised with an understanding of Lebanon's twisted political situation, my interviewers' suggestion of terrorism financing going on through La Shish did not make sense to me. Of course—and I was thinking pretty rapidly on my feet now—my brother may have suggested things that simply were not true in order to enhance his position. If he had lied to them, well, that sort of game was a huge house of cards. Any lies he told suggesting terror links between Hizballah and La Shish would be uncovered and damn him twofold. So, I wagered to myself, these guys are shooting in the dark. Besides, I reasoned, Talal had immigrated to the United States close to a decade prior to the formation of Hizballah. Given his hedonistic lifestyle, I had seen no evidence of him being politically radicalized here in the United States. He was definitely more interested in chasing young women around his posh restaurants than he was in funding Hizballah.

Still, the two agents had their rather pathetic pictures. I would later learn that these pictures of the Shi'a cleric had been taken at a highly publicized and videotaped event. In fact, Talal had one similar picture framed and displayed at his business. Apparently, Talal, who had donated to a charity that benefited Shi'a orphans in southern Lebanon, was being recognized as a keynote speaker at the event. The cleric was indeed associated with Hizballah, the Lebanese political party that currently exercises de facto control over Lebanon's government and enjoys both massive local funding and state sponsorship from the oil-rich coffers of Iran. Historically, Hizballah's military wing had conducted numerous terrorist attacks and, as a result, in 1999 was placed on the US State Department list of Foreign Terrorist Organizations. After Hizballah's condemnation of the September 11, 2001, attacks, it was removed from the terrorism list but later returned. As Hizballah developed a social services arm, the military and religious elements of the organization began to define themselves differently. The presence of the old cleric at the charity event was not all that unusual—or even threatening. As an intelligence professional, my feeling was that, given their influence, it would be stranger *not* to have a Hizballah representative present at such a ceremony.

Lebanese people are generous, and they are world travelers. As a child, I attended many celebrations in honor of Lebanese who had immigrated overseas and donated to charities in Lebanon. Elaborate festivities and traditional dances, designed to make the donors feel like royalty, were common. I could only imagine what off-base conclusions these Detroit investigators, probably lacking any cultural understanding of such events, would draw. Did they jump to the conclusion that Talal was playing a meaningful financial role in supporting an organization that operated a standing army that had successfully expelled Israeli forces from southern Lebanon? It seemed to me they had done just that. Did they know about the work being done by many ordinary Lebanese to ease the burden of the orphans of that war? Of that, I was fairly certain, they had no clue.

I knew at that point that the agents were trying to tie Talal to terrorism, and, given their brusque treatment of me, I began to worry about the unaccountable behavior I had witnessed while at the FBI. In fact, government records would later show that even after a second raid of Talal's residence in September 2005, no actual evidence of terrorism was obtained, nor was incriminating evidence of terrorism ties ever found in the nearly four years of tapped phones, intercepted faxes, and closely monitored bank activities. I was shocked to learn that after the initial raid on his businesses and homes, Talal was permitted by investigators in Detroit to repeatedly travel out of the United States with the full knowledge of the FBI and the case prosecutors—knowledge provided, no doubt, by Fadi, their informant. In fact, a few weeks after the April 2005 raid, Talal emptied out his home and shipped its contents to Lebanon, leaving behind nothing but a few pieces of old furniture. He also shipped vehicles to Lebanon. If that was not a sign that he was planning to depart from the United States with the intention of building a new life in Lebanon, I don't know what would be. Indeed, he finally skipped town in September 2005 for Lebanon, a country that, fortunately for him, had no extradition treaty with the United States.

If one accepts the story line of the Detroit investigators, Talal had sent millions of dollars to Lebanon. Permitting him to travel to Lebanon, where he could enjoy this stored fortune, represents an egregious disregard for the kind of proper investigation owed to the citizens of the United States. In fact, the only logical explanation for his unimpeded departure is the prosecutors' desire to get rid of him so he would be unable to challenge their unfounded terrorism accusations in the form of media innuendos. Moreover, it turns out that Fadi, the prosecutors' lone informant, had cautioned Talal, via Lola, that he, Talal, would be indicted in the near future. I believe the Detroit gang wanted Talal out of the picture so they could carry out their plan without challenge. After all, Talal had the money necessary to defend himself against bogus accusations.

I was becoming more impatient with the interview by the second. My growing fear, as I sat in the now nearly empty cafeteria, was that incompetence, ignorance, and—dare I say it?—racism were sustaining this investigation. Some of those fears would be confirmed at Lola's detention hearing in May 2006. Lola had been arrested pursuant to the tax-evasion indictment. During her detention hearing, the Detroit US Attorney's office trotted out their hodgepodge of a "terrorism" story in what they must have considered a safe venue. The upshot of the testimony of the prosecution's FBI Middle East "expert"—a person with neither academic qualifications nor experience in the region—was not pretty. Lola's defense attorney quickly took apart the testimony. The hearing was ultimately so humiliating for the prosecution that the Detroit attorneys would never again raise a terrorism allegation in any forum where they could be challenged or required to produce a shred of supporting evidence.

As the two agents conferred over where to go next with their questions, I summed up my take on the situation. The agents' lack of understanding of the incredibly broad scope of duties and responsibilities in my division was evident from their judgment that I should have recognized the individual in the photo. Then they became hostile to me rather than working to determine how, or if, I could assist in their investigation. Finally, they asked a series of brief, out-of-context questions to which I had difficulty formulating complete and constructive responses. For example, they asked, "How do you feel about Talal Chahine?" and "Do you know what religion your sister is?" The tone of the latter question clearly indicated that they viewed her conversion to Islam as a form of wrongdoing. All things considered, I was ready to end the interview then and there.

Then they asked me whether I had ever taken classified materials out of CIA Headquarters. My response to that was to immediately terminate the interview. The question had not been couched in the context of their investigation: the agents had completely failed to demonstrate any awareness of the rules and regulations governing the transport and control of classified materials by CIA case officers. In the clear absence of intelligent preparation on their behalf, I recognized the pointlessness of continuing to simplify my answers to suit their level of understanding. My only recourse was to close out the meeting. Given that simplified answers could later be misrepresented as something other than an attempt to be cooperative, it seemed the only safe choice. I stood up, told them we were through, and wished them well. As I turned and walked away, my gut told me something was rotten at the heart of this investigation.

As I walked back to my desk, I could not help but recall a story I had once heard about FBI interviews. On one of my few visits to Detroit after becoming an FBI agent, my brother brought over some friends who were allegedly interested in asking me questions about the FBI, but who mainly hoped to catch a glimpse of my service weapon. One of these guys immediately asked me how I, as an Arab, could work for the US government—after all, he offered, the government hates Arabs. A second guy then chimed in and told me that he had a friend who had once genuinely wanted to assist the FBI when they came to interview him. He had been bullied and threatened by the FBI agents, and he had subsequently vowed to never talk to the FBI again and had shared his humiliating experience with the rest of the Arab community. I interrupted immediately and told the young men gathered there that the government does not hate Arabs and that FBI agents were trained heavily in interviewing skills. I told them that I found it hard to believe that FBI agents threatened or bullied anyone, but I admitted there are always a few bad apples in any organization. After much debate, I asked them to give the FBI another chance and not to judge the entire FBI on one misunderstanding. At the time, I sincerely believed what I was saying. But now, after my scary interview, I had little doubt that the Detroit FBI field office had earned its tarnished reputation in Detroit's Arab community.

I was very disappointed by my interview experience. Here was an organization I had served loyally and defended to anyone who criticized it. CIA officers who knew I was a former special agent with the FBI often shared with me their experiences with the Bureau. Most of these experiences were negative, ranging from stories about the FBI's loose handling of classified information to accounts of agents intimidating foreigners whom they interviewed overseas, to bad judgment calls after excessive alcohol consumption. I always took it upon myself to defend FBI agents' inexcusable behavior. I would explain that law enforcement was a task different from the gathering of intelligence, and that the FBI and CIA ultimately have different missions. I defended the Bureau against foreign intelligence operators who described it as a "bunch of clowns." I was not sure whether my love for the Bureau, my first real American family, prevented me from believing these stories, but I always found an excuse for it.

That night, I shared my interview experience with Gordon. I told him that I was concerned about the ignorance of these FBI agents and that I knew from investigations such as the Brian Kelly or the Steven Hatfill cases, where the FBI wrongfully accused Kelly of espionage and Hatfill of spreading Anthrax in the D.C. area, that things can definitely go wrong, very wrong. I confided my worry that there would likely be no accountability whatsoever for the Bureau agents who were attempting to paint me as a supporter of terrorism.

"Are you kidding me, Nada?" Gordon looked at me with surprise.

"Nope, not at all. That interview is just the tip of some really bad mojo. I can feel it," I said.

Gordon challenged me. He was incredulous that any agency would come after me. To him, I was sterling. I was brave and did things by the book, sometimes to a fault.

"Answer this," he challenged me. "How many FBI agents have conducted successful extraordinary renditions? A handful. How many FBI agents have conducted three renditions? Only you. How many successful terrorism *prosecutions* have you spearheaded? Not those bullshit indictments that are so popular and easy to get, I mean actual go-to-court convictions? Your FBI record of service is unprecedented. Few agents have contributed to the FBI the way you have. And you have done even more for the CIA! How many CIA officers served in a war zone while pregnant? How many were shot at? How many saved lives? These agents may be ignorant, but the CIA and the Justice Department can't possibly ignore your record of service or doubt your future contributions. And, how many native Arabic speakers with proven law-enforcement and intelligence experience and who are now learning Farsi do you think the government has?"

"One?" I cut in.

"These novice agents," Gordon continued, "the ones who conducted this interview, may well be ignorant of your work record, but no amount of stupidity is going to change the facts of your service and leave you vulnerable to an accusation of supporting terrorists."

I was touched by Gordon's pride in me, but I didn't have the heart to tell him my sneaking suspicion that making sense is not always the way the Justice Department works. Nonetheless, I promised him I'd hope for the best; I would focus my efforts on my upcoming assignment. I really wanted to get back to field work—and I looked forward to using my Farsi.

DERAILED

I felt like someone had stabbed me in the back. A senior CIA official had just told me that my Farsi-related assignment had been canceled. I wasn't going anywhere except to . . . Detroit! I was told that I would be a witness in a legal matter relating to my sister.

It did not make sense to me that such an eagerly anticipated assignment had been canceled. I reasoned that I could easily fly back to the United States if I were to be summoned as a witness, which I doubted I would. I was confused in that, as far as I could tell, the regulation cited for keeping me in the United States didn't actually seem to apply to a case where an operative might act as a witness. So I hired an attorney, referred to us by one of Gordon's mentors, who successfully challenged the internal Agency regulation. Quickly, the deputy director of operations decided instead to use his "personal discretion" to cancel my assignment.

I felt let down by my own people and by the Agency I served. Worse, I was mightily puzzled about my future course of action.

In a knee-jerk reaction, upset with the CIA for canceling my assignment, I reapplied to work for the FBI. When I later consulted with Gordon, he agreed with me that it was impulsive, and he pointed out that my reasons for leaving the FBI had not changed. Deciding it was best to wait and see what happened at the CIA, I asked my supervisor to send me to Farsi school full time. When the Agency agreed, I assumed the whole witness issue question and the odd regulation ploy would be temporary. So, there I was, trusting in the Agency and happy in the knowledge that learning Farsi would provide me with key skills for many a future assignment. There wasn't a single Agency case officer who was both a native Arabic speaker and a fluent Farsi speaker. My mastery of this new skill would create a powerful new capability for the US government in its attempts to obtain intelligence directly related to Iranian intentions and practices in the Middle East. As always, I was proud to serve my country.

DECISION MADE 12

"Nada, please do not do it for my sake," Gordon beseeched me. "I don't care about the money or losing my job; you have to stand up to these cowardly racists. We will sell our house, live with friends if we have to; I will work construction jobs. We will make things work. For God's sake, you are going to plead guilty to something you did not *do!*"

I told Gordon, plain and simple, that I had no choice. I intended to plead guilty to charges that were untrue.

I hadn't yet told him the full history of my changing feelings. My decision was made. The Prouty family had suffered more than two years of hell and that, I felt, was enough. Elements of the government I had grown close to and had sacrificed for had betrayed me. Left me, the spy, out in the cold. These prosecutors were driven by ambition. Their shortsightedness and their hubris—a bad combination—went on and on. I walked around feeling their knife driven into my heart.

I was a changed person. Pleading guilty filled me with righteous indignation, which was strangely energizing. I was forced to reevaluate my entire belief system—specifically, the huge amount of trust I had put in my government. "Married to the job" was not a cliché in my case. The CIA and the FBI had trusted me with their most sensitive operations and deepest secrets, and I had repaid that trust by placing my life and, at one time, the life of my unborn child on the line. And just like that, all that trust was gone?

A WALK IN MY SHOES

After my Gulf assignment was canceled, I began to study Farsi on a full-time basis. I was hopeful that common sense would prevail and that I would be heading overseas sooner rather than later. I immersed myself in Farsi and eventually tested at a "Level 4" (out of 5), indicating native fluency in reading, writing, and speaking Farsi. As I dreamed of how I would put my new capabilities to use and how I could better collect intelligence using my new skills, I had no idea my efforts were for naught. The prosecution in Detroit had decided I was guilty. Guilty of what, it appeared, they were not entirely sure. They just needed time—and a little imagination—to try to find something that would pass for evidence long enough to extort a plea out of me.

On February 27, 2007, Detroit AUSA Kenneth Chadwell called me directly on my mobile phone. He said he had called my attorney but hadn't received a return call, and rather than wait for a communication from any representative of the global law firm representing me, decided to call me directly. I insisted that I was still represented by counsel, but Chadwell expressed skepticism and pressed on with questions. After my cafeteria interview experience with the Detroit FBI agents, which I had told Chadwell about, I insisted that I could talk to him only in the presence of my attorney. My attorneys agreed that this call was extremely aggressive and a possible violation of both the Michigan and Virginia Bar Association regulations regarding contact with an individual known to be represented by counsel, but they would not support my desire to submit a formal complaint, claiming that such a complaint would create a "negative" atmosphere with the US Attorney's office in Detroit.

On March 5, 2007, the US Attorney's office, in another aggressive move, contacted me by sending me a letter to my home, revealing that I was the target of an investigation and seeking to arrange a meeting with me. My attorneys again declined to react to this action in any way other than to open a discussion regarding my meeting with the US Attorney's office to resolve their concerns.

Later that month, while sitting at my desk at the CIA Farsi School, I was suddenly pulled out of my class and escorted out of the building. I was told that I was under investigation and was being put on administrative leave. Two armed security personnel escorted me to my vehicle and brought me my purse. I felt like a piece of garbage. I'd been tossed out on the street without any opportunity to answer, or indeed even know, the charges and accusations against me.

On May 24, 2007, I traveled to Detroit to meet with the FBI and the prosecutors. I was eager to face my accusers. During the flight, I tried to fathom the reasons for the prosecutors' inappropriate contact with me, but I drew blanks. Once again, I thought of my brother and the whole Talal mess, wondering if it was all related to my brother's role in the tax-evasion case. What if my brother, who I knew was still serving as the Detroit office's criminal informant, had misled them? Well, if he had, he had, and more the sad story for him. But I believed I was protected by truth and that anything involving me would be proved baseless. With the facts on my side, I would be able to explain any fiction or ambiguity my brother might have raised; I might even educate them regarding the incredibly complicated international investigations that were the backbone of my career.

The flight from Washington was a short one, as was the taxi ride from the airport to the US Attorney's office. When the meeting started, the FBI agent I had previously met at CIA headquarters was there. That worried me. I thought, however, that with several mindful observers in the room, this agent's ignorance would not get him far. The government representatives informed me that they had about fifteen issues to discuss with me, most related to the FBI computer system I used on a daily basis during my years at the FBI.

When the questioning began, the lead agent asked me to explain why I had searched a specific name—which he provided—on the FBI system. I recalled the name and immediately told the agent that I had intended to recruit this person, given his potential access to targets of interest to the FBI. The agent repeated with the same line of questioning, and for each individual search, I explained the respective reasons behind them. From time to time, I looked over at the AUSA. I was growing more apprehensive with the reaction to my questioning, and they seemed to share my apprehension. I was surprised to see them so upset; I had expected to see relief as I addressed each concern. I then realized the FBI agent's questioning of these searches revealed his complete misunderstanding of my casework and my assigned responsibilities. The FBI computer system is notoriously inaccurate, and its shortcomings are the subject of many inspector general reports. (The August 2003 Executive Summary of the FBI Office of the Inspector General report states that "the ACS system is likewise prone to human error with documents concerning highly sensitive operations, being made available to any user because of improper uploading or inadequate restriction codes." This report and the March 2002 Department of Justice Review of FBI Security Programs both hold the FBI responsible for deficiencies in ACS training, inadequate controls and security flaws, susceptibility of the system to error, and universal view of the system as unfriendly and difficult to operate.)

In short, it appeared that the Detroit office's ignorance about the computer system's flaws, as well as their inexperience with the nature of my work, had led them to invest massive resources in a dead end. But strangely, at that point, the agent changed the way he was asking me questions. He stopped giving me specifically helpful details about my document viewing and instead gave me a few thin points of unhelpful data, such as the date of the document or a broad description of the subject as, say, "an investigation into terrorism." It was totally unrealistic to expect me to recall why I had viewed an isolated document out of the tens of thousands I had accessed in my career. When I pressed for more information about some of the documents under consideration, the agent identified one of these documents as related to the terrorist group Hizballah, but he did not elaborate further.

Much to my disappointment, I had to inform the investigators—who had boasted at the start of our meeting that they knew "every detail" of my career—that I had been assigned to and had worked a number of headline-grabbing Hizballah cases. I ticked off a list, including the William Buckley kidnapping and the Khobar Towers bombing, adding that I had, on innumerable occasions, helped out the squad that handled Hizballah matters. Their desks happened to be adjacent to our squad's desks. I finished my short bio—doing their work for them, essentially—by informing my interrogators that I had once traveled to the Detroit area and met with a Detroit asset on a matter relating to an international terrorism/potential Hizballah informant.

There, I thought. *There's your information. What next?*

I was shocked and horrified when the lead agent replied that, after examining all documents relating to me, he was confident I had *not* traveled to Detroit. He was calling me a liar—or worse. At that point, I knew the "investigation" was little more than a witch hunt. I now saw the men in the room as extraordinarily dangerous. Despite possessing great authority, they were not being held responsible for getting even fundamental facts right. I had indeed been in Detroit. I could prove it.

I had viewed tens of thousands of documents on this FBI system. Now, without being shown a specific document or provided with sufficient information to determine how a selected document may have related to my work, I was unable to explain some of these documents to my interviewers' satisfaction. Based on my experience as a special agent, it is standard FBI practice to either show a person a questioned document or give them a surplus of facts and opportunities to explain their relationship to a document. Anything less than that hinders an investigation—there is no reason to hide the contents of a document you are convinced a person has already seen. The investigatory goal should be to establish an unambiguous relationship between a person and a document, not to quiz the user on their powers of recall.

But now I saw a flash of excitement in the eyes of the lead agent—and I realized his goal for our meeting. I had personally witnessed the threat of "You are going down, guilty or not" at the Washington field office during many investigations—the investigation of exonerated anthrax suspect Steven Hatfill being one of the more egregious instances—and I knew exactly what was happening. Because I had extensive security clearances and was still employed by the CIA in a sensitive position, there were no security barriers that would prevent me from seeing a document the computer indicated I had already seen. So the only reason they were not showing me the document in question was because they were deep into the hunt—and I was the quarry. They were hoping, no doubt, that I would give myself away somehow.

Despite my best efforts to be thorough in the matter before us, investigators refused to give me basic clarifying information on the documents in question, such as what query I had entered in the FBI database to bring up the document. I asked if the query was the name of one of my subjects. No answer. I asked what the computer indicated I had been working on that day. No answer. Each quarter, bureau agents were required to report our statistics, and I noted to my examiners that the records would show that I had reported statistics relating to my travel to Detroit or to any of my cases with connections to Detroit. Was the document under review related to a case I helped the Hizballah squad with? How long was the document up on the screen? Was this one of the many documents that I, like numerous other agents, pulled up accidentally, given the FBI ACS system's documented shortcomings? None of my questions were answered, and my voiced doubts about the proper functioning of the ACS information system were summarily brushed aside. It became increasingly clear that the investigators were using the most unreliable tools possible in trying to characterize my computer usage.

At the conclusion of the meeting, I realized with a sinking heart that they had no interest in the truth. The prosecution's agenda had already been set, and the results of this meeting would no doubt be twisted to fit it. All they had to do was ignore the inconvenient facts that I had worked an international terrorism case in Detroit and that I had done extensive work on Hizballah over the course of my FBI career.

The prosecutors also chose to ignore both a two-year background investigation that required the travel of an FBI agent to Lebanon and three successful counterintelligence investigations that focused on my FBI computer usage as part of granting me a sensitive compartmented information (SCI) security clearance while I worked at the Washington field office. Years after I left the Bureau, these investigators, removed from the facts by both distance and time, concluded that I had briefly viewed a single mysterious document without authorization. I would never learn what that document was.

With the paucity of facts in support of their investigation, the prosecutors focused on putting as much pressure as possible on me. In addition to the routine tactic of draining my finances via hundreds of thousands of dollars in attorneys' fees, they started a carefully calculated attack campaign against me and my family. The key to their campaign was avoiding any form of judicial authority or oversight. If they had been forced to bring their facts before a judge at this point, I would have gotten the opportunity to rebut their unfounded accusations before they had put into place the points of leverage necessary to extort a plea.

In July 2007, after receiving written approval for the trip from the CIA, I traveled to London on vacation. Part of my agreement at that time was to provide the CIA with my travel itinerary and contact details. I traveled with Gordon, Eva, and my sister Rula. Upon our return to Dulles International Airport, we were all held in custody for some time and my passport was confiscated. Detroit-based agents that I had never before met flew to Washington and illegally detained us under the guise of a "routine border search," giving us what is affectionately referred to in FBI parlance as the "full harassment package." Over Eva's loud cries, the agents searched our luggage and questioned me about a "current Lebanese passport" they claimed they were trying to locate. There was no such passport. My Lebanese passport had expired in the early 1990s, and I had never renewed it. The investigators apparently imagined that I had been secretly traveling outside the United States using my Lebanese passport. That prosecutorial fantasy was put to rest when they subpoenaed all my passports—a move that backfired when the results of the subpoena proved I had traveled only on my US diplomatic, official, and tourist passports following receipt of my citizenship in 1994.

TRIAL BY PUBLICITY

In the next phase of the prosecution, the Detroit attorneys requested that we meet again in Detroit, this time with Gordon present. Gordon initially declined to participate, but the prosecution pressed for him to attend and noted ominously to our attorneys that Gordon and I were facing "a family decision." This threat suggested that the Detroit attorneys were ready to go after Gordon, another in their series of threats that were meant, in the long run, to force me to capitulate to any terms they set before me.

In Detroit, on July 27, 2007, the prosecution admitted that I had largely addressed the concerns they had raised the first time I'd met with them, but they then proceeded to introduce what they described as "new evidence." Their self-congratulatory mien was sickening. Proudly dredging up my twenty-year-old naturalization violation—the so-called green card marriage that I had previously disclosed in writing on my 1997 FBI application and for which the statute of limitations had long expired—they noted that they were within the law to charge me with a felony for every use of my US passports and even for every cashed paycheck for which the passport had been used for identification. (The law in this instance allows that, although the naturalization charge had passed the statute of limitations, it could be construed that the passports I held had been illegally obtained and were therefore not valid. Use of an invalid passport is a felony.) So, every time I had traveled internationally for the FBI or the CIA was now an instance the prosecution could use to force me to my knees. The hundreds of felonies associated with this ploy would mean many years in prison and hundreds of thousands of dollars in fines. AUSA Chadwell and company admitted that the scheme was ambitious, but they assured both me and my attorneys that Justice intended to litigate every single charge to the maximum extent possible if I did not agree to take their new plea, a plea that would force me to waive the statute of limitations on the naturalization fraud charge. Waiving this right would mean losing my citizenship; I would then be set up for deportation, an end that, it was becoming clear to me, was Chadwell's goal for the case. What better publicity and proof of my guilt than to strip me of my citizenship and send me back to Lebanon? It would be a great sound bite for the media while padding the career vitas of team prosecutors. Chadwell and his colleagues promised to land on me with both feet if I refused this new deal.

Arrogance and ambition can be unlimited in the closeted world of the federal Justice Department. The Detroit AUSA made it clear that in the process of prosecuting me, they would also destroy my husband's career in government—only my signature on their handcrafted plea bargain would save Gordon, an exemplary public official, from this fate. They had originally wanted Gordon present in Detroit so they could threaten him to his face.

Then, in a bizarre coda, AUSA Chadwell promised everyone present that "within six weeks," he would prove that I was "a spy for Hizballah." My attorney, confident that there was no evidence of spying, suggested we wait out the six weeks and then discuss a plea, but Chadwell's supervisor quickly jumped into the conversation and said the government's demands were on the table and there was no reason to wait any longer.

While I weighed threats of extended prison time and a ruined family against the farcical plea agreement deal Chadwell waved at me, in September 2007, the prosecution arrested my sister Rula via a spurious complaint that they would abandon just five days later. With Lola away serving her sentence for tax evasion—she had been given an eighteen-month sentence back in May—Rula was caring for Lola's children. Absent some smart defensive maneuvers by Rula, who had foreseen just this kind of coercion, Lola's children would most likely have entered the public welfare system. Clearly, the prosecution's strategy was to add another layer of fear by bullying my sisters' families. The threat of taking children away from parents and threatening to split up families dovetailed perfectly with the threats against me. If I refused Detroit's plea bargain, my sisters' children faced being lost in a maze of uncaring foster families or, worse, forced deportation.

The prosecution also included an attack on the first roommate I had in America, Samar—a decorated Marine Corps captain who was using her native Arabic language skills to save lives while serving a second tour in the combat zones of Iraq. In September 2007, under the direction of the FBI, the Marine Corps placed Samar under detention in Baghdad and transported her in shackles to Florida. The US Marine Corps Central Command (MARCENT) were informed only that Samar was being held under a classified investigation. Facing shadowy national security claims and bowing to the anxiety present in the post-9/11 environment, the Marines quickly washed their hands of Samar and handed her over to the overzealous prosecutors. For an organization that prides itself on never leaving a Marine behind, Samar's Marine fellows not only left her behind but also pushed her down. In Florida, Samar asked for legal representation and was told "there was no one available." Facing the same threat of hundreds of felony charges, and with a spouse also in government service, Samar pleaded guilty to similar immigration violations weeks later, in early November. The prosecutor who had examined Samar's record of service may have revealed the real basis of Samar's prosecution when he commented that given Samar's accomplishments in Iraq, she might have reached the rank of general one day. In that closed circle of prosecutors, a female Arabic-speaking general would be little more than a freak—surely the Detroit AUSA did not want an Arab in such a sensitive position.

Finally, the most odious threat raised its head. My attorneys informed me that deportation to Lebanon was an avenue the Detroit prosecutors would be exploring if I did not take their plea deal. AUSA Chadwell was very specific in one of our last meetings that the US Attorney's office would be making public the fact that I served in the CIA. That point was not negotiable in any way. Deportation to Lebanon as an acknowledged employee of the CIA, to a country then under the de facto control of Hizballah, was a direct and immediate threat to my life.

Threat and domination take many guises in bureaucracies, but what I saw developing here was especially galling in that the AUSA clearly perceived it as their *right* to impose threats. It was their *right* to bully me. And I had no rights: I could only *obey*. Such was the tenor of my case at this point. Going to trial on hundreds of felony charges, a trial that could last half a decade and cost us millions of dollars, which we didn't have, could also destroy Rula, end Gordon's career, and leave Lola's children vulnerable and unsupported. In addition to putting my daughter Eva's life in danger while serving in Iraq, a guilt I still live with daily, the past two years had been extremely stressful for Eva. I would sometimes find Eva (then under the care of a nanny) under the table trembling and crying when I got home from work. Putting her under similar stress for the indefinite future was not something I could face in good conscience.

I thought about the prosecution's plan to destroy me, someone who had made a youthful mistake but who had openly disclosed that mistake in the course of her FBI application. Someone who, since that mistake, had devoted her life to serving the United States with an unchallenged record of impeccable service—service unmatched by those who sought to harm me. I realized that, ironically, as a national security worker, I was an easy target. Because my work was highly classified, I could not defend myself in public; furthermore, I did not have control of the exonerating information I needed. The purported evidence against me—nonexistent, as it turned out—was labeled "secret," and the convenient cloak of "national security" was used to hide it from those who might have questioned it and used it effectively to expose the smear campaign against me.

My ethnicity was certainly another reason the prosecutors pursued me. As Chadwell put it to me, "In a post-9/11 environment, you could be found guilty by simply being an Arab." *Is this his operational motivation?* I wondered. "Do you want to be away from your daughter for a long time?" he added. At my initial meeting with him in May 2007, he made the bizarre statement that "All Shi'a in Detroit are supporters of Hizballah." These kinds of statements had earned him a reputation his superiors were well aware of, and they clearly accepted and endorsed his openness about his suspicions toward Arabs. It was yet another problem with the bureaucracy that had me pinned against the wall that such statements were taken as the utterances of a *rational* individual. This was enough to convict me in the minds of many: I was guilty of being an Arab in a politically charged environment; it stood to reason that no one was going to stand up for me.

Finally, I had to consider the role my brother might have played in all this. Having a criminal informant who was ready to even family scores by telling agents and prosecutors what they wanted to hear must have given the prosecution a tremendous level of comfort. Relaying his statements, accurate or not, to a grand jury or using them in a judicial proceeding gave them a strong veneer of credibility, provided they were careful never to expose him to cross-examination. Having a snitch ready to tell investigators whatever they wanted to hear was invaluable, and the prosecutors would use it to maximum advantage.

MOMENT OF (UN)TRUTH

I had to make a decision. If I did not take the plea deal the prosecution had crafted, I would be exposing myself to a possible death sentence; certainly, I would be destroying the lives of my family. In hindsight, I believe the prosecution's ultimate plan was to have me "disappear" in Lebanon, a place where the truth could be buried forever. But at that time I had to make my decision about the plea bargain, and I knew I owed it to my family to take the deal. What I owed to myself was to expose the truth. I would need to lose this battle to secure a chance of winning the war.

Winning the war, for me, meant eventually telling my story to the world. The prosecution's blatant lies, omissions of fact, and misrepresentations to the media, as well as the egregious flaws in the indictment instrument itself, gave me hope that I would one day be exonerated. For political reasons that I discovered later, their indictment document had been rushed, and it contained glaring mistakes. For instance, it listed the wrong dates for the document I had allegedly viewed without authorization and for the date of my divorce.

The accurate date of my divorce from Christopher Deladurantaye was April 12, 1995. Their filing incorrectly listed the date as January 17, 1995. During the plea discussions, the prosecution provided my attorneys with the date that I had allegedly viewed the document as June 4, 2003. Looking at my calendar, I discovered that that date was two days prior to a long-scheduled CIA "entry on duty" (EOD) polygraph set for June 6. As any government employee who is subject to routine polygraph examinations can tell you, you are on your very best behavior when you know a polygraph is scheduled. In the prosecution's filing, the alleged viewing date was incorrectly listed as June 24, 2003. Significantly, the standard CIA question of whether I had ever misused the FBI ACS computer system was part of the June 6, 2003, polygraph. I successfully passed the test.

The indictment document also contained half-truths, clearly designed to tell only parts of the story—the parts that appeared to bolster the prosecution's flawed conclusions. The government filed documents stating that I had taken classified information home. Of course, they failed to mention that I had requested and received permission from my supervisor, after discovering the documents misfiled in a utility closet, to take the documents home and organize them. In fact, I was a card-carrying, authorized, FBI courier of classified information. I routinely transported classified information in the Washington Metro area as well as between the United States and the Middle East on numerous occasions during my travels overseas.

Last, and perhaps most egregious, was the prosecution's preposterous claim that I had not worked Hizballah cases—despite the fact I had described my Hizballah cases to them months earlier. My record of case assignments and awards for Hizballah-related work were irrefutable. As time would show, this lie was a critical element in the prosecution's media campaign, a lie so essential that it persists on DOJ websites to this very day.

The basis of the prosecution's "She's a mole!" campaign was that I had passed information regarding Hizballah to Talal Chahine—despite the fact that years of investigation and millions of taxpayer dollars spent had failed to produce a scintilla of actual evidence.

They fabricated this tale of a slithering Lebanese infiltration of the intelligence services, and the press went along for the ride. The One Percent Doctrine had found a voice, and prosecutors continued to beat that drum, refusing to correct future press releases. The scolding they received from the judge in my case and the multiple independent investigations that confirmed my innocence only made them circle their wagons tighter. Between a barrage of press releases, television and newspaper interviews, and carefully selected investigation details leaked to the media, the prosecution was successful—for some time—in prosecuting me in the court of public opinion.

On November 13, 2007, in a federal courtroom in Detroit, I pleaded guilty to one count each of criminal conspiracy, which has a maximum penalty of five years in prison and a $250,000 fine; unauthorized computer access, which has a maximum penalty of one year in prison and a $100,000 fine, and naturalization fraud, which has a maximum penalty of ten years in prison and a $250,000 fine.

On the same November day, the Department of Justice press release inaccurately stated that I had pleaded guilty to "accessing a federal computer system to unlawfully query information about my relatives." This claim was utterly false. The three counts the prosecution demanded I plead guilty to were a pair of immigration-related charges and one misdemeanor count of viewing a single document (never shown to me) that they specifically identified as "DE74791" allegedly "relating to a Hizballah-based investigation." In my plea hearing, I spoke to the absurdity of this document charge and told the judge, "Although I don't have a recollection of the date, or the time, or the information, I accessed the file."

In the same release, then-Assistant Attorney General Kenneth L. Wainstein stated the following:

> This defendant engaged in a pattern of deceit to secure U.S. citizenship, to gain employment in the intelligence community, and to obtain and exploit her access to sensitive counterterrorism intelligence. It is fitting that she now stands to lose both her citizenship and her liberty.

Wainstein's inflammatory statements weren't supported by the evidence available at that time and have been completely disproved by every element of the US government that has independently examined my case. But they weren't designed to shed light, merely to throw fuel on the fire. Months later, the prosecutor at my sentencing hearing would give the lie to Wainstein's claim that it was fitting I should lose my liberty by stating that "it was clear in the way the plea was written (by the U.S. Government) that Ms. Prouty does not have to be incarcerated."

Similarly, Brian Moskowitz, special agent in charge of the ICE (Immigration and Customs Enforcement) office, stated in the November 2007 press release that "Nada Prouty's guilty plea should serve as a solemn warning to those who say they've pledged their allegiance to the United States and then made the conscious decision to place America's interest at risk." The statement is pure smokescreen. The only thing I did consciously place at risk repeatedly was my life and my liberty for the safety of America and her citizenry. Neither of these men had ever served the United States in the way I had. I was astounded to see them malign the nature of my service in order to gain media attention.

Confusion in the prosecutorial ranks started to surface when other, less tightly scripted officials started commenting on the case. In a November 14, 2007, *Washington Post* article, an FBI spokesman stated, "Prouty underwent a full background investigation before she was hired, including interviews with her current and former husband and with family and friends in Lebanon." But, according to a November 15, 2007, *Detroit Free Press* article, "[Prouty] divorced [her first husband] in 1995. That was the last time Chris Deladurantaye heard from Prouty until federal agents knocked on his door a few months ago." Something was missing here. Did the FBI, as part of my background check, not meet with Deladurantaye for the interview prior to my hiring? After all, they sent an agent to Lebanon. Would they not have had a Detroit agent drive across town to interview Deladurantaye?

On November 14, 2007, then-US Attorney Stephen Murphy was interviewed on Fox News. In response to a question regarding how my background investigation had been conducted, Murphy advised his listeners that "vetting doesn't catch everything. And when a person is here since 1991, via fraud, you know, you've got some history there that can be built up to make things look legitimate." Notwithstanding that he had the wrong year for my arrival in the United States, Murphy gave an implausible excuse for the FBI's inability to conduct a simple background investigation on a marriage listed on the first page of my FBI application. Murphy then tried to deflect attention from this inconvenient line of questioning, which was rapidly straying from the prosecution's storyline: "Whether she was taking a little bit of stuff or a lot of stuff, it is a federal crime and that's what we've prosecuted her for." Leaving aside Murphy's unwillingness to take responsibility for determining the facts of my case, he effectively spun my extorted plea to viewing a single mystery document as proof of "taking a lot of stuff," thereby advancing the espionage fantasy and giving a clueless press carte blanche to question my patriotism. Once again, I was reminded how easy it is for insinuation and innuendo to pass for logical argument and reasoned debate.

The impact of these statements was devastating to me and my family. Media camped outside my home for a week in November 2007, harassing us and pointing their cameras in the windows. I was branded a traitor, with the lowest blow coming from the *New York Post,* who dubbed me "Jihad Jane" in a November 20 poison-pen article. The inflammatory rhetoric passed for fact for thousands of curious readers. Soon, many of my former colleagues in the FBI and CIA washed their hands of me.

My immediate thoughts that November went to my family's safety. My address had been released to the public, my property was invaded by journalists spurred by sensationalist claims, and my neighbors were harassed for interviews by local television stations. At one point I called the local police department when a nearby media station began filming through my glass front door. I was told that if I was "Nada Prouty," they would be "unable to help me." My back was against the wall, and I constantly worried about someone hurting my husband or our daughter. Some of our neighbors warned their children against playing with Eva, and these children told Eva they would not play with her "because your mother is bad." When I dropped Eva off at school, her teacher would scramble away so fast that I didn't even have a chance to speak with her about the distress my daughter was feeling. I worried about someone learning where Eva went to school and kidnapping her or harming her.

The essence of my dilemma recalled a scene in the 2005 movie *Syriana* in which an embattled CIA officer, played by George Clooney, gets an earful of down-home D.C. wisdom from the powerful businessman set on ruining him. "In Washington," the businessman says, "you are innocent until indicted." I was living proof of that sad truth.

IN THE CLEARING STANDS A BOXER

Betrayal is, no doubt, one of the worst of human experiences. Although I was intimately familiar with betrayal at a young age, thanks to my parents, I still felt utterly shocked at my colleagues' abandonment of me. I was disappointed that I was being used by federal prosecutors for what I concluded to be their personal gain, but I was crushed by how quickly some friends at the Bureau and at the Agency disavowed me—the same friends I would have taken a bullet for. I felt alternately incensed and humiliated. My pride had been manipulated by others and turned to feelings of shame.

I found, somehow, in those darkening days of late fall the ability to tell myself that I would fight this. Vowing to stand up to my accusers and with true friends reaching out to me from all corners of the world, I felt my determination surge again. I vowed to dedicate my future to exposing the truth. The attack the prosecutors had crafted was complete, was a noose around my neck, but the one thing they did not count on was my commitment to never give up, to fight to the last breath.

As my court sentencing date loomed, I felt like I was preparing to enter a boxing ring. I was ready to understand my "enemy," to roll with the initial flurry of punches that this early round would land on me. I was moved by Gordon's and by Eva's love to remain standing. I would outlast their attacks. I would, I believed, win in the later rounds. I would move cautiously and take them by surprise. Receiving the media attention they so aggressively sought and despite my agreement to their plea deal, the prosecution continued their attacks. While I stood gagged by the court and by secrecy restrictions, the prosecution had been able to use my silence to discredit me and bury my record of public service. Flush with this success, they appeared to feel they existed above the requirements of the law and of prosecutorial ethics.

I did see a glimmer of hope when I learned that Senators Chuck Grassley and Kit Bond had asked, in a letter written and dated November 14, 2007, and addressed to then-attorney general Michael Mukasey, for an accounting of my case. I figured that the more honest scrutiny my case received, the better my chance to make the truth public. I was disappointed, however, at the eventual outcome of this request. The following January, FBI officials responded to the letter in a closed-door meeting with Senate investigators. I never did learn the results of this meeting, but I remember hoping at the time that the FBI would not be able to fool Congress as they had fooled the media and the public.

AFTERMATH

In December 2007, the prosecution filed a superseding indictment, ostensibly against Talal Chahine, but that had more to do with me than with him. In this document, the Detroit prosecutors blatantly lied, listing five cases that they claimed I had accessed without authorization—an outrageous accusation even by their low standards. I was never actually charged with viewing these documents, but the innuendo got the prosecutors what they wanted: the media again picked up my story, and the prosecution's vilification of me was back in the spotlight.

Also at the end of December, USAA Federal Savings Bank froze our joint checking account and invalidated our debit and credit cards without warning. When confronted, the bank produced a series of dubious letters and by-laws and argued that their hands were tied. Our protests eventually convinced them to at least restore Gordon's access to our accounts on the condition my name be removed from the account. My investment accounts, however, were to remain unavailable to me, and my access to the bank was denied. After multiple letters back and forth, federal regulators agreed that the restriction of access to my account was a violation of Federal Reserve regulations but declined to assist us in any way. As an investigator, I could tell the bank had been served with one of the infamous "National Security Letters" that permits the FBI to secure data and institute policy without judicial oversight, most often under the aegis of a terrorism investigation. Because I had signed waivers to permit the government to access my financial information, whereby they would have been able to view my records without alerting me, the National Security Letter wasn't even necessary; it was a move designed to cause me and my family as much pain as possible. With the bulk of our funds frozen, we were reduced to begging from friends to buy milk for our daughter and put gas in the car so Gordon could go to work. With bills around every corner, we struggled to make our mortgage payments, and it dawned on me that that was yet another layer to this attack. Missing a mortgage payment could impact Gordon's security clearance and keep him from being employed. Yes, there's a reason they call it hardball!

All this was a call to arms of sorts. I knew I would fight to clear my name and to regain my citizenship. But December held at least one positive note for us. I learned that I was pregnant in December, and I was thrilled with the idea of having a second child. Knowing how close I was to my sisters, I wanted Eva to have a sibling. I felt blessed with our soon-to-be new baby girl. This pregnancy was just as physically challenging as my first, and I wanted to do some things differently. I wanted to be prepared for my new daughter's arrival, and I included Eva in the planning. Together, we got the baby room ready and had long chats about what it would be like with her sister around. With all the stress that surrounded us, I was touched by Eva's nurturing instincts, her love, and her caring ways. I was relieved to see that, despite all the madness, Eva was growing into a loving, happy child. I felt proud that I had been able, for the most part, to shelter her from the situation we were facing. I knew I would feel even more pride if I could, before the birth of this second child, fight my way out from under the cloud that hung over me. And the first step in that road back was around the corner—my sentencing hearing in May.

EXONERATED 13

On May 13, 2008, I kissed my daughter goodbye and left for the airport to fly to Detroit, where I would learn the results of my sentencing and come face to face with my future. I was not sure when I would see her next, and I felt a sharp pain from the guilt I had bottled up during my service in Iraq. I had put her life in danger, believing that it was my duty as a citizen to help create a better future for all children in America. Now I might be forced to live apart from her. My heart pounded as I jetted toward the city where I had first lived as a young and hopeful student, fleeing a crazy family and a war-torn homeland. Regardless of what lay ahead, I was ready to continue to fight for my family.

And so, on May 14, 2008, Federal District Judge Avern Cohn fined me $750, begrudgingly voided my citizenship, and spoke in critical tones about the nature of the prosecution's case. The judge did not have any discretion in canceling my citizenship as it was required by the structure of the plea deal. But the disparity between my light sentence and the maximum penalties encompassed in the charges speaks for itself.

The result of the sentencing was better than I had ever dared hope. In his closing remarks, Judge Cohn stated the following:

> This is a highly unique situation. The essential offense, which you committed, was marriage fraud. You engaged in a sham marriage to obtain citizenship and to avoid having to return to Lebanon. Your desire not

to return to Lebanon, given the conditions which existed there in the early 1990s, is understandable. You also improperly accessed a computer available to you at your workstation. As to that offense, you did not print out anything, nor did you tell anyone what you read. The personal circumstances, as noted, that led to the sham marriage occurred almost twenty years ago. Since that time you have rendered extraordinary services to the United States as an agent of the FBI and in the employ of the CIA. At no time did you ever compromise or jeopardize the integrity of any work assignment to improper behavior or inappropriate conduct. As a citizen you served your country honorably and effectively and at times in situations which exposed you to personal danger. The media accounts of your case, perhaps prompted by the excessiveness of the press releases issued by the United States Attorney's Office, have grossly distorted the circumstances of your case. You and your family have suffered, and will continue to suffer, as a result of an error in judgment made nineteen years ago, including loss of citizenship and loss of employment.

I was ecstatic that the judge had seen through the smoke to the real facts of my case. The government team quickly scattered out of the courtroom, heads hung low, muttering "no comment" to the press they had so adeptly and thoroughly manipulated. There would be no gloating and trading of high-fives, as there had been four months earlier when I was forced to plead guilty to charges the government knew to be untrue. So began my life as a stateless person.

On March 12, 2008, the director of security for the CIA, Charles S. Phalen, issued an exoneration letter on my behalf addressed to the prosecutors in my case. The letter was the result of two weeks of debriefing sessions followed by multiple polygraph tests conducted by the CIA. In the letter, Phalen emphatically states that "the Agency did not identify any information that Mrs. Prouty cooperated or engaged in unauthorized contact with a foreign intelligence service or terrorist organization." The letter was an unclassified summary that twenty-seven-year CIA veteran Robert Grenier, former chief of the elite Counterterrorism Center, would later detail in a *60 Minutes* interview that would air in March 2010. Greiner would note on *60 Minutes* the following with respect to my case: "There was a full investigation which included multiple polygraph examinations. . . . She was completely exonerated." When asked how thorough these investigations are and how seriously they are taken, Grenier would state on national television that, "You cannot imagine how seriously the CIA would take an investigation like that."

WHAT GOES AROUND COMES AROUND

But before all that good news would finally come my way, my life in limbo slowly unfolded. Starting in June 2008, following my exoneration and Judge Cohn's blistering dressing-down of the prosecutors in my case, the Detroit prosecutors began to work on protecting their erroneous statements and media releases. They knew the truth by this time, and I believed it was their obligation to set the record straight for the American people. I also knew the pace at which the government works and figured that this would take some time. I recognized that the prosecutors in my case had to do a good deal of damage control, if not figure out how to spin the affair in their favor.

I took this opportunity to finally relax and reconnect with my family; the past two years had been really hard on all of us. My sister Rula decided to treat us to a Disney vacation, and I remember thinking how Disney's Fantasyland didn't hold a candle to the surreal fantasy my life had become.

When we got back from Florida, I received a letter from the local immigration office requesting that I report to their office in two days. When I did, I was informed that I was now considered a deportable alien and was required to report monthly with my bags packed, ready to be prepared to depart the United States. They told me that ICE was actively seeking to remove me to an unidentified country other than Lebanon. I told them that, based on my prior government service in national security, deportation would jeopardize not only my personal safety but the security of my classified knowledge as well. I was told that if I had any concerns, I should contact the

United Nations and seek removal from the United States, to a possible destination of my choice, prior to the ICE taking action. There were other restrictions too. I was told that I must ask for permission to travel outside of a fifty-mile radius from my home. If I violated this restriction, I would be subject to arrest. I did not understand why, after I had been cleared of having any association with my country's enemies, I was facing such harsh monitoring conditions.

The only thing I could think of was that they were trying to force me out of the United States. As long as I was here, I would be living in a fifty-mile jail cell. Why did ICE—and I was sure ICE was taking orders from other government operatives who were behind these moves—want me to leave the United States when they knew that, given the sensitive operations and cases I had worked, it would be potentially contrary to the interest of the United States?

On my more frustrating days, I thought about starting life somewhere else. I even considered the possibility that I would be forced to go to Lebanon and face my destiny there. Living under confinement sounded unbearable, but the alternatives were bleak. I did not want to jeopardize any ongoing intelligence operations, so I feared being forced into a situation where Hizballah operatives tortured the information out of me. I assure you this was no hysterical fear—it would be a very real possibility, were I to end up deported, that I might fall into enemy hands. At these moments I flashed on the horrible ordeal that William Buckley, the CIA's Beirut station chief who was kidnapped by Hizballah terrorists in Beirut in 1984, had faced at the hands of his killers.

But all things considered, I realized I would rather start a new life in a new country, someplace where I would actively work to mitigate my vulnerability, than live under the circumstances I was now being forced to deal with. Was that what the US government wanted? I was beginning to suspect that there was more to my stateless status and the threats to deport me than the classic trajectory, which I had seen unfold on several occasions while working for the FBI, of "indict, force a guilty plea, gather your statistics and accolades, and move to your next target." Thus, it did not surprise me when I read, in an

August 14, 2008, press release, that US Attorney Stephen Murphy, the Justice Department official who had overseen my prosecution, was now using my guilty plea and my proscribed status to bolster his national security credentials. Murphy was someone who wanted to move up the career ladder by using his accomplishments in the war on terror, and what better way for him to proceed, or so he must have thought, than to publicize that he had been instrumental in putting me out of government service.

In the midst of all this, I was blessed with a near-perfect birth. On September 12, 2008, Gordon, Eva, and I welcomed our new bundle of joy, Elizabeth (Ella) Gordon Prouty into our family circle. Gordon doted on her, and seeing both girls resting on Daddy's shoulder brought joy to my heart. Ella's birth gave me still another reason to continue fighting. My restored dignity and my complete exoneration were gifts I wanted to bestow on both Eva and Ella. I knew this dream would not be an easy one to realize, and I was ready for what came next. I was waiting for the Detroit prosecutors to defend their indefensible actions. I knew it was only a matter of time before more attacks on me would surface, and those suspicions were soon confirmed.

I was further convinced that there was something more behind DOJ's investigation when I read an October 28, 2008, Department of Justice press release that lionized the prosecutors in my case for their "elimination of vulnerabilities to the nation's security within the intelligence community and [for] uncovering numerous compromises in classified national security investigations into the activities of the designated foreign terrorist organization, Hizballah."

More shocking than this whitewash of my case, and more telling of the forces behind attacks on me, was a December 2008 report from the US Attorney's Office of the Eastern District of Michigan, which blatantly and boastfully lied about the office's "accomplishment." The report concluded that my case was "the only known case of an illegal alien infiltrating U.S. intelligence agency with potential *espionage* implications pertaining to a foreign terrorist organization." Here again, I saw the power of insinuation, not just of my evil intentions in viewing classified material, but also in the damning claim that I had, from the moment of my immigration to the United States, been bent on a premeditated course of espionage.

The final attack came in March 2009, nearly a year after my sentencing. AUSA Chadwell contacted my attorneys and demanded that I surrender my 1994 naturalization certificate, threatening me with a felony conviction if I failed to surrender the certificate and any copies. A felony charge and conviction would violate the terms of my supervision, permit ICE to take me into custody immediately, and generate a new order for deportation—one not withheld. I had long ago misplaced the naturalization certificate, and I realized that the copy of the certificate that ICE had sent me (as part of a Freedom of Information Act request) was very possibly a setup. With this last threat, I decided that my tactic of simply ignoring the continued attacks was not working.

With a good deal of exonerating information now public, I reached out to government officials and members of Congress for help in addressing my untenable situation. I worried that the continued legal attacks, public press releases, and misleading statements would eventually succeed in forcing me out of the United States and foreclose any assistance I might receive. Most neutral observers who heard the facts of my story were shocked that a successful FBI/CIA career could be destroyed by an ill-advised marriage I made as a teenager, especially given my disclosure of this mistake to the FBI at the time of my initial hiring. Many individuals were sympathetic, and some did all they could to help; unfortunately, their efforts were to be blunted by the seemingly never-ending campaign of threats and lies orchestrated by the prosecution. I was still without a powerful ally. I needed someone with stature and respect in my corner.

With the end of 2009 approaching, and with no hope in sight, I recognized that I needed more help than I had been able to secure from fair-minded individuals in the government. Checks and balances certainly were not going to rescue me, but there were other options. The cornerstone of the campaign against me was continued manipulation of the media. The prosecution in Detroit had gone to extraordinary lengths to silence me in the run-up to their malicious campaign, and those efforts continued. I realized that I had to tell my story to the American people—myself.

Having lived for the previous five years moving anonymously about in the shadows—a necessary precaution for an officer in the National Clandestine Service—I initially recoiled at the idea of taking my case to the media. After the nasty headline stories following my plea hearing, I was contacted by virtually every mainstream news organization. Some sought comments, while others wanted interviews. After my plea hearing I was still under a gag order, a restriction not suffered by the prosecution. But even when the gag order was lifted, I had planned to rectify my case privately, while doing everything possible to protect the cases and assets that had formed the foundation of my life.

But my efforts to work with government officials once the fanfare of my sentencing had subsided were less than effective. I was still the subject of an ongoing campaign threatening additional prosecution and subsequent deportation. The personal risks to me were grave, but, because of the publicity generated by the prosecution, the threat to US national security was immeasurable. I needed to do everything in my power to put the issues surrounding my case into the hands of the American people. I printed out a list of potential media outlets with their contact information and, for the first time ever, carefully looked it over. I was hesitant and anxious. My experience with the media thus far, limited to the coverage following my plea hearing, had not been positive. I needed an organization that had experience with complex government investigations and that would invest real resources in the story until they were satisfied they had uncovered the truth. I spoke to a number of contacts with media experience and, hoping against hope, graded a list of organizations. In what seemed like a bit of a reach, I put *60 Minutes* at the head of the class.

GONE IN 60 MINUTES

Soon after my media grading session, I prepared a package of information for the producers at *60 Minutes* that included all my exonerating evidence. I provided it to a producer and waited ten days or so to hear back from him. While waiting, I thought about the reasons *60 Minutes* would be a good place for my story to be told. They were an undeniably professional outfit, and they cast their stories in a manner that made people think critically about the relationship between individuals and overreaching systems of power and privilege. Nonetheless, I feared they might not grasp the truth at the heart of my complex story. There was always the possibility that by reaching out I could cause irreparable damage to my already mischaracterized case.

When they did call, I was informed that they were interested enough to look into the matter, but I was told they would only later decide whether the case was worthy of an airing. They thanked me politely for the background material I had sent them, but added that they would be independently verifying any documents or information I shared with them. I knew the impression they must have of me. According to the rest of the media, I was a spy, and I wouldn't be surprised if they thought me guilty until their research raised a reasonable doubt. Their objectivity confirmed my confidence in their investigatory skills. "Trust but verify" was how I had worked with my sources, and I was glad to see that the professionals at *60 Minutes* conducted business similarly.

As with any major news organization, I assumed *60 Minutes* would have its share of law enforcement and intelligence sources to turn to when investigating my case. I expected that professional researchers would study the case and provide the show's producers with lists of questions to be answered. From day one, I had told the producer and his associates to feel free to ask me any question about anything—that nothing was off limits. I tried to encourage them by repeatedly telling them that the more they looked into the matter, the better it was for me. With that understanding, I spent January and February in 2009 answering dozens and dozens of questions relating to my case work, my family, my travels, and my personal history. I was elated to see the level of detail the researchers employed; they left no stone unturned. The Detroit prosecution had looked only at information that corroborated their self-serving narrative; having the professionals at *60 Minutes* digging into all aspects of my case was very encouraging.

But all these positive feelings disappeared when I got a call from one of the show's producers. In no-nonsense terms, he revealed to me the possibility that "secret evidence" existed proving I was a Hizballah spy. In the story he had been told, this evidence was so sensitive it couldn't be used in court, but it had been used to negotiate a plea deal from me. Furthermore, his source claimed that I had been told of the existence, but not the content, of this evidence. The producer was then told that, confronted with the existence of secret evidence, I had waived the statute of limitations on my naturalization charge and had accepted a plea that could potentially result in a sentence proportionate to the sentence I would receive based on those crimes alleged by the secret evidence.

As soon as I heard the origins of the producer's necessarily confrontational questions (I knew the show had to be as thorough as possible), I immediately knew who was feeding this story to him. The prosecutorial team had worked hard to silence me since 2007. They had taken outrageous measures to accomplish their goal, including continued threats of lengthy prison time, a media campaign of misleading leaks, the threat of deportation to Lebanon, and threats against my family and loved ones. And now, I believed, prosecutors were playing hardball with *60 Minutes,* advising the show to drop the segment because the prosecution in my case had information that could torpedo my on-air defense and make all claims of objectivity on the part of the show mere lies.

This new tactic was creative. The only previous time I had heard of "secret evidence" that could not be used in court, it was invoked not to protect the United States but to defend a corrupt and totalitarian third-world government. Although my heart was pounding at this point, I patiently explained to the producer that I was aware of many national security cases where defendants were tried in a court of law without restrictions on the nature of the evidence presented against them. For God's sake, I told him, Attorney General Eric Holder stated in November 2009 that Khalid Sheikh Mohammad

(KSM) was going to be tried in Manhattan. According to a Google search, KSM had been caught in Rawalpindi, Pakistan, in 2003, transported to a secret facility where he was waterboarded over a hundred times, and then transported to Guantanamo Bay. But all this secret interrogating would not be a part of his case. Holder's desire to prosecute this case in a New York court highlighted the fact that the Justice Department had confidence in their capabilities to try an individual fairly in a court of law without revealing secure sources and classified methods.

I told the producer that there was no secret evidence in my case, that the claim was bogus, and that the prosecution had used a series of escalating threats that started with the draconian multiple felony charges for passport use, followed by the threats against my husband's career and my family members' future, then culminating in the threat of deportation overseas—with the clear implication of my death—to force my plea agreement. I did not hear from the producer for days; with growing pessimism, I assumed 60 Minutes had bought into the idea of "secret evidence." If an organization as capable as 60 Minutes would fall for this trick, I was doomed.

Day after silent day passed, and I began to accept defeat. When the phone rang one day and I heard the producer on the other line, I was almost too nervous to speak. He was asking hard questions again, but I could tell he had worked through the "secret evidence" claim and discarded it as a fiction. 60 Minutes was ready to move forward with the story. As their investigation wound down, we agreed on dates and locations for filming.

On the first day of the interviews, I was extremely anxious. I did not know what questions were coming, and I hoped their months of investigation had led them to full understanding. The interviews were taped over three days, culminating in a multi-hour interview under television lights and surrounded by cameras—a literal hot seat. The questions covered the FBI cases I had worked, my service in Iraq, and, of course, the legal case against me. The night before the final interview, I had nervously jotted down some notes to help me recall the exact timeline of events, but when Scott Pelley began asking me questions, I took a deep breath, put the paper aside, and let go of my anxiety. I felt as if I was reaching out as one American to all other Americans, and I wanted to sound like myself. I wanted to answer questions from the heart, not from a script, so I let my heart do most of the talking. I felt buoyed after the interview, but strangely, I could not recall any of my answers when Gordon later asked me about it. I simply felt a huge weight had been lifted off my shoulders. For the first time in a long while, I was at peace.

On March 28, 2010, I waited to watch my interview with a mixture of excitement and fear. I had set out to share my side of the story with my fellow citizens, the only path open to me after the prosecution had for so long manipulated the media and, in turn, the people. I hoped that my sincerity would show through. I hoped, too, that the preposterous lies spread by the prosecution would now, at last, be properly rebutted on the national stage. Most of all, I hoped that people would finally be able to make up their own minds as to the depth and sincerity of my service to America's intelligence and law-enforcement agencies.

Although we had no inkling how my story was to be reported, Gordon and I celebrated then. It is almost impossible for me to overstate how much I wanted everyone to know that I loved my country, that I loved the vibrancy of American society. I lived every day in awe of the remarkable way in which, for me, American individualism managed to avoid, for the most part, cliquish separatism, evolving instead toward shared community. I wanted the viewing audience to know that America had literally saved me—given me shelter from the storm of civil war and the endlessly bickering factions that, to this day, plague the formation of a truly civil society in the nation of my birth. I hoped that in some small way, the interview had made people think about what it meant to be an American and to be an American patriot.

As soon as the episode was over, the phone started ringing. Friends and family called to express their support and their pride in my decision to go public with my case. A call that especially resonated with me was a call from a neighbor who confessed that she had been duped by the initial media coverage of my story; she offered sincere apologies for avoiding me for the past two years. Her call meant a lot to me, and it presaged many similar calls and conversations to come.

In the weeks following the *60 Minutes* broadcast, my life changed dramatically. I started to receive fan mail. People started up petitions and websites for me, and friendly neighbors called out to me by name. One of the most touching post-interview moments happened at a session of Eva's gymnastics class. When Eva and I arrived at the facility, I saw a person running across the gymnasium carrying a bouquet of flowers. As he approached, I realized he was the parent of one of Eva's classmates and the flowers were for me. He handed me the bouquet and told me he had never met an American hero before and that he wanted to thank me for my service to America. I was touched by his generosity of spirit. I also received a call from an executive placement firm with a number of security consulting offers. *Ha!* I thought, *My expertise is still marketable.* That, too, made me smile. Moreover, I was overwhelmed by the flood of positive comments on the *60 Minutes* website. The comments made it clear that my faith in my fellow citizens had not been misplaced. And, to tell the truth, these positive comments were a potent antidote to the hate mail I had come across in the "Comments" appended to articles in papers like the *Detroit Free Press* and online blog sites. The more positive and, frankly, more rational *60 Minutes* comments gave me hope that the ordeal I had gone through would end with recognition of my patriotism and my dedication to American interests:

Nada, you are an American Hero. Thank You!

This is just an abomination to what this country stands for. We Americans should be eternally thankful that people like her, despite being a foreigner, have protected this "great" nation against the beasts out there. And this is how we repay her?

Give this woman her citizenship. She put her life on the line for this country. Yea, she broke the law when she was nineteen. She should be forgiven for that because of her service to this nation.

Wow! Did this lady get bad legal advice! She needs a Presidential pardon, restoration of her citizenship and to get her back to work!

I am proud to have been served by you and express my gratitude for all that you have done for this misguided country of ours. . . . You my dear are an American. And I bestow upon you citizenship in my country. For this country is run by "We the people," not the fools in Washington. Welcome to the new USA where your service is appreciated and honored.

With my side of the story now circulating in prime time, I immediately saw a shift in public opinion. This opened new doors for me. The prosecutors' efforts to keep me silent had now publicly backfired: the facts of my story stood in shocking contrast to the fictions prosecutors had so carefully crafted. And the prosecutors were in for a shock, one I would be happy to see them suffer. Supportive government officials who were already helping in my case were able to get enough traction after the *60 Minutes* interview to successfully change my immigration status.

Two moments in the time that followed now stand out in my memory.

First, on November 12, 2009, FBI Assistant Director of Counterterrorism James McJunkin was scheduled to provide the Senate Select Committee on Intelligence (SSCI) with the results of the two-year FBI damage assessment conducted after my prosecution. While the results of this meeting are not in the public record, it is apparent that McJunkin's testimony authenticated the facts previously stated by Judge Cohen. Specifically, there was "no damage" and "no compromise" to any FBI investigation, operation, or human asset. Had there been a scintilla of evidence to support the outlandish claims made in Detroit, the SSCI would have never agreed to support a path to naturalization and eventual return of my citizenship.

Second, and most tellingly, on December 23, 2010, I was notified of the unprecedented decision made by the attorney general, the director of the CIA, and the Secretary of Homeland Security to grant me permanent resident alien (PRA) status, the first step to re-obtaining my citizenship. This decision, I believe, speaks for itself. Level-headed and high-ranking professionals, reviewing the mismanaged investigation that had resulted in my coerced plea agreement and in recognizing the gross manipulation of the facts by the prosecution, moved to set the matter straight. In granting me PRA status, the US government sent a powerful broadside into the smug aura surrounding the Detroit prose-cutorial team. Their plan to smear me to generate self-serving headlines was now exposed. Agencies in which the prosecution's lies had once found support recanted when they finally secured the opportunity to review the facts for themselves. There were plenty of opportunities for anyone with any kind of incriminating evidence to challenge or derail the decision to grant me PRA status to come forward—but no one did. Clearly, a new path to citizenship for me would simply not have been possible if any real evidence existed that I had betrayed my country.

With the stroke of a pen by Attorney General Holder, CIA Direc-tor Leon Panetta, and DHS Secretary Janet Napolitano, nine months after the *60 Minutes* airing, I was a legal resident and enjoyed the honor of becoming an American once again.

THE PEOPLE HAVE SPOKEN

As I read the overwhelmingly positive media accounts of my case as featured on *60 Minutes,* one specific article stood out in sharp contrast to these heartfelt responses. In a *Detroit Free Press* article dated March 28, 2010, Michigan Congressman Mike Rogers, a Re-publican member of the House Intelligence Committee and a former FBI agent, claimed he had been "briefed" on my case. Rogers, the article stated, had told the paper, concerning the veracity of my side of the story, that he "didn't believe her." The article went on to say this: "Rogers said he believes Prouty passed classified information to Chahine—which Prouty denies. He also doesn't believe the computer inquiries were legitimate."

Why had Rogers commented on what he "believed" instead of the facts of the case? Who was he citing when he said he had been briefed on my case? When was he briefed last? Was he not aware of the multiple exonerations offered on my behalf? Where was he getting his information? Where was the evidence in support of his strongly held beliefs?

As a former investigator, contradictory behavior—believing something in spite of evidence to the contrary—does not sit well with me. I tossed and turned in bed and was unable to fall sleep the night after I had read the *Free Press* story. I eventually decided to get up and do some research on Rogers. First, I Googled his name and pulled up dozens of documents. When I started scanning and reading these documents, one jumped out at me. It was a September 2006 report from the political watchdog group Alliance for Justice on the subject of Stephen Murphy, the US attorney whose Detroit tax-evasion case against Talal Chahine had somehow turned into a root-out-the-Hizballah-mole circus my case eventually became. As I read the document, I had a moment of stunning clarity regarding the true nature of my prosecution. Rogers had been vocal about my case from day one; indeed, his choice of words mirrored the public smear campaign of the Murphy team's prosecution. My case ended up garnering a lot of media attention for Rogers—and for Stephen Murphy, just as Murphy was seeking a federal judicial appointment. The Alliance for Justice report showed that Murphy had been donating and raising money for Rogers's political campaigns for years. When one more search quickly confirmed that Murphy didn't reside in Rogers's district, it raised an interesting question: Was Rodgers, in order to bolster the prosecution's "Hizballah spy" story, rewarding Murphy by launching vociferous and fear-mongering attacks on me?

Their mutual interests and allegiances certainly would have made the use of my case to further their political and professional careers an attractive option. So, as I sat there at the computer doing my research and thinking about alliances and political turf wars, I came to truly appreciate the role politics had played in my persecution. I believe the Rogers–Murphy relationship is the first layer peeled off this complex plot, and I am confident that with time more and more layers will be peeled to expose the entire truth.

IN THE END IS MY BEGINNING, AGAIN

Although personal gain, the ethnic insularity of various government agencies, and my vulnerable position as an Arab-American national security employee were all factors that contributed to the unprofessional nature of my prosecution, I now realize the impact of "politics" in my case. I now understand the rushed plea deal filled with inaccuracies, the overzealousness of my accusers, and the overreaching public campaign against me as each having political origins and future political ramifications. I understand, for example, why the prosecutors did not push for a cooperation agreement. Asking for such an agreement would have fulfilled a simple professional responsibility, to determine whether any operations or human assets had been compromised.

I now understand why the prosecution neither showed me specific documents nor provided me with enough information to recall the reason I viewed these documents. I now understand why they allowed Talal to travel outside the United States. I now understand why they wanted me in Lebanon. Finally, I now understand who my true adversaries were—and it wasn't the foreign forces I'd been fighting all this time.

As satisfying as it is to find the truth, I remain quite concerned about the nature of the conversation in this country about citizenship and patriotism and sacrifice. When I was on the front lines, both at the FBI and for the CIA, I naïvely thought all government servants shared the same unselfish goals—the welfare of America and its people. But my ordeal has taught me otherwise. For individuals back home to make their own career goals the motivating factor behind their pursuit of justice is, frankly, not the sort of motivation that one expects from freedom- and democracy-loving Americans—citizens of the country the rest of the world is supposed to emulate when it comes to liberty and justice. Suspicion and fear mingled with threats of punishment are not hallmarks of a healthy civil society. Such behaviors represent a very close-minded approach to the world; one might even say xenophobic.

Believe me, I know such behaviors well. I saw them everywhere in the fractured Lebanon of my youth. In that Lebanon, and in much of the Arab world then and now, political society—the repressive state, warring factions, etc.—always had the upper hand in relation to civil society. Among other things, this distribution of power meant that Arab governments were quite efficient at defining and punishing their internal enemies. My prosecution brought into stark relief the possibility that the politicizing of the war on terror would create similar "internal enemies" here in America. Such enemies are, more often than not, patriotic Americans who happen to have what some, in their ignorance, see as "different" names and faces. It's not overt racism in the classic sense, but rather a troubling kind of suspicion of non-white, non-ethnically Western European, and non-Christian individuals. Such suspicion promotes ignorance, which is a very real threat to American freedom and enlightened civil society.

Having said that, I know, having worked next to the outstanding, chivalrous, and dedicated members of the FBI, the CIA, and the US military, that our intelligence and law-enforcement agencies are, for the most part, made up of exceptional individuals who are selfless in their dedication and patriotism.

More than twenty years ago, I escaped the war-torn country of my birth and an abusive family and came to America to get an education. I was counting on this education to be a bulwark against a Lebanese culture hostile and demeaning to women. What I did not count on was falling in love with America and with America's cherished ideals, with democracy, freedom, and equality, as well as the open society—a society where debate and reason and creativity are qualities held in high esteem by the very laws of the land. I eventually realized I could not return to Lebanon—that it was no longer a country for me. So I was determined to stay here, in America, and to add, if I could, to the wonder I felt in its presence.

In return for these treasures, I decided many years ago that I wanted to offer my services to my new country, to show my appreciation for all the opportunities I had been offered. I went to school and worked hard and was honored to do so. And then I found a home at the FBI and later at the CIA. When I say I found a home, I really mean I found a home, for my biological family (my sisters being one exception) and my homeland had ceased to be for me sources of mutual respect and love. I looked at my colleagues at both the FBI and the CIA as family in a very real sense. Such, I believe, is a common feeling for immigrants who come to America from countries wracked by war or famine or genocide.

When my patriotic service was twisted into grotesque lies to advance the personal interests of individuals who had never faced the dangers I had, individuals who had never accomplished the kinds of missions assigned to me, my faith in America was tested. Ultimately, the actions of these few could not deter my love for my country or my commitment to use America's honored tradition of a free press to tell my story. Inaccurate headlines and hooligan comments by my detractors could not make me less a patriot, nor could such actions diminish the truth of my efforts in the service of justice. I value my American freedoms because I remember what it was like not to enjoy these freedoms. And by the same measure, I now enjoy a newborn appreciation for the wisdom of the American people. When elements of the government I honorably served launched their baseless attacks, I went to the people themselves for redress. That struggle was a long one, and I wandered in the dark for a while. But I gradually reclaimed my light. Because of what I believed in and because of how I was buoyed by the best qualities of the American character, I remained—and I remain—uncompromised.